Making the EMU

Making the EMU

The Politics of Budgetary
Surveillance and the
Enforcement of Maastricht

James D. Savage

OXFORD
UNIVERSITY PRESS

OXFORD
UNIVERSITY PRESS

Great Clarendon Street, Oxford OX2 6DP

Oxford University Press is a department of the University of Oxford.
It furthers the University's objective of excellence in research, scholarship,
and education by publishing worldwide in

Oxford New York

Auckland Bangkok Buenos Aires Cape Town Chennai
Dar es Salaam Delhi Hong Kong Istanbul Karachi Kolkata
Kuala Lumpur Madrid Melbourne Mexico City Mumbai Nairobi
São Paulo Shanghai Taipei Tokyo Toronto

Oxford is a registered trade mark of Oxford University Press
in the UK and in certain other countries

Published in the United States
by Oxford University Press Inc., New York

First published in 2005

First published in paperback 2007

British Library Cataloguing in Publication Data

Data available

Library of Congress Cataloging in Publication Data

Data available

ISBN 978-0-19-927840-4 (Hbk.)

   978-0-19-923869-9 (Pbk.)

1 3 5 7 9 10 8 6 4 2

Typeset by SPI Publisher Services, Pondicherry, India
Printed in Great Britain
on acid-free paper by Biddles Ltd., King's Lynn, Norfolk

For Lenore, again with love

Preface

The idea that the integrity of the budgetary data employed for the Maastricht Treaty's convergence process and excessive deficit procedure rests on a set of accounting rules is rather chilling. This is, after all, the world of Enron, Parmalat, and Adecco accounting, where creative bookkeeping is practised by private and public institutions worldwide. Oversight organizations such as the Security and Exchange Commission in the United States appear hopelessly compromised, efforts at harmonizing global private sector accounting rules between Europe and the United States, as well as within Europe, drag on for years, while the European Commission is charged by its own audit chief with exaggerating the quality of its finances. Yet, this is exactly what has occurred. The European Union entrusted the credibility of the member states' critical budgetary figures to a relatively minor agency in the European Commission, which harmonizes these data with a set of accounting rules that were never intended for such a purpose. This book examines just how this came to be, and what effect the Treaty's surveillance procedure has had on the making of the EMU and the enforcement of Maastricht and the Stability and Growth Pact.

The minor agency in question is Eurostat, and it is this supranational institution that serves as the *entrée* to our broader understanding of the politics, administration, and organization of the surveillance procedure. Eurostat, however, is far more well known for its recent scandals in the awarding of fraudulent contracts, rather than for its rectitude in monitoring member states' budgetary activities. Furthermore, when one thinks of the Commission's role in EU macroeconomic policy coordination, its Directorate General for Economic and Financial Affairs (ECFIN) comes first to mind, far overshadowing Eurostat. Nonetheless, it is Eurostat, not ECFIN, which creates supranational law and binding rulings on the size and the constitution of member state budgetary accounts for the surveillance procedure. Attention is now directed away from the Treaty's Stage II convergence period, during which member states qualified for EMU status and that lasted from 1994 through 1998, to the turmoil taking place with the Stability and Growth Pact. This disruption stems initially from Portugal's efforts in 2001 at masking its budget deficit through questionable accounting, and, more currently, from France and Germany's lack of compliance with the excessive deficit procedure. Yet, in order to comprehend fully the nature of this turmoil in Stage III, which activated the European Central Bank and euro currency and continues to consolidate economic and monetary union, Eurostat's national accounts rulings during Stage II must first be considered. These decisions enabled three and possibly four member states to gain EMU status, and they may make it possible, in more contemporary circumstances, for member states to reduce substantially or even eliminate their excessive deficits. Thus, this study is organized chronologically, with significant attention paid to the logic and method of the European Union's national accounts decision-making process. My effort extends beyond simply saying that the Commission made such-and-such a ruling at a particular time, by increasing the transparency of its technical nature for the reader. At times, this means employing national accounts and budgetary references, though I have attempted to make this technical language as accessible as possible for the reader.

This research was supported by a Fulbright–European Union Public Affairs fellowship, which enabled me to spend a semester with Eurostat's Unit B-4, the key group of staffers responsible for the Treaty's surveillance procedure during the Stage II convergence process, who continue to play a central role in Stage III monetary union. Thanks to the generosity and encouragement of Yves Franchet, Eurostat's Director General at that time, I was granted complete access to Eurostat's files, meetings, and personnel. Although Franchet's involvement with Eurostat's fraudulent contracting resulted in his resignation, there is no evidence at this time to suggest that these activities influenced the conduct of the surveillance procedure, certainly during the Stage II convergence process. Repeated contact with Eurostat since then has enabled me to follow the agency's most recent activities and national accounts rulings affecting the member states' deficit and debt calculations. During my stay with the Commission, I conducted frequent formal and informal interviews on a daily basis with Eurostat. In addition, I interviewed personnel at ECFIN, the European Central Bank, the European Court of Auditors, and numerous European Union member state national statistical institutes and central banks. Except for very rare instances, I have refrained from identifying those whom I interviewed. These individuals are civil servants who work in sensitive positions of a highly political nature, and their candor and generosity may best be thanked by avoiding linking their identities with their direct comments.

I am indebted to a number of people who assisted me during the years it took to complete this work. Gerard Alexander, John Duffield, Erica Gould, John Gilmour, Jeff Legro, Herman Schwartz, David Waldner, and Joseph White provided invaluable comments on various chapters. Aiding me yet one more time, as he has throughout my career, Nelson Polsby supported my application for a Fulbright fellowship. I would also like to recall the late Aaron

Wildavsky, whose last research on budgeting examined the Maastricht Treaty. In some small way I would like to think that my work complements his research. Beverly Crawford extended a warm invitation to present my research at the University of California at Berkeley's Center for German and European Studies. I am very grateful to these staff members of Eurostat's Unit B-4 who tolerated my endless questions: Luca Ascoli, Eduardo Barredo, Denis Besnard, Christine Coin, John Delaney, Jean-Pierre Dupuis, Dieter Glatzel, and Hubertus Vreeswijk. Special thanks go to Luca and Jean-Pierre, who have been especially generous with their time and technical assistance. Margaret Nicholson served as a very able and helpful host for the Fulbright Program in Brussels. The amazing Dominic Byatt of Oxford University Press offered continuous support and encouragement, which made the publication of this study possible. The Arendt family extended their friendship as well as kind and generous hospitality that ensured that our stay in Luxembourg proved to be a most pleasurable experience: Jacques, Rita, Christine, Fanny, Max, and Andre. Finally, this book is dedicated to my wife, Lenore, who is my loving helpmate and fellow world traveler.

Contents

List of Tables

List of Figures

List of Abbreviations

CBO	Congressional Budget Office (United States)
CMFB	Committee on Monetary, Financial, and Balance of Payments Statistics
EEC	European Economic Community
EC	European Commission
ECA	European Court of Auditors
ECB	European Central Bank
DG ECFIN	Directorate General II for Economic and Financial Affairs
ECJ	European Court of Justice
ECOFIN	Council of Economic and Finance Ministers
EMI	European Monetary Institute
EMU	Economic and Monetary Union
ESA	European System of Integrated Economic Accounts/European System of Accounts
ESS	European Statistical System
EU	European Union
FAWP	Financial Accounts Working Party
GAO	General Accounting Office (United States)
GDP	Gross Domestic Product
IDB	Inter-American Development Bank
IMF	International Monetary Fund
INSEE	National Institute for Statistics and Economic Studies (France)
MOF	Ministry of Finance
NCB	National Central Bank
NSI	National Statistical Institute
OECD	Organization for Economic Cooperation and Development
OMB	Office of Management and Budget (United States)
SNA	System of National Accounts (United Nations)
UN	United Nations

Enforcing Maastricht: The Significance of Treaty Surveillance

Hence we must conclude that it is as difficult to compare social expenditure as it is to estimate the relative wealth of the Union and of France. I would add that it would even be dangerous to attempt it. When statistics are not based on strictly accurate calculations, they mislead instead of guide. The mind easily lets itself be taken in by the false appearances of exactitude which statistics retain even in their mistakes, and confidently adopts errors clothed in the forms of mathematical truth.

(Alexis de Tocqueville, *Democracy in America*)

We may next turn to the organization of finance. Several of the offices of a state, if not all, handle large sums of public money. There must accordingly be a separate office for finance which receives and audits the accounts of other offices, and is only concerned with this one function. The holders of this office go by different names in different places—auditors, accountants, examiners, or advocates of the fisc.

(Aristotle, *The Politics*)

In March 1998, the European Monetary Institute (EMI) and the European Commission (EC) issued their eagerly awaited convergence reports that identi-fied which European Union (EU) countries qualified for membership in the new Economic and Monetary Union (EMU).[1] The Maastricht Treaty on European Union established a broad set of economic criteria required of successful appli-cant countries. Clearly, though, for most of the EU's fifteen member countries their domestic politics focused on reaching the Treaty's famous budgetary deficit and debt reference values of 3 and 60 percent of the Gross Domestic Product (GDP). Thus, the fate of the most important treaty in recent European history

---

[1] European Monetary Institute (1998). "Convergence Report: Report Required by Article 109j of the Treaty Establishing the European Community," Frankfurt, March 1998; European Commission (1998). "Convergence Report 1998: Prepared in Accordance with Article 109j(1) of the Treaty," Brussels, March 25.

turned on the budgetary status of separate, sovereign nations and the statistical calculation of these figures. Yet how could the Institute's authorities, the Commission, and other European public officials be certain that the criteria had truly been met? Many of the EU countries experienced intense political conflict as they pursued economically constrictive fiscal policies in 1996 and 1997, and success in becoming a first-round EMU member could make or break political careers. Would the EU's political leaders be easily seduced into submitting misleading budgetary figures under these circumstances? In Germany, the politics of the day demanded "drei punkt null" not "drei punkt eins," and if Germany's support for the EMU could be undermined by a tenth of a percent, so too might the entire EMU experiment. Moreover, how could the Institute and Commission decide whether these budgetary data were not only accurate but also consistent and harmonized among the EMU applicant countries? As de Tocqueville's observation regarding the difficulty of comparing the statistics of the United States to those of France suggests, would a 3 percent deficit in Belgium be equivalent to one in Italy or France? How could the Treaty's most politically sensitive provisions be protected from manipulation so that the integrity of the Maastricht process would assure an often skeptical European public, international financial markets, and world press? How, indeed, would EU officials ensure that the member states complied with the Treaty's fiscal convergence criteria? Without credible budgetary statistics, how could Maastricht be enforced?

Although scholars have extensively analyzed the Maastricht Treaty and efforts at member state compliance, the Treaty's critical surveillance procedure itself surprisingly has remained largely unexamined. Instead, much of the academic literature, particularly the scholarship that examines the Treaty's Stage II convergence process assumes that little or no centralized effort was made to ensure that member state compliance occurred in any regulated fashion. Indeed, several analyses of EU member state behavior during the convergence process assume that government compliance with the Maastricht deficit and debt criteria, as in the cases of Italy, Germany, and France resulted largely from "confidence tricks" as well as "emergency measures and budgetary accounting gimmicks."[2] These comments certainly question whether the Maastricht Treaty offered any meaningful influence on member state budgetary policies, and imply that the EU's leadership and the European Commission essentially

---

[2] Vincenzo Chiorazzo and Luigi Spaventa (1999). "The Prodigal Son or a Confidence Trickster? How Italy Got Into EMU," in David Cobham and George Zis (eds.), *From EMS to EMU: 1979 to 1999 and Beyond*. London: Macmillan Press, p. 150; Jurgen von Hagen and Rolf Strauch (1999). "Tumbling Giant: Germany's Experience with the Maastricht Fiscal Criteria," in David Cobham and George Zis (eds.), *From EMS to EMU: 1979 to 1999 and Beyond*. London: Macmillan Press, p. 70. Desmond Dinan writes,

turned a blind eye to the member states, leaving them free to do whatever they desired to comply with the fiscal reference values. They furthermore reflect a lack of understanding about exactly how the Commission evaluated these budgetary and accounting maneuvers.

Another set of assumptions exist about the member states' budgetary figures themselves. The member states' deficits, for example, are said to be easily comprehensible and conveniently interchangeable from one member state to another, due to a deficit being a "clearly recognizable and quantifiable figure." "The figure of the deficit expressed as a percentage of GDP," one scholar noted, "is a relatively easily comparable piece of data."[3] Economists, in particular, have produced a number of formal models assuming that accurate, reliable, and readily accessible information exists about member state deficits in order to theorize about the "optimal" stability pact, the need for "prudent" budgetary margins, and hypothesize about how governments should optimally manage their budget deficits within the Treaty's deficit and debt values.[4] These various assertions, however, raise questions as to whether these budgetary data are indeed conveniently available and easy to interpret.

This book argues that the Maastricht Treaty created a surveillance procedure that proved to be critical, at times decisive, in the making of the EMU by determining which countries gained entry into the EMU. Understanding the

France's creative accounting was successful; Germany's was a failure. The Commission allowed France to apply a huge one-off payment from France Telecom in 1997 against the country's deficit ... Yet whereas the German government had sneakily tried to revalue the Bundesbank's gold reserves in order to meet the convergence criteria, Italy's center-left Olive Tree coalition government had taken such politically courageous steps as introducing tough austerity measures and levying a special tax to help cut the budget deficit.

What Dinan does not explain is how the Commission arrived at its decisions that allowed France to gain from the France Telecom payment or Italy to gain from the eurotax, while rejecting the gold revaluation efforts of Germany, Belgium, and Italy. Desmond Dinan (1999). *Ever Closer Union*. Boulder: Lynne Rienner, pp. 472–3. Alison Watson warns: "Coordination may be needed to ensure standardization of policies among the Member States. For example, 'creative accounting' by Member States (i.e. the shifting of expenditures, revenues, and obligations from one level of government to another) in order to meet the fiscal criteria should be discouraged." Alison M. S. Watson (1997). *Aspects of European Monetary Integration*. New York: St. Martins, p. 124. On the importance of budgetary rules and monitoring, see Vito Tanzi and Ludger Schuknecht (2000). *Public Spending in the 20th Century*, ch. 8. New York: Cambridge University Press.

[3] Alberta Sbragia (2001). "Italy Pays for Europe: Political Leadership, Political Choice, and Institutional Adaptation," in Maria Green Cowles, James Caporaso, and Thomas Risse (eds.), *Transforming Europe*. Ithaca: Cornell University Press, p. 83.

[4] Roel Beetsma and Harald Uhlig (1999). "An Analysis of the Stability and Growth Pact," *Economic Journal*, 109, 546–71; Alessandra Casella (1999). "Tradeable Deficit Permits: Efficient Implementation of the Stability Pact in the European Monetary Union," *Economic Policy*, 29, 323–61; Jorgen Drud Hansen and Jan Guldager Jorgensen (1999). "How to Play Safe in Fiscal Policy Under the Stability and Growth Pact," *European Union Review*, 4, 37–52; Thomas Dalsgaard and Alain de Serres (1999). "Estimating Prudent Budgetary Margins for 11 EU Countries: A Simulated SVAR Model

surveillance activities of Eurostat, an obscure agency in the EC, is the key to answering these questions about how the EU influenced the fiscal policies of the member states, how it created harmonized and credible budgetary data, and how it attempted to control what it regarded as member state budgetary gimmickry. Following the Treaty's delegation of authority for the activation of budgetary surveillance, Eurostat gained unexpected influence over the procedure, particularly during the convergence process leading up to monetary union. Prior to the EMI and EC assessments of member state compliance, Eurostat issued its own top secret report, "Statistics on Convergence Criteria: Assessment by Eurostat."[5] This document, based on Eurostat's collection and analysis of member state budgetary data, provided the authoritative evaluation of whether the applicant countries truly fulfilled the Treaty's budget requirements. More than just confirming budgetary compliance, Eurostat's painfully hard-won reputation for political independence, adherence to professional standards, and transparent decision-making helped to counter fears that the outcome of the fiscal convergence process was predetermined or fraudulently manipulated. Thus, this little-known supranational organization, acting within the sphere of its technical competence, enforced the Maastricht Treaty and helped determine the future of the EMU. An examination of Eurostat, however, extends beyond the March 1998 decision date for determining which member states qualified for EMU membership. The European System of Integrated Economic Accounts (ESA), as administered and interpreted by Eurostat, remains the standard for the excessive deficit procedure and the Stability and Growth Pact, and it is the basis for establishing the short-term financial statistics that are necessary for any future fiscal integration that might occur in the EMU.

The Maastricht Treaty and its surveillance procedure, therefore, significantly advance the pace of institutionalization and Europeanization. First, the Treaty itself extends the series of "grand bargains" agreed to by the member states to further EU political and economic integration. Second, the Treaty empowers the EC to act as the guardian of the Treaty, furthering EU institutionalization by way of its delegated rule-making and rule-interpreting authority. Third, through Eurostat's creation of a information compliance system, these rules extend the dense, embedded network of EU laws and regulations that directly influence the

---

Approach, Economics Department Working Paper 216," OECD, ECO/WKP(99)8; Barry Eichengreen and Charles Wyplosz (1998). "The Stability Pact: More Than a Minor Nuisance?" 26, 67–113; Michael J. Artis and Marco Buti (2001). "Setting Medium-Term Fiscal Targets in the EMU," *Public Finance & Management*, 1, 34–57; Alessandro Missale (2001). "Optimal Debt Management with a Stability and Growth Pact," *Public Finance & Management*, 1, 58–91.

[5] Eurostat (1998a). "Statistics on Convergence Criteria: Assessment by Eurostat," Luxembourg, March 25.

behavior of the member states, set the agenda for future policy discussions, and lock in the member states' policy-makers into transnational society. Fourth, despite significant incentives to seek self-interested rulings on the status of their national deficit and debt levels, the member states themselves identify with the integrity of the procedure, participate in its development, and promote the use of these rules in member state policy-making. Fifth, as a result, the member states are encouraged to comply with EU policies and incorporate EU national accounting rules into domestic practices, thus contributing to Europeanization and EU integration. Focusing on Eurostat, therefore, accomplishes more than simply shedding light on the Maastricht Treaty's little known but crucial surveillance procedure. It expands our understanding of how the member states achieved fiscal convergence, how the actions of the EC continue to influence the budgetary behavior of the member states, and how the Treaty's surveillance procedure for both Stage II economic convergence and Stage III monetary union promotes integration through institutionalization and Europeanization.

As the following sections of this chapter indicate, this study employs principal–agency theory to analyze, first, the delegation of authority from member state principals through the Treaty to surpranational agents to conduct the procedure; second, the dynamic relationships taking place among the parties involved in the surveillance process; and, third, how autonomy and institutional design influence the credibility of the surveillance procedure. Theories on treaty compliance offer a variety of monitoring techniques to assess member state behavior. The Maastricht Treaty itself should be viewed as a macrobudgetary rule, comparable to similar rules enacted in the United States and Japan. These macrobudgetary rules present their own surveillance challenges, given the technical nature of national budgetary accounts and procedures. European integration theories illuminate the broader implications of the Maastricht surveillance procedure. Collectively, these theories raise questions about the nature of delegation, supranational agency rule-making, treaty compliance and enforcement, techniques of surveillance, and EU integration.

1.1   Monitoring, Principal–Agency, and Institutional Autonomy

A defining characteristic of the EU is the delegation of authority from member states to supranational organizations.[6] From any number of theoretical

---

[6] See, for example, Mark A. Pollack (2003). *The Engines of Integration*. New York: Oxford University Press; Mark A. Pollack (1997). "Delegation, Agency, and Agenda Setting in the European Community," *International Organization*, 51(1), 99–134; Mark A. Pollack (2002). "Learning for the Americanists (Again): Theory and Method in the Study of Delegation," *West European Politics*, 25(1), 200–19.

perspectives, one of the most important of these delegated administrative responsibilities is the EC's role as treaty guardian. Both neofunctionalists and intergovernmentalists recognize the special significance of this duty. In neofunctionalist integration theory, the Commission possesses special boundary spanning functions, capabilities, and tasks, including treaty guardianship, all of which promote integration among EU member states. For intergovernmentalists, member states act as the prime-movers and pace-setters for integration, leaving supranational organizations in a distinctly subordinate, if not marginalized status. Yet, intergovernmentalists recognize that for state actors to bargain effectively and create binding agreements among themselves, the Commission's guardianship activities, such as monitoring member state behavior, may at times be useful in providing relevant information to principal state actors.

The unique significance of treaty guardianship, as opposed to other Commission tasks, is reflected in the work of scholars who employ principal-agency theory in the analysis of delegated relations between member state principals and supranational organization agents. Because of the urgency to create credible commitments in the case of treaties, the Commission is hypothesized to be largely autonomous, to the point where the notion of agency is replaced by some theorists with the idea of trusteeship and full institutional independence. Still, from an integovernmentalist, rational understanding of institutional design, member states may still build extensive oversight capabilities into treaties, if not outright controls, to restrict agents, even when the need exists to create credible commitments. These possibilities raise the following questions: What was the nature of the Treaty's delegation to the Commission? Does the Commission act as agent or a truly autonomous trustee in its surveillance duties required by the Maastricht Treaty? Moreover, viewed over time, have the member state principals expanded their controls over the Commission, or has the Commission extended its degree of independence since the initiation of the surveillance procedure? The framework for answering these questions requires a brief review of the relevant elements of principal–agency theory.

The act of EU delegation to supranational organizations takes place because these bureaucratic agents offer their member state principals certain functional benefits and special institutional capabilities that enable the principals to overcome their own administrative deficiencies and information asymmetries. These benefits include the provision of unique political, policy, and technical expertise; the management of supranational programs and regulatory activities; the application of rule-making and rule adjudication skills; and the monitoring, surveillance, and enforcement of treaties. Especially for purposes of treaty guardianship, delegation helps to fulfill the desire of principals to establish the credibility of their policy- and rule-based commitments by way of an independent monitoring and enforcement of actor compliance. Moreover, delegation may serve the interests of the member state principals if they delegate unpopular and politically difficult responsibilities to these agents, rather than absorb the blame themselves. In this way, delegation enables principles to engage in blame-avoidance as well as credit-claiming behavior with their electorates. Hazards exist, however, for a principal when it delegates autonomy to an agent. An agent may possess its own priorities, agendas, bureaucratic imperatives, organizational turf issues, and policy preferences, which can produce action that runs counter to the interests and intent of the principal. This opportunistic behavior, also known as agency loss, takes the form of agency drift and agency slippage, where drift or shirking refers to the agent pursuing its own preferences rather than the principal's, and slippage refers to incentives created by the principal that actually induce the agent to act contrary to the principal's preferences. Agency loss is reinforced by the agent's special technical skills, bureaucratic expertise, and agenda-setting powers that can enable the agent to hide preferences, intent, information, and administrative action from the principal.[7]

These tendencies may be countered by the principal in a variety of ways. The principal may design rules or contracts that specify the nature of the intended delegation, screen potential agents to determine their likely compliance with the contract, conduct oversight hearings, exercise budgetary and auditing control, monitor agent behavior, and impose sanctions and distribute rewards. The political, economic, and administrative price paid by the principal to minimize agency loss, such as setting up a monitoring regime, are known as agency costs. These transaction costs become more expensive as the number of both principals and agents multiply, and as the agent's efforts to avoid these constraints increases. An agent reporting to multiple principles, for example, may be able to play them off against each other, as when the principals issue contradictory and vague rules of behavior. Similarly, the presence of multiple agents increases the

---

[7] D. Roderick Kiewiet and Mathew D. McCubbins (1991). *The Logic of Delegation*. Chicago: University of Chicago Press. On agents seeking autonomy and hierarchical control: Terry Moe (1985). "Control and Feedback in Economic Regulation: The Case of the NLRB," *American Political Science Review*, 79(4), 1094–116; Terry Moe (1987). "An Assessment of the Positive Theory of 'Congressional Dominance,'" *Legislative Studies Quarterly*, 12(4), 475–520; B. Dan Wood (1988). "Principals, Bureaucrats, and Responsiveness in Clean Air Enforcements," *American Political Science Review*, 82(1), 213–34; and the exchange of comments in, Brian J. Cook and B. Dan Wood (1989). "Principal-Agent Models of Political Control of Bureaucracy," *American Political Science Review*, 83(3), 965–78. On adverse selection, see Dirk-Jan Kraan (1996). *Budgetary Decisions*. New York: Cambridge University Press.

principal's monitoring and sanctioning tasks, which favors the agents' ability to avoid detection and punishment. Consequently, though some scholars posit that principals rationally and successfully anticipate agent behavior in the design of institutional rules, there may be an element of contingency and unpredictability in this behavior, due to the agent's own set of incentives and organizational imperatives, and in the sometimes limited ability of principals to control agents. Much of a principal's success in controlling agency drift thus depends upon its prescient anticipation of agency behavior, and the design and structuring of a principal–agency relationship by way of a binding contract. To constrain an agent's behavior, the contract may include the presence of feedback loops and noninstitutional surveillance mechanisms, such as "fire alarm" warnings by interested third parties, the press, and financial capital markets who alert principals to divergent agent behavior. These warnings enable the principal to learn from and then repair the flaws in the institutional design that permit agency drift to occur.[8] The capacity of both the principal and agent to learn from repetition and experience so that they might maximize their relative positions, plays a significant role in the dynamics and evolution of their relationship.

The degree of control the principal seeks to exercise in this relationship, however, depends upon the political responsibilities, functions, and organizational tasks assigned to the agent. In the EU, the member state principals have assigned to the Commission, the European Court of Justice, the European Central Bank, and the European Court of Auditors a variety of tasks, some of which require significant institutional autonomy for them to conduct their duties successfully.[9] Specifically in the case of the Commission, that organization's delegated responsibilities include initiating legislative and policy proposals to the European

---

[8] Mathew D. McCubbins and Thomas Schwartz (1984). "Congressional Oversight Overlooked: Police Patrols Versus Fire Alarms," *American Journal of Political Science*, 2(1), 165–79; Ronald B. Mitchell (1994*b*). "Regime Design Matters: International Oil Pollution and Treaty Compliance," *International Organization*, 48(3), 425–58; Ronald B. Mitchell and Patricia M. Keilbach (2001). "Situation Structure and Institutional Design: Reciprocity, Coercion, and Exchange," *International Organization*, 55(4), 891–917; Mancur Olson (1973). *The Logic of Collective Action*. Cambridge, MA: Harvard University Press. On the rational design of institutions, see Barbara Koremenos, Charles Lipson, and Duncan Snidal (2001). "The Rational Design of International Institutions," *International Organization* 55(4), 761–99, and a response: John S. Duffield (2003). "The Limits of 'Rational Design,' " *International Organization*, 57(3), 411–30.

[9] Jonas Tallberg (2000). "The Anatomy of Autonomy: An Institutional Account of Variation in Supranational Influence," *Journal of Common Market Studies*, 38(5), 843–64; Mark Thatcher (2002). "Delegation to Independent Regulatory Agencies: Pressures, Functions and Contextual Mediation," *West European Politics*, 25(1), 125–47; Robert Elgie (2002). "The Politics of the European Central Bank: Principal-Agent Theory and The Democratic Deficit," *Journal of European Public Policy*, 9(2), 186–200; Mark Thatcher and Alec Stone Sweet (2002). "Theory and Practice of Delegation to Non-Majoritarian Institutions," *West European Politics*, 25(1), 1–22; Jonathan Bendor, A. Glazer, and T. Hammond (2001). "Theories of Delegation," *Annual Review of Political Science*, 4, 235–69; Mark A. Pollack (2002).

Council and European Parliament, managing the EU budget and carrying out EU policies, creating and regulating implementing rules, and serving as the guardian of EU treaties. Although the EU member states delegate authority, they nevertheless exercise control over their agent by retaining final legislative authority, by approving the EU budget, and by imposing the comitological oversight committee system on the Commission's regulatory, management, and rule-making efforts.[10]

Yet, when it comes to its responsibility as the treaty guardian, where the Commission monitors and acts to ensure the member states' compliance with fundamental EU laws, the Commission is presumed to be left relatively autonomous. The member states recognize the guardian function requires institutional freedom if the integrity of these basic rules and the reputations and credibility of the member states are to be preserved. Reputations and credibility are important not only because of the legitimacy and status they confer, but also because damaged reputations and credibility can provoke defensive and even hostile behavior from other actors. The greater the degree of independence and autonomy exercised by a monitoring organization in such a critical role, the more likely it will be perceived as an honest broker, with its analysis and conclusions more likely accepted as legitimate and trustworthy. Similarly, if a monitor's autonomy is compromised, the parties involved may regard its findings with suspicion and doubt, possibly rejecting them altogether, with the resulting lack of trust potentially undermining the agreement binding the parties together in the first place. As Jonas Tallberg observed, "Monitoring of compliance is of limited value if those whose compliance is being monitored in turn control the monitor."[11]

When the Commission carries out its unique treaty guardian functions, which includes the surveillance of member state treaty compliance, Giandomenico Majone suggests that the logic of principal-agency fails to define fully this special relationship with the member states.[12] Rather than

"Learning from the Americanists (Again): Theory and Method in the Study of Delegation," *West European Politics*, 25(1), 200–19; Daniel P. Carpenter (2001). *The Forging of Bureaucratic Autonomy*. Princeton: Princeton University Press; John D. Huber and Charles R. Shipan (2003). *Deliberate Discretion? The Institutional Foundations of Bureaucratic Autonomy*. New York: Cambridge University Press.

[10] Alexander Ballmann, David Epstein, and Sharyn O'Halloran (2002). "Delegation, Comitology, and the Separation of Powers in the European Union," *International Organization*, 56(3), 551–74; Thomas Christiansen and Emil Kirchner (eds.) (2000). *Europe in Change: Committee Governance in the European Union*. Manchester: Manchester University Press.

[11] Jonas Tallberg (2002a). "Delegation to Supernational Institutions: Why, How, and with What Consequences?" *West European Politics*, 25(1), 23–46, p. 29.

[12] Giandomenico Majone (2001). "Two Logics of Delegation: Agency and Fiduciary Relations in EU Governance," *European Union Politics*, 2(1), 103–22.

acting as an simple agent, the Commission behaves and is treated as a trustee; it assumes something resembling a fiduciary responsibility on behalf of its member state principals. In this sense, a complete transfer of full delegational authority, autonomy, and political independence takes place from the principal to the trustee, especially in those cases where the principal is incapable or unable to manage its affairs, or when, because of overt and obvious conflicts of interest, it is inappropriate for it to do so.

Thus, principal-agency theory sheds light on the dynamics of hierarchical relationships between member state principals and supranational EU organizations. What remains to be seen is the exact nature of those relationships. In the case of the Maastricht Treaty, does the Commission, which for purposes of Stage II convergence effectively means Eurostat, serve as an agent or a trustee? What is the extent of its authority? What is the nature of its relationship with the member states? Furthermore, principal-agency relationships are dynamic rather than static in nature. Principals and agents both learn from and adapt to each in what appears to be an ongoing struggle for control and autonomy. So, as the convergence process develops in Stage II from 1994 through 1998, how, if at all, do principals and agents attempt to extend oversight on the one hand, and agency preferences on the other? How is this struggle played out in the context of treaty surveillance? To answer these questions, it is important to understand in greater detail the theoretical issues surrounding the processes and techniques of treaty monitoring and compliance.

1.2   Treaty Monitoring and Macrobudgetary Surveillance Techniques

The techniques and challenges of Eurostat's monitoring of the member states' budgetary status are perhaps best understood by international relations scholars who study treaty construction, and the intimate relationship between monitoring and treaty compliance.[13] Ronald Mitchell offers a reasonable definition

---

[13] Oran R. Young (1979). *Compliance and Public Authority*. Baltimore: Johns Hopkins University Press; Abram Chayes and Antonia Handler Chayes (1991). "Compliance Without Enforcement: State Behavior Under Regulatory Treaties," *Negotiation Journal*, 7(3), 311–30; Abram Chayes and Antonia Handler Chayes (1993). "On Compliance," *International Organization*, 47(2), 175–201; Abram Chayes and Antonia Handler Chayes (1995). *The New Sovereignty: Compliance with International Regulatory Agreements*. Cambridge, MA: Harvard University Press; Petros C. Mavroidis (1992). "Surveillance Schemes: The GATT's New Trade Policy Review Mechanism," *Michigan Journal of International Law*, 13(2), 374–414; Ronald B. Mitchell (1994a). *International Oil Pollution at Sea: Environmental Policy and Treaty Compliance*. Cambridge, MA: MIT Press; Nancy W. Gallagher (1999). *The Politics of Verification*. Baltimore: Johns Hopkins University Press; George W. Downs, David M. Rocke, and Peter N. Barsoom (1996). "Is the Good News About Compliance Good News About Cooperation?"

of compliance as "an actor's behavior that conforms to a treaty's explicit rules."[14] From a realist perspective, treaties are imposed by hegemonic states and it is in their interest to promote a working monitoring and verification process so that they are informed of whether relatively less powerful states are compliant. From a neoliberal perspective, treaties are pluralistically collaborative efforts, where the monitoring and verification of compliance validates a state's conformity to shared group member goals, and by way of this validation a state may truly claim credit in both the domestic and international arenas for its actions.[15] Furthermore, viewed from both perspectives, the act of verification of compliance or noncompliance usually initiates a treaty's formal reward and punishment provisions, and in this way compliance itself is encouraged when an actor state's behavior is monitored and verified. In the case of the Maastricht Treaty, verification of compliance effectively determined EMU membership and noncompliance sets in motion the sanctioning provisions of the Treaty and the Stability and Growth Pact.

Verification, however, ultimately depends upon a treaty's monitoring and oversight process. These processes may vary tremendously as to their transparency, information requirements, number of state and extra-state actors involved, independence of the monitoring authority, and extent of actor state self-monitoring. Although treaties may provide for some form of an actor state's self-report of behavior, the claim of compliance is most compelling and believable when verification is performed in some independent fashion. This means that the actor state's behavior is observed and the information required for verification is gathered by some, and perhaps several, external and independent

International Organization, 50(3), 379–406; Xinyuan Dai (1998*b*). "International Institutions, Domestic Constituencies and Compliance with Environmental Agreements," "International Institutions and National Compliance: The Domestic Constituency Mechanism," and "Information Systems of Treaty Regimes," unpublished manuscripts, University of Chicago; Peter M. Haas (1998). "Compliance with EU Directives: Insights from International Relations and Comparative Politics," *Journal of European Public Policy*, 5(1), 17–37; John Setear (1997). "An Iterative Perspective on Treaties: A Synthesis of International Relations Theory and International Law," *Harvard International Law*, 37, 139–230; John Setear (1997). "Responses to Breach of Treaty and Rationalist International Relations Theory: The Rules of Release and Remediation in the Law of Treaties and the Law of State Responsibility," *Virginia Law Review*, 83, 1–126; Douglass C. North (1990). *Institutions, Institutional Change and Economic Performance*. New York: Cambridge University Press; Elinor Ostrom (1990). *Governing the Commons*. New York: Cambridge University Press.

[14] Ronald B. Mitchell (1993). "Compliance Theory: A Synthesis," *Review of European Community and Institutional Environmental Law*, 2(4), 327–34, p. 328.

[15] Arild Underal (1998). "Explaining Compliance and Defection: Three Models," *European Journal of International Relations*, 4(1) 5–30; Beth A. Simmons (1998). "Compliance with International Agreements," *Annual Review of Political Science*, 1, 75–93; Beth A. Simmons (2000). "International Law and State Behavior: Commitment and Compliance in International Monetary Affairs," *American Political Science Review*, 94(4), 819–35.

monitors. Mitchell refers to this monitoring as a "compliance information system," which "consists of the actors, rules and processes that collect, analyze and disseminate information on violation and compliance."[16]

Mitchell identifies two reasons for creating such systems. Treaties employ them, first, to determine the presence of "effectiveness-oriented" behavior, which measures how effective the collective group members' actions are at achieving regime goals. In this case, data collection is usually of a collective or cumulative nature, is used for general information purposes, and poses relatively little threat to a particular state. Consequently, the incentive for state cooperation with the monitoring system is generally positive and the state's willingness to provide accurate self-reported data is high. Under these least contentious of circumstances, the differences between parties and conflicts of interests are far less fundamental, and differences are resolved by appealing to norms, shared principles, and processes, without resorting to the enforcement of group cohesion and member compliance by an external or central actor imposing sanctions.[17]

The second purpose Mitchell identifies is ascertaining the presence of "compliance-oriented" behavior, which determines whether an individual group member complies with the collective's treaty goals. In this case, the data collected by the compliance information system are employed as part of a process

---

[16] Mitchell (1993). "Compliance Theory: A Synthesis," *Review of European Community and Institutional Environmental Law*, 2(4), 330. Also, Ronald B. Mitchell (1998). "Sources of Transparency: Information Systems in International Regimes," *International Studies Quarterly*, 42, 109–30.

[17] Duncan Snidal (1985). "Coordination Versus Prisoners' Dilemma: Implications for International Cooperation and Regimes," *American Political Science Review*, 79(4), 923–42, p. 932. Snidal cites as an example of a nonconfrontational coordination game, the "standardization of measurement systems," where "any role for centralized authority in coordination problems is less likely to be less concerned with enforcement than with codification and elaboration of an existing or latent convention and with providing information and communication to facilitate the smooth operation of the convention." This "standardization of measurement systems" describes a common, yet critical administrative task in the creation of monitoring and inspection regimes. This is certainly true for the Maastricht Treaty. Consequently, as Snidal acknowledges, differences of opinion and interest may occur in developing such codes of standardization, to the point that the interaction among parties may come to resemble that of a more contentious collective action game. "Cooperation [among parties] in the coordination game depends upon the surrounding social-political context . . . .This provides a significant insight to the nature of coordination games," as "coordination is a fundamentally different problem when viewed in the small than when viewed in the large." (p. 932) In other words, when viewed "in the large," the Commission's delegated authority in its treaty guardian role reflects institutional autonomy, trusteeship, and the cooperative coordination of interests. Yet, within the actual administration of the surveillance process itself, what Snidal would label "in the small," there may exist significant political and bureaucratic differences. These differences, in turn, influence the creation, interpretation, and application of the rules employed in the monitoring and enforcing of EU treaties. Also see Robert H. Bates (1988). "Contra Contractarianism: Some Reflections on the New Institutionalism," *Politics & Society*, 16(2–3), 387–401.

of imposing sanctions for state noncompliance. As a result, the level of coopera-tion and the quality and integrity of self-reports are likely to be low, while differ-ences over technical standards, methods of data collection, and data analysis will be great. These conflicts stem from the intrinsic asymmetric information prob-lems and the resulting tensions that often occur between the monitor who col-lects and analyzes data, and the entity being monitored that provides self-reported data. As the number of actors in the collective increases, so too does the difficulty of overcoming these asymmetries of information. Surveillance becomes more difficult and the likelihood of imposing appropriate sanctions to collect necessary data increases. The Maastricht Treaty clearly falls in Mitchell's second category, yet in both the effectiveness and compliance models a state's willingness to cooperate with the monitoring system is a function of its incen-tives to cooperate, the value of the collected information for its own purposes, its capacity to cooperate, and the quality of the system itself.

There are two broad and contrasting schools of thought about how best to achieve treaty compliance through monitoring. The first, labeled the "mana-gerial school," claims that high rates of treaty compliance are possible without relying upon sanctions for noncompliant behavior. When it occurs, noncom-pliance stems from the lack of precise rules that outline the terms of the treaty, as well as deficiencies in a political actor's institutional, administrative, and economic capacities. To remedy these problems, Chayes and Chayes contend that compliance rates may be improved through rule clarification, building institutional capacity, and the selection of effective policies rather than the application of sanctions. Monitoring plays a central role in this approach because it identifies when rule clarification is necessary and noncompliance results less from willful behavior than institutional incapacity. When moni-tors encounter problems in gathering data and information for purposes of verifying state behavior, these problems, too, stem from the lack of clarity in data requirements and state capacity.[18]

The second approach, known as the "enforcement school," is based upon rationalist assumptions of solving collective action problems through monitoring and the application of sanctions to induce compliance. Downs, Rocke, and Barsoom challenge the idea that "deep" treaty compliance com-monly occurs without the actual application or at least threat of imposing

---

[18] For an example of the management school of compliance, see Abram Chayes and Antonia Handler Chayes (1991). "Compliance Without Enforcement: State Behavior Under Regulatory Treaties," *Negotiation Journal*, 7(3), 311–30; Abram Chayes and Antonia Handler Chayes (1993). "On Compliance," *International Organization*, 47(2), 175–201; Abram Chayes and Antonia Handler Chayes (1995). *The New Sovereignty: Compliance with International Regulatory Agreements*. Cambridge, MA: Harvard University Press.

sanctions.[19] Monitoring provides participants with the necessary information on compliant and noncompliant behavior, which helps determine when to apply sanctions. Consequently, monitoring and verification may very well be a contentious process, requiring sanctions by monitors to collect necessary data. This fits the case of the Maastricht Treaty, where a member state's "compliance-oriented" behavior towards the Treaty's "convention" is determined through the codification and statistical analysis of harmonized economic and budgetary data.

What these theories indicate is that when compliance-oriented behavior is under scrutiny, monitoring will be a contentious and arduous task, with the enforcement and managerial schools of compliance recommending competing strategies of sanctioning in contrast to capacity building and rule clarification. These strategies, however, may come together in the case of the EC's role as treaty guardian. Tallberg hypothesizes that the EU fuses the managerial and enforcement schools, as both capacity building and the application of sanctions are common attributes of the EU's compliance efforts.[20] The Commission, for example, builds institutional capacity by clarifying treaty rules and providing bureaucratic assistance and administrative training to the member states, but it also monitors treaties and applies sanctions, with the aid of the European Court of Justice, against transgressing member states. Thus, another set of questions raised about the Maastricht Treaty's surveillance procedure is whether its monitoring process reflects the managerial approach, the enforcement approach, or some combination of the two, and, if so, how? How might Eurostat apply sanctions against member states, and how does it build institutional capacity while clarifying the Treaty's rules for harmonizing budgetary statistics? How do the member states participate and respond to this surveillance? What, in fact, are the difficulties the Commission faces in conducting this surveillance of the member states' budgetary activities?

1.2.1   Compliance Information Systems and Macrobudgetary Rules

The significance of compliance information systems and the challenges they confront when monitoring government budgets may be better understood when examined in the institutional context of what students of budgeting and

---

[19] For an example of the enforcement school, see George W. Downs, David M. Rocke, and Peter N. Barsoom (1996). "Is the Good News About Compliance Good News About Cooperation?" *International Organization*, 50(3), 379–406.

[20] Jonas Tallberg (2002). "Paths to Compliance: Enforcement, Management, and the European Union," *International Organization*, 56(3), 609–43.

economic policy describe as "macrobudgetary rules." Throughout the 1980s and 1990s, many of the industrial democracies coped with rising budget deficits by adopting similar institutional reforms, including the enacting of overarching rules that imposed deficit, debt, and spending restrictions on their budgetary processes.[21] In the United States, as shown in Table 1.1, these macrobudgetary

Table 1.1 Macrobudgetary rules of the United States, Japan, and the EU

	United States	Japan	European Union
Rules	Gramm–Rudman–Hollings—1985 and 1987 Budget Enforcement Act—1990 Balanced Budget Act—1997	Fiscal Structural Reform Act—1997	Maastricht Treaty—1992
Budgetary goals	Combination of deficit and balanced budget targets/ Expenditure caps/ PAYGO requirements	Deficit and debt targets	Deficit and debt targets
Spending restrictions	Multi-year spending caps	Multi-year programmatic spending limits	None
Budgetary coverage	Applies to central government	Applies to central government	Applies to combined central and local governments of each EU member
Monitoring agents	For GRH: GAO/OMB/CBO For BEA: CBO/OMB For BBA: CBO/OMB	Ministry of Finance/Board of Audit	European Commission/ European Monetary Institute
Sanctions	Sequester	None specified	EMU membership denied/Stability Pact financial penalties

[21] In response to their fiscal imbalances, government budgetary processes became more centralized, "top down," and "front loaded" to reduce the influence of interest groups and budgetary claimants. Macrobudgetary rules and guidelines set at the beginning of the budgetary process constrained micro-decisions undertaken throughout the remainder of the process. Governments employed hard targets, spending ceilings, and caps to limit spending; calculated long-term inflationary and program costs through baseline budgeting; created new legislative committees and support agencies to provide spending and cost information to decision-makers; enacted budget resolutions and reconciliation devices to control entitlements and social provisions; and strengthened the powers of finance ministers to constrain spending decisions. Budget balanced and deficit control reasserted

laws included the Balanced Budget and Emergency Deficit Control Act of 1985, better known as Gramm–Rudman–Hollings, the Budget Enforcement Act of 1990, and the Balanced Budget Act of 1997. The Japanese enacted the Fiscal Structural Reform Act of 1997, and the EU adopted the Maastricht Treaty. These rules provide for treaty- or statute-based budgetary goals expressed in terms of deficit and debt limitations. The Maastricht Treaty and the Structural Reform Act, for example, set deficit spending constraints at 3 percent of GDP, as the Japanese explicitly borrowed the Europeans' goal for their own law.[22] The

themselves not only as norms, but, more importantly, governments codified these norms in the form of macrobudgetary rules, reformed institutional procedures, and redesigned institutional arrangements. On these institutional changes and reforms, see: James Poterba (1994). "State Responses to Fiscal Crisis: The Effects of Budgetary Institutions and Politics," *Journal of Political Economy* 102, 799–821; James Poterba (1995). "Balanced Budget Rules and Fiscal Policy: Evidence for the States," *National Tax Journal*, 48, 329–36; James Poterba (1996). "Budget Institutions and Fiscal Policy in the U.S. States," *American Economic Review*, 86, 395–400; James Poterba and Jurgen von Hagen (1999). *Fiscal Institutions and Fiscal Performance*. Chicago: University of Chicago Press; Jurgen von Hagen and I. J. Harden (1994). "National Budget Processes and Fiscal Performance," *European Economic Reports and Studies*, 3, 311–408; Rolf R. Strauch and Jurgen von Hagen (2000). *Institutions, Politics and Fiscal Policy*. Dordrecht: Kluwer Academic Publishers; Aaron Wildavsky (1980). *How to Limit Government Spending*. Berkeley: University of California Press; Aaron Wildavsky and Larry R. Jones (1994). "Budgetary Control in a Decentralized System: Meeting the Criteria for the Fiscal Stability in the European Union," *Public Budgeting & Finance*, 14, 7–22; Aaron Wildavsky and Eduardo Zipico-Goni (eds.) (1993). *National Budgeting for Economic and Monetary Union*. Dordrecht: Martinus Nijhoff; Jurgen von Hagen (1991). "A Note on the Empirical Effectiveness of Formal Fiscal Restraints," *Journal of Public Economics*, 44, 199–210; Allen Schick (1983). "Incremental Budgeting in a Decremental Age," *Policy Sciences*, 16, 1–25; Allen Schick (1986). "Macro-Budgetary Adaptations to Fiscal Stress in Industrialized Democracies," *Public Administration Review*, 46, 124–34; Allen Schick (1988). "Micro-Budgetary Adaptations to Fiscal Stress in Industrialized Democracies," *Public Administration Review*, 48, 523–33; Allen Schick (1990). "Budgeting for Results: Recent Developments in Five Industrial Countries," *Public Administration Review*, 50(1), 26–34; and James D. Savage (2001). "Budgetary Collective Action Problems: Convergence and Compliance Under the Maastricht Treaty on European Union," *Public Administration Review*, 61(1), 43–53.

[22] The Japanese MOF drafted the Structural Reform Act based upon its understanding of the Maastricht formula, which was that the way to determine the deficit target was to multiply the debt as percent of GDP figure by the estimated GDP growth rate. In 1997, Japan's debt stood at 90 percent of GDP and the estimated growth rate for that year was 3 percent. Multiplied together, the result was 2.7 percent, which when rounded out at 3 percent became the deficit target employed in the act. Remarkably, Canada, too, adopted Maastricht's 3 percent deficit goal, but in a more informal manner. The deficit target served as an internal guideline for the MOF during the drafting of its 1994–8 budgets, when at last the Canadians successfully brought their 1998 budget into surplus. Thus, the deficit target never became a formal law, and is therefore not shown in Table 1.1, which outlines the macrobudgetary rule provisions for the remaining Group of Seven nations and the EU. The Canadians never bothered with a formula; their borrowing of the Maastricht target was strictly a matter of politics and convenience. The target was first identified in the fiscal policy chapter of the Liberal Party's 1993 platform, and it was borrowed, as one Canadian observer put it, "off the rack." Clearly, there was never any technical or economic consideration as to the target's specific applicability for Canada's economy. "It was," recalled former Deputy Finance Minister C. Scott Clark, "very much a political choice." Prime Minister Jean Chrétien made the connection with Maastricht explicit, Clark

Americans and the Japanese imposed spending restrictions in the form of multi-year spending caps and multi-year programmatic spending limits. Furthermore, each of these macrobudgetary rules specified the scope of their budgetary coverage, with the Maastricht Treaty encompassing a broader definition of the levels of government affected by the rules. The rules also created monitoring units to develop compliance information systems to verify whether the state actors fulfilled the terms of the macrobudgetary rule. In the American and European cases, this verification triggered the application of appropriate sanctions.[23] When its system is disabled, the macrobudgetary law itself may be critically compromised.

Consider, briefly, the failure of the Americans' Gramm–Rudman–Hollings law. That law required the Congressional Budget Office (CBO) and the Office of Management and Budget (OMB) to take "snapshots" or estimates of the deficit, and report to the General Accounting Office (GAO) the amount of variation from that year's deficit target. The GAO, in turn, reviewed and certified these estimates and, if necessary, initiated sanctions, which took the form of across-the-board budgetary "sequesters" or cuts. Yet, the law itself encouraged "fakery" and "rosy scenarios," as it excluded nearly 70 percent of expenditures from sequestration and it incorporated a $10 billion "cushion" above the deficit target, thereby limiting the threat that punitive sequesters would be activated. What crippled the law, however, was the Supreme Court's ruling that the GAO's role was unconstitutional, as the law required that a legislative

noted, when, after coming to power, Chrétien declared, "This is what they are doing in Europe, and this is a good basis for us in Canada." Interview with Scott C. Clark, April 23, 2001. Remarkably, neither the Japanese nor the Canadians actually contacted the EU to determine how well the deficit targets worked for the EU. Another fascinating feature of the 3 percent deficit target was that the idea for it originated in France in 1982 while Jacques Delors was finance minister, then it became incorporated into the Maastricht Treaty, and later it spread to the Japanese and Canadians, without much consideration as to whether what made sense in France in the early 1980s also applied to these other countries.

[23] The lack of sanctions in the Japanense law may reflect that this type of budgetary rule truly is unique in Japan's modern history. The 1997 Act produced the first major changes in the Japanese budgetary process since the 1947 Finance Law, which was created under American supervision during the occupation. In addition to the deficit target, the law for the first time introduced multi-year programmatic spending caps and targets into the process, rather than relying upon annual, incremental budgeting. Perhaps because this type of law was something of an experiment for the Japanese and especially for the MOF, and because it was adopted in the midst of a recession, leaving the Japanese unsure as to their ability to comply fully with its demands, the law lacked the more powerful sanctions of its European and American counterparts. For background on the 1997 law, see James D. Savage (2000). "A Decade of Deficits and Debt: Japanese Fiscal Policy and the Rise and Fall of the Structural Reform Act of 1997," *Public Budgeting & Finance*, 20(1), 96–112. On the 1947 law, see James D. Savage (2002). "The Origins of Budgetary Preferences: The Dodge Line and the Balanced Budget Norm in Japan," *Administration & Society*, 34(3), 261–84.

branch agency assume an executive branch function, thus violating the Constitution's separation of powers. As a result, the Court's decision excluded GAO from the monitoring process. Without the honest broker monitoring role played by the politically independent GAO, the budgetary snapshots proved to be untrustworthy and the sequester was activated only when politically agreeable to the executive branch. The law's failure to produce balanced budgets only intensified public skepticism towards the entire budgetary process.[24]

Extensive budgetary compliance information systems are necessary, for as observers of budgetary politics have long noted, politicians and bureaucrats are experts at avoiding the very macrobudgetary rules they create. They develop rosy scenarios, where revenues are exaggerated, expenditures minimized, or economic projections distorted. They engage in "strategic misrepresentation," the use of endless accounting tricks and fakery in the calculation and classification of budget categories.[25] To evade or manipulate their own budgeting constraints, governments create special taxing districts with their own powers to raise revenues and spend money, they rely upon nonguaranteed borrowing and off-budget spending, they employ capital budgets to accommodate higher spending levels, they borrow from pension funds, shift tax collection and expenditure dates, and extend fiscal years beyond the normal calendar. In response, governments typically employ a variety of surveillance techniques for verifying the integrity of budgetary data and compliance with budgetary rules. These techniques have long been considered by public administration scholars as a form of organizational control, and by legislative studies experts as oversight. They include legislative and external agency review, public hearings, accounting, auditing, program evaluation, and a reliance on such informal information sources as the media, interest groups, and back-channeled information leaks.[26]

---

[24] On the cynicism created by Gramm–Rudman–Hollings, see Joseph White and Aaron Wildavsky (1989). *The Deficit and the Public Interest*, chs. 19–22. Berkeley: University of California Press.

[25] On budgetary gimmickry, see Joseph White and Aaron Wildavsky (1980). *The Deficit and the Public Interest*, chs. 19–22. Berkeley: University of California Press; Larry R. Jones and K. J. Euske (1991). "Strategic Misrepresentation in Budgeting," *Journal of Public Administration Research and Theory*, 4, 437–60; Roy Meyers (1994). *Strategic Budgeting*. Ann Arbor: University of Michigan Press.

[26] An example of classic public administration literature where budgets and auditing are employed by the center to control the periphery is Herbert Kaufman (1960). *The Forest Ranger: A Study in Administrative Behavior*. Baltimore: Johns Hopkins University Press. Also, Peter M. Blau and W. Richard Scott (1962). *Formal Organizations*. Scranton: Chandler, esp. chs. 6 and 7. On legislative oversight, Morris Ogul (1976). *Congress Oversees the Bureaucracy*. Pittsburgh: University of Pittsburgh Press. For an example of auditing and accounting used as control devices in a principal-agency relationship, see Jonathan Bendor, Serge Taylor, and Roland Van Gaalen (1985). "Bureaucratic Expertise Versus Legislative Authority: A Model of Deception and Monitoring in Budgeting," *American Political Science*

These theories on treaty compliance offer insight into the techniques of monitoring. Eurostat may employ some or all of these techniques in its budgetary surveillance of the member states. Yet, which are used and to what effect? How intrusive must the Commission be in a member state's budgetary affairs to determine its degree of compliance? Furthermore, how might Eurostat's rule-making authority to harmonize budgetary data influence member state budgetary activities and administrative practices, in ways that further European integration? To answer this last question, which addresses how the Commission's surveillance function promotes EU integration, it is important to consider integration theory in greater detail.

1.3   EU Integration: Institutionalization and Europeanization

1.3.1   Institutionalization

Theories of European integration are commonly divided into neofunctionalist and intergovernmental schools of thought. Amy Verdun, for example, identifies at least thirteen theories that she locates along a neofunctionalist and intergovernmental continuum, based on two considerations. As expected, the neofunctionalist end of the continuum reflects theories that emphasize the significance, if not primacy, of supranational and non-state actors in leading integration. These theories generally view the process of integration as one stemming from the automatic spillover effects from one functional policy arena to the next, often in a deliberate path-dependent fashion. The intergovernmentalist end of the continuum, by contrast, locates theories that look to states as the dominant force behind integration, and consider integration to be a more indeterminate and unpredictable process. Verdun notes that one of the more recent and prominent theoretical efforts to combine neofunctionalism and intergovernmentalism is Alexander Stone Sweet and Wayne Sandholtz's conception of institutionalization.[27]

Review, 79(4), 1041–60. Lindner warns, however, that not all scholars are equally sensitive to the need for data control and monitoring. He notes, "In their model von Hagen/Harden do not discuss the institutional details of the micro-execution of budget-lines and subsequent auditing methods, but focus exclusively on the budgetary decision-making process and the ability of actors to reverse budgetary decisions in the implementation stage." Johannes Lindner (2001). "Linking Institutions with Outcomes: An Institutionalist Assessment of the EU Budgetary Procedure," paper for the ECSA Seventh Biennial International Conference, May 31–June 2, p. 4.

[27] Amy Verdun (2002). "Merging Neofunctionalism and Intergovernmentalism: Lessons from EMU," in Amy Verdun (ed.), *The Euro: European Integration Theory and Economic and Monetary Union*. New York: Rowman & Littlefield, pp. 9–28; For other reviews of integration theories, see Ben Rosamond (2000). *Theories of European Integration*. New York: St. Martin's Press; and Kenneth Dyson

Institutionalization refers to the ongoing movement towards supranational governance as a consequence of the growing embeddedness and expansion of EU rules that constrain and guide member state behavior. The rise of supranational authority, as exercised by such institutions as the Commission, the European Court of Justice, the European Central Bank, and the European Court of Auditors, stems from the delegated authority member states grant to these and other EU organizations because they provide unique and beneficial collective gains to the member state principals. Stone Sweet and Sandholtz posit that the central, animating collective gain sought is the reduction in transaction costs generated by the increase in cross-border economic activity and communications. These transaction costs include "customs and other border controls, differing technical standards, divergent health and environmental regulations, distinct systems of commercial law, diverse national currencies, and so on."[28] These costs, in turn, are significantly mitigated by the transnational policies pursed by the EU's supranational organizations to harmonize and set standards, provide dispute resolution mechanisms, and regulate economic and other activity. Each of these integrating and institutionalizing activities is largely realized by the creation and clarification of rules. The greater the level of transborder activity, the greater the need and demand for such rules to resolve conflict and ambiguity among the member states. The states, to be sure, also play key roles in this dynamic of rule-based EU institutionalization.[29] Particularly when creating the grand bargains of EU treaties, member states engage in interstate negotiation and delegate supranational agency and autonomy. The degree of delegated autonomy and trusteeship increases as these supranational organizations engage in their regulatory oversight, judicial review, and treaty guardianship functions, each of which requires the institutional capacity to monitor behavior and apply

(2002). "Introduction: EMU as Integration, Europeanization, and Convergence," in Kenneth Dyson (ed.), *European States and the Euro*. New York: Oxford University Press, pp. 1–30. On institutionalization, see Wayne Sandholtz and Alec Stone Sweet (eds.) (1998). *European Integration and Supranational Governance*. New York: Oxford University Press; and Alec Stone Sweet, Wayne Sandholtz, and Neil Fligstein (eds.) (2001). *The Institutionalization of Europe*. New York: Oxford University Press.

[28] Alec Stone Sweet and Wayne Sandholtz (1998). "Integration, Supranational Governance, and the Institutionalization of the European Polity," in Wayne Sandholtz and Alec Stone Sweet (eds.), *European Integration and Supranational Governance*. New York: Oxford University Press, p. 11. Also see Alec Stone Sweet, Wayne Sandholtz, and Neil Fligstein (eds.) (2001). *The Institutionalization of Europe*. New York: Oxford University Press.

[29] On the intergovernmentalist interpretation of integration, see Andrew Moravcsik (1998). *The Choice for Europe*. Ithaca: Cornell University Press; and Andrew Moravcsik (1999). "A New Statecraft? Supranational Entrepreneurs and International Cooperation," *International Organization*, 53(2), 267–306.

sanctions to promote compliance with EU rules. Consequently, the following dynamic emerges:

As supranational organizations acquire and wield autonomy, they are able to shape not only specific policy outcomes but also the rules that channel policymaking behaviors. As supranational organizations and rules emerge and solidify, they constitute transnational society by establishing the bases for interaction and access points for influencing policy. As transnational society endures and expands, the organizations and rules that structure behaviors become more deeply rooted as "givens," taken for granted as defining political life.[30]

In this sense, then, institutionalization consolidates neofunctionalist and intergovernmental interpretations of integration, even as it reflects a path-dependent, historical institutionalist mode of development where contingent historical choices become locked in and self-reinforcing.[31] Thus, at critical historical moments, the grand bargains created by self-interested member states lead to the rise of these rule-creating, sometimes highly autonomous supranational organizations. The "rootedness" that emerges from their rules, begins, in turn, to influence and set the agenda for future grand bargains, locking Europe into a path of increasing integration.

This understanding of institutionalization raises several questions about how the Commission's surveillance procedure promotes integration. What is the nature of the Commission's delegated authority? Eurostat, acting as the EU's supranational agent, should be able to trace its delegated responsibilities to the grand bargains that serve as the EU's ultimate source of authority. In order for it to advance institutionalization, do Eurostat's activities add to the body of supranational rules? These rules should contribute to the resolution of cross-border differences, which, for purposes of determining compliance with the Treaty, means harmonizing and resolving technical variations in the

---

[30] Stone Sweet and Sandholtz (1998). "Integration, Supranational Governance, and the Institutionalization of the European Policy," in Wayne Sandholtz and Alec Stone Sweet (eds.), *European Integration and Supranational Governance*. New York: Oxford University press, p. 11.

[31] On path dependency and historical institutionalism, see James Mahoney (2000). "Path Dependence in Historical Sociology," *Theory and Society*, 29, 507–48; Paul Pierson (2000). "Increasing Returns, Path Dependence, and the Study of Politics," *American Political Science Review*, 94(2), 251–67; Paul Pierson (1998). "The Path to European Integration: A Historical-Institutionalist Analysis," in Wayne Sandholtz and Alec Stone Sweet (eds.), *European Integration and Supranational Governance*. New York: Oxford University Press, pp. 27–58; and Paul Pierson and Theda Skocpol (2000). "Historical Institutionalism in Contemporary Political Science," in Ira Katznelson and Helen V. Milner (eds.), *Political Science: The State of the Discipline*. New York: W. W. Norton & Company, pp. 693–721.

calculation of budgetary deficits and debt. Do these rules further contribute to the sense of "rootedness" that helps lock-in the behavior of member states, at least in the technical areas of Eurostat's responsibilities?

1.3.2 Europeanization

Coinciding with EU institutionalization is the integrating process of Europeanization.[32] Europeanization refers to the influence and effect of EU formal rules, procedures, regulations, and practices on the member states' political institutions and public policies, which are reinforced by informal policy networks, organizational cultures, and personal relationships. These pathways of Europeanization are initially activated by formal requirements. Particularly noteworthy among these requirements are the grand bargains of EU treaties, as well as "legal practices, rulings of the European Court of Justice, EU directives and policy mandates." This "downloading" of "a European model" consisting of EU rules, principles, norms, and "integration through law," reflects hierarchical "top-down" adaptational pressures on the member states.[33] Rational incentives on the one hand, and constructivist institutional socialization and learning on the other, often work together simultaneously to promote the acceptance of EU practices and preferences. In this way, over time, member state elites themselves begin to learn new roles, identities, and interests, and adopt and incorporate EU rules and norms into domestic practices, policies, and institutions, thereby furthering the rate of Europeanization.

Member states vary, of course, in terms of their degree of Europeanization. Where EU rules and practices prove to be incompatible or run counter to domestic policies and institutions, adaptational pressures experienced by the member states will be more intense, causing them to be more resistant and noncompliant. These conditions reflect a "misfit" occurring between the member state and the EU. By comparison, when domestic preferences coincide or easily "fit" with those of the EU, both the degree of adaptational pressure and the cost of compliance will be relatively low, leaving the member states more willing and able to comply with EU rules.

---

[32] On Europeanization, see Maria Green Cowles, James Caporaso, and Thomas Risse (eds.) (2001). *Transforming Europe: Europeanization and Domestic Change.* Ithaca: Cornell University Press, esp. Thomas Risse, Maria Green Cowles, and James Caporaso, "Europeanization and Domestic Change: Introduction," pp. 1–20. Also, Gerda Falkner (1999). "Interest Groups in a Multi-Level Polity: The Impact of European Integration on National Systems," Robert Schuman Centre for Advanced Studies, EUI Working Paper RSC 99/34.

[33] Kenneth Featherstone and Claudio M. Radaelli (eds.) (2003). *The Politics of Europeanization.* New York: Oxford University Press.

For some scholars, the force of Europeanization's influence on a member state is only truly tested when initial policy or institutional misfits occur. As Borzel and Risse note, "In brief, misfit and resulting adaptational pressures constitute the starting point for any causal mechanism discussed in the literature. . . . Policy misfits essentially equal compliance problems."[34] The member states' own constraints in terms of domestic institutional arrangements and structures, administrative capacity, leadership, policy styles, preferences, and resources, and cognitive and normative frameworks, all affect their degree of fitness or misfitness with Europeanization. Furthermore, to be effective, Europeanization must occur at the administrative as well as the member states' macro institutional level. According to Knill, studies of Europeanization take into account agency-based "embedded core patterns of national administrations."[35] Europeanization is more likely to be successful when adaptational pressures complement rather than challenge these core patterns, which include organizational practices, rules, traditions, and cultures. Radaelli notes that at least four possible reactions to Europeanization are possible, including member state transformation, absorption, inertia, and retrenchment.[36] Transformative change is equivalent to systemic or fundamental alterations in member states' institutions or policies; absorption reflects member state accommodation without transformation, particularly in circumstances where adaptive pressures prove to be relatively minimal; inertia refers to a lack of change stemming from significant misfit between the member state and the EU; and retrenchment refers to member state response where divergence in behavior and outcomes rather than convergence is promoted due to extreme misfitting conditions.

These responses suggest that Europeanization is a dynamic process, where the member states may do more than simply react passively to the EU's constraining mandates. Dyson and Goetz point out that the EU's constraints may work to the advantage of member state elites in ways that promote, modify, or retard Europeanization.[37] Member state political leaders may employ these pressures strategically to advance the changes at the national desired by the

---

[34] Tanja A. Borzel and Thomas Risse (2003). "Conceptualizing the Domestic Impact of Europe," in Featherstone and Radaelli (eds.), *The Politics of Europeanization*. New York: Oxford University Press, pp. 57–80.

[35] Christoph Knill (2001). *The Europeanisation of National Administrations: Patterns of Institutional Change and Persistence*. New York: Cambridge University Press.

[36] Claudio M. Radaelli (2003). "The Europeanization of Public Policy," in Featherstone and Radaelli (eds.), *The Politics of Europeanization*. New York: Cambridge University Press, pp. 27–56.

[37] Kenneth Dyson and Klaus H. Goetz (2004). "Living with Europe: Power, Constraint, and Contestation," in Kenneth Dyson and Klaus H. Goetz (eds.), *Germany, Europe and the Politics of Constraint*. New York: Oxford University Press, pp. 3–35.

EU in the face of domestic opposition. They may also seek to "upload" their own rules, practices, and preferences to the EU level, thus modifying or reducing the adaptational pressures placed upon them. Further complicating the simple top-down model, Dyson notes, is the changing macro political and economic conditions associated with the expansion of the EU into Eastern Europe, Europe's weakened economy, and diminishing returns of economic benefits to the larger member states, particularly Germany.[38] These events may lead member states to be less cooperative or even oppose, and thereby retard, Europeanization. Thus, the rate of Europeanization reflects a dynamic and ongoing process between the EU and the member states.

Europeanization raises several questions about the surveillance procedure. Does surveillance consist of a simple top-down process where the Commission downloads its rules to the member states? What, if any, are the bottom-up, uploading responses of the member states? Is there a variation of fitness and misfitness among the member states due to the adaptational pressures they experience in their willingness and ability to comply with the surveillance procedure? Does Europeanization extend to both the policy and the administrative levels of the member states, where the member states adopt EU values and administrative practices that are associated with EU surveillance techniques?

1.4   Outline of the Book

This book attempts to answer the questions posed by the various theories presented in this chapter by examining the surveillance procedure created by the Maastricht Treaty, and its role in the creation of the EMU and the enforcement of the Treaty and the Stability and Growth Pact. The framers of the Treaty clearly understood that compliance depended in part upon the EU's access to transparent and harmonized budgetary and economic data. These data would be used to determine whether a range of soft and hard sanctions would be imposed against noncompliant actors. The Treaty delegated to the European Commission the responsibility for the gathering of these data as part of an ongoing monitoring and surveillance procedure. The degree of autonomy and trusteeship granted by the Treaty, however, went unstated, leaving this matter, as well as the politics of creating and implementing a compliance information system, to be tested as the monitoring process emerged over time.

---

[38] Kenneth Dyson (2004). "Economic Policies: From Pace-Setter to Beleaguered Player," in Dyson and Goetz (eds.), *Germany, Europe and the Politics of Constraint*. New York: Oxford University Press, pp. 201–29.

Chapter 2 of this study employs principal-agency theory to analyze the crafting of the Treaty's rules on budgetary reference values and the actual delegation of surveillance authority to the European Commission. Within the Commission, Eurostat emerged as the lead agency in the surveillance after its entrepreneurial leadership fought a successful bureaucratic battle with the Commission's Directorate General for Economic and Financial Affairs. To fulfill its organizational task, Eurostat mobilized the member states' participation in the surveillance procedure, incorporated them into its decision-making process, and helped build the institutional capacity of the EU's epistemic statistical community. At the same time, Eurostat took action to gain the political and bureaucratic independence it required to gain status as a largely autonomous, trustee-like, supranational monitoring agency.

Chapter 3 examines the techniques of surveillance employed by Eurostat during the surveillance process to develop a compliance information system, including the development of the member state self-reporting form required by the Treaty, the use of the European System of Accounts that served as the Treaty's standard for measuring the member states' deficits and debt, the role of on-site inspections, and the assumption of trust that guided Eurostat's analysis of the member states' budgetary data. An example of ESA's logic is offered in a detailed analysis of a national accounts categorization of public enterprise privatization. This important interpretation of ESA prevented the member states from employing revenues derived from certain types of privitization in the calculation of their deficit figures. These techniques not only enhanced Eurostat's surveillance capacities; they furthered the agency's efforts to obtain independence in its decision-making.

Chapters 4 and 5 review the creation of European statistical case law by Eurostat and the member states, represented in the Committee on Financial, Monetary, and Balance of Payments Statistics. By examining Eurostat's rules and rule-making process, we learn, first, that by clarifying the statistical measures for calculating the member state's deficits and debt, these case law rulings provide a regulatory basis for guiding the member states in what constitutes acceptable budgetary behavior for complying with the Maastricht Treaty. The presence of these rulings and their direct affect on the member states' fiscal decisions runs counter to the notion advanced by some scholars that "the Commission was able to judge whether a country had hit the target levels, but it had virtually no impact on how the states were to reach those levels."[39]

---

[39] This widespread understanding of the member states' fiscal independence from centralized EU influence during the convergence period is expressed, for example, in Mark Hallerberg (1999). "The Importance of Domestic Political Institutions: Why and How Belgium and Italy Qualified for EMU,"

These rulings, in any event, comprise some of the most controversial decisions made by the Commission during the Stage II convergence period, including the rulings on whether the economic transactions of France Telecom, the German and Italian gold revaluations, and the Italian euro-tax would produce urgently needed revenues for their governments. The process of making these rulings at times proved to be quite controversial, and defined the relative decision-making authority of the Commission and the member states for the surveillance procedure. The development of this process suggests that rather than being static in nature, a principal–agency relationship may very well be flexible, dynamic, and adaptive depending upon the exigencies of the moment. Moreover, the integrity of Eurostat's rule-making process, which simultaneously acts as a dispute resolution procedure, sets the stage for assessing the credibility of the entire surveillance procedure. As shown in Chapter 4, Eurostat's rulings determined the EMU status of at least three EU member states, while during the post-convergence Stage III period considered in Chapter 5, Eurostat's certification of the member states' budgetary data helps to determine whether the Stability and Growth Pact's penalty process will be activated against noncompliant EMU member governments.

Finally, Chapter 6 employs principal–agency theory to assess the autonomy and credibility of Eurostat's decision-making in light of scandals occurring at the highest levels of the organization. The Treaty's surveillance procedure's expansion of EU rules, which empower supranational organizations and encourage member state compliance with collective policies and goals, are considered for their influence in furthering EU integration through institutionalization and Europeanization.

unpublished manuscript, November 4, p. 25. Hallenberg's excellent work on the compliance of EU countries with the Maastricht Treaty notes that Eurostat produces harmonized budgetary data, but he holds to the view that "direct fiscal policy coordination at the EU level was, and remains, limited in its direct effect." See Hallenberg's "EU Institutions and Fiscal Policy Coordination, 1991–2001," May 27, 2001, paper prepared for the 2001 European Community Studies Association Meeting, Madison, Wisconsin, p. 2 and pp. 9–10, and his *Domestic Budgets in a United Europe: Fiscal Governance from the End of Bretton Woods to EMU*. Ithaca: Cornell University Press, 2004.

2

Treaty Delegation and the Institutional Structure of Budgetary Surveillance

The Maastricht Treaty's framers clearly understood that compliance with the agreement's fiscal provisions depended in part upon the Council of Economic and Finance Ministers' (ECOFIN) access to transparent budgetary and economic data consistent with the harmonizing standards of the European System of Economic Accounts. These data would be employed to determine if a range of soft and hard sanctions would be imposed on noncompliant actors, the most significant of these being the denial of Economic and Monetary Union (EMU) membership. The Treaty and its supporting legislation delegated to the European Commission (EC) the responsibility for administering the European System of Accounts and gathering, analyzing, and evaluating these data as part of an ongoing monitoring and surveillance process. Yet, though the Treaty provided the overarching design of this process, events proved that its implementation would hardly be automatic in nature or its outcome predetermined. What went unstated during the drafting of the Maastricht Treaty was the tremendous effort that would be required on the part of all major actors to build the institutional capacity and undergo the organizational learning necessary to realize this compliance information system. To fulfill its organizational task, the Commission mobilized a unique epistemic community consisting of networks of national accounts experts who served in the EC, the European Union (EU) member states, and international organizations throughout the world. Moreover, completely unanticipated and contingent was the emergence of entrepreneurial leadership and bureaucratic politics within the Commission that determined which EC organization would take the lead in the surveillance procedure and guide this epistemic community throughout the EMU fiscal convergence process. Before examining some of these unforeseen events, it is first necessary to review the relevant surveillance provisions of the Maastricht Treaty, its related Protocol and secondary legislation, and the Stability and Growth Pact.

2.1   Designing the Maastricht Treaty's Budgetary Reference Values

The inclusion of deficit and debt targets in the Maastricht Treaty reflected the widespread concern that the new EMU could be undermined by governments conducting unstable fiscal policies. Germany, in particular, influenced by its own legacy of hyperinflation, expressed reservations about admitting nations into the EMU with a history of incurring large, chronic deficits financed by way of inflated currencies and high levels of debt.[1] Moreover, a diverse set of national budgetary positions characterized by large deficits would impede the run-up to monetary union, given their consequences for exchange rates. As Guglielmo Caporale explains, "If a large amount of public sector debt is issued denominated in one currency, this will change its equilibrium nominal exchange rate, and put downward pressure on it, which will have to be offset by market intervention or higher interest rates. . . . A budget deficit is commonly associated with a current account deficit. . . . Therefore large budget deficits will often raise the risk premium on the currency of the country."[2] In response, the framers of the EMU sought to limit the likelihood of these adverse consequences by constraining the size of member nations' budget deficits and debt. In 1989, the Delors Report, the blueprint for the future Maastricht Treaty authored by former French Finance Minister Jacques Delors, declared, "the large and persistent budget deficits in certain countries has remained a source of tension and has put a disproportionate burden on monetary policy. . . . access to large capital markets may . . . facilitate the financing of economic imbalances." As a result, the report urged that "binding

---

[1] Peter B. Kenen (ed.) (1996). "Making EMU Happen, Problems and Proposals: A Symposium," *Princeton Studies in International Finance*, (1997) Essay 199; Thomas Banchoff (1997). "German Policy Towards the European Union: The Effects of Historical Memory," *German History*, 6(1), 1 60–7.

[2] Guglielmo Maria Caporale (1992). "Fiscal Solvency in Europe: Budget Deficits and Government Debt Under European Monetary Union," *National Institute Economic Review*, 5(1), 69–77. For discussion on the strengths and weaknesses of the economic and political logic underlying the Maastricht Treaty, see: William H. Buiter, Giancarlo Corsetti, and Nourile Roubini (1992). " 'Excessive Deficits': Sense and Nonsense in the Treaty of Maastricht," Center for Economic Policy Research, Paper 750; Barry Eichengreen (1992). "Should the Maastricht Treaty Be Saved?" *Princeton Studies in International Finance*, Essay 74; Barry Eichengreen (1996a). "A More Perfect Union? The Logic of Economic Integration," *Princeton Studies in International Finance*, Essay 198; Barry Eichengreen (1996b). "Sensible EMU: How to Avoid a Maastricht Catastrophe," *The International Economy*, 3(1), 16–17; Andrew Hughes Hallett and Peter McAdams (1996). "Fiscal Deficit Reductions in Line with the Maastricht Criteria for Monetary Union: An Empirical Analysis," Center for Economic Policy Research, Paper 1351.

rules . . . [consisting of] effective upper limits on budget deficits of individual countries" be established, as "uncoordinated and divergent national budgetary policies would undermine monetary stability and generate imbalances in the real and financial sectors of the Community."[3]

The Maastricht Treaty adopted many of the Delors Report's recommendations and incorporated its own famous budget constraints, as urged by the Germans, Dutch, Danes, and British.[4] The Treaty states in Article 104 as shown in Table 2.1, that EMU member states "shall avoid excessive government deficits," where excessive was defined in the Treaty's Protocol as no more than 3 percent of Gross Domestic Product (GDP) for budget deficits and no more than 60 percent of GDP for the national debt. (Note: The numbering of the Treaty articles throughout this text reflects the Amsterdam Consolidated Version of 1997, which incorporated the Treaty on European Union into the Treaty Establishing the European Community.) The ceilings were not absolute, however, and the Treaty refers to them as "reference values." The Treaty declared that a country might still qualify for membership if the level of deficit and debt as a percent of GDP "has declined substantially and continuously and reached a level that comes close to the reference value." Moreover, the ECOFIN Council, which would determine whether the deficit and debt were excessive, must consider whether the deficit reflects operating or investment expenditures, and the "medium-term economic and budgetary position" of the government.

The key discussions over what constituted proper reference values occurred in the European Community's Monetary Committee.[5] Representatives from Germany and Holland both firmly supported the idea that deficits in the current account or operating budget should be prohibited. This proposal was rejected because of the difficulty of separating capital or investment expenditures and debt from the operating budget. Furthermore, such a limitation would cripple anti-cyclical policies during recessions. France and Italy defended the use of high-employment or cyclically adjusted budgets, but this idea too was rejected because of measurement problems. Multi-year budget targets were ruled out due to their dependence on fiscal estimates rather than actual revenue, expenditure, and debt figures. Consequently, annual budget deficits and debt levels, as measured by ratios to GDP, became the reference values for fiscal convergence.

[3] Peter B. Kenen (1995). *Economic and Monetary Union in Europe*. New York: Cambridge University Press, pp. 14–15.

[4] Andrew Moravcsik (1998). *The Choice for Europe*. Ithaca: Cornell University Press.

[5] Kenneth Dyson and Kevin Featherstone (1999). *The Road to Maastricht*. Oxford: Oxford University Press.

Table 2.1 Treaty establishing the European Community,[a] Article 104

1. Member States shall avoid excessive government deficits.
2. The Commission shall monitor the development of the budgetary situation and of the stock of government debt in the Member States with a view to identifying gross errors. In particular it shall examine compliance with budgetary discipline on the basis of the following two criteria:
   (a) whether the ratio of the planned or actual government deficit to gross domestic product exceeds a reference value, unless
      — either the ratio has declined substantially and continuously and reached a level that comes close to the reference value;
      — or, alternatively, the excess over the reference value is only exceptional and temporary and the ratio remains close to the reference value;
   (b) whether the ratio of government debt to gross domestic product exceeds a reference value, unless the ratio is sufficiently diminishing and approaching the reference value at a satisfactory pace.
      The reference values are specified in the Protocol on the excessive deficit procedure annexed to this Treaty.
3. If a Member State does not fulfill the requirements under one or both of these criteria, the Commission shall prepare a report. The report of the Commission shall also take into account whether the government deficit exceeds government investment expenditure and take into account all other relevant factors, including the medium-term economic and budgetary position of the Member State.
      The Commission may also prepare a report if, notwithstanding the fulfillment of the requirement under the criteria, it is of the opinion that there is a risk of an excessive deficit in a Member State.
4. The Committee provided for in Article 114 shall formulate an opinion on the report of the Commission.
5. If the Commission considers that an excessive deficit in a Member State exists or may occur, the Commission shall address an opinion to the Council.
6. The Council shall, acting by a qualified majority on a recommendation from the Commission, and having considered any observations which the Member State concerned may wish to make, decide after an overall assessment whether an excessive deficit exists.
7. Where the existence of an excessive deficit is decided according to paragraph 6, the Council shall make recommendations to the Member State concerned with a view to bringing that situation to an end within a given period. Subject to the provisions of paragraph 8, these recommendations shall not be made public.
8. Where it establishes that there has been no effective action in response to its recommendations within the period laid down, the Council may make its recommendations public.
9. If a Member State persists in failing to put into practice the recommendations of the Council, the Council may decide to give notice to the Member State to take, within a specified time-limit, measures for the deficit reduction which is judged necessary by the Council in order to remedy the situation.

Table 2.1 *Continued*

In such a case, the Council may request the Member State concerned to submit reports in accordance with a specific timetable in order to examine the adjustment efforts of that Member State.

10. The rights to bring actions provided for in Articles 226 and 227 may not be exercised within the framework of paragraphs 1 to 9 of this Article.

11. As long as a Member State fails to comply with a decision taken in accordance with paragraph 9, the Council may decide to apply or, as the case may be, intensify one or more of the following measures:
    — to require the Member State concerned to publish additional information, to be specified by the Council, before issuing bonds and securities;
    — to invite the European Investment Bank to reconsider its lending policy towards the Member State concerned;
    — to require the Member State concerned to make a non-interest bearing deposit of an appropriate size with the Community until the excessive deficit has, in the view of the Council, been corrected;
    — to impose fines of an appropriate size.
    The President of the Council shall inform the European Parliament of the decisions taken.

12. The Council shall abrogate some or all of its decisions referred to in paragraphs 6 to 9 and 11 to the extent that the excessive deficit in the Member State concerned has, in the view of the Council, been corrected. If the Council previously made public recommendations, it shall, as soon as the decision under paragraph 8 has been abrogated, make a public statement that an excessive deficit in the Member State concerned no longer exists.

13. When taking the decisions referred to in paragraphs 7 to 9, 11 and 12, the Council shall act on a recommendation from the Commission by a majority of two-thirds of the votes of its members weighted in accordance with Article 205(2), excluding the votes of the representative of the Member State concerned.

14. Further provisions relating to the implementation of the procedure described in this Article are set out in the Protocol on the excessive deficit procedure annexed to this Treaty.
    The Council shall, acting unanimously on a proposal from the Commission and after consulting the European Parliament and the ECB, adopt the appropriate provisions which shall then replace the said Protocol.
    Subject to the other provisions of this paragraph the Council shall, before 1 January 1994, acting by a qualified majority on a proposal from the Commission and after consulting the European Parliament, lay down detailed rules and definitions for the application of the provisions of the said Protocol.

[a] Amsterdam Consolidated Version, June 1997, harmonized the Treaty on European Union and the Treaty Establishing the European Community.

The origins of the two values, especially the 3 percent deficit figure, is particularly interesting. The 3 percent deficit reference value originated in France, where it was adopted by the Mitterrand government in 1982 at the recommendation of Finance Minister Jacques Delors to impose fiscal rigor. As Delors recalled,

3 percent [was] a realistic target for the adjustment of the French economy. At 3 percent, if you make a distinction between ordinary spending and investment spending, you could consider that in a European country the part of the budget devoted to the preparation of the future is at least 3 percent, more then, if you include all the spending for education, and so on.

So, as Delors noted, the 3 percent deficit target adopted at Maastricht was "of French origin," and reflected an allowance for investment spending. Meanwhile, the 60 percent debt target was the "result of discussion inside the group of ministers of finance in charge of the preparation of the Maastricht Treaty."[6] The debt reference value was selected because it was the approximate average of the combined EU governments' gross debt, which for the fifteen

---

[6] Interview with Jacques Delors, March 30, 2001. Delors' observations are consistent with Dyson and Featherstone's interpretation of events. They write,

The criteria, procedure, and sanctions to avoid excessive deficits played a major part in French negotiating objectives. . . . the [French] Finance Ministry saw the need to establish a new basis of credibility for EMU in the financial markets. Hence it introduced the concept of a 3 per cent budget-deficit criterion into the negotiations. . . . Mitterrand was prepared to concede on this issue by two arguments coming from the Foreign Ministry: that the President had actually endorsed the 3 per cent figure in 1982; and that tough criteria would be a signal of French seriousness and determination to the Germans.

Kenneth Dyson and Kevin Featherstone (1999). *The Road to Maastricht.* Oxford: Oxford University Press, pp. 240–1.

On the selection of the debt reference value, see Lorenzo Bini-Smaghi, Tommaso Pado-Schioppa, and Francesco Papadia (1994). "The Transition to EMU in the Maastricht Treaty," *Princeton Studies in International Finance*, Essay 194, especially pp. 27–31. They also write that the 3 percent figure "was consistent in the long term with the 60 percent level for the debt-to-GDP ratio under the hypothesis of a 5 percent long-term rate of growth for nominal GDP," p. 30. Alison Watson offers a similar story, such that the debt figure was the national average figure. She goes on to note, however:

Other economists argue that the figure of 60 per cent has been derived from a well-known formula which determines the level of budget deficit (conditioned on the future nominal growth rate of GDP) needed to stabilise government debt. This formula demonstrates that, in order to stabilise the government debt at 60 per cent of GDP, the budget deficit must be brought to 3 per cent.

Alison M. S. Watson (1997). *Aspects of European Monetary Integration.* New York: St. Martins, see ch. 5, "The Convergence Criteria: Budgetary Conditions," p. 123.

The long-term nominal GDP growth rate in this formula is also 5 percent. A helpful reviewer adds, "In dynamic terms, if the nominal GDP growth rate is 5 percent per annum, and the annual deficit is 3 percent of GDP, then the ratio of public debt to GDP will converge on 60 percent. This formula gives us two ways to measure the true deficit. We measure government cash balances directly on an annual basis. Or we can measure the debt-to-GDP ratio."

member countries stood at 57 percent of GDP. The Monetary Committee focused on gross debt level because for several EU member states there existed no reliable measure of net debt. The 3 percent deficit figure also coincided with an economic formula that determines what the deficit level must be in order to stabilize the debt level at 60 percent of GDP, based upon the EU's assumed long-term nominal GDP growth rate of 5 percent. In any case, some governments objected to precise deficit targets and argued for greater fiscal flexibility, particularly as looking at single year deficit and debt levels ignored broader economic and fiscal conditions. As a compromise, the 3 and 60 percent targets became "reference values" rather than exact ceilings.[7]

2.2   The Maastricht and Stability and Growth Pact Sanctions

The Maastricht Treaty created incentives for governments to engage in creative accounting and gimmickry. Although the Treaty set deficit and debt convergence reference values, an initial, but ultimately misleading, inspection suggests it permitted governments to pursue these targets at their own discretion, with the reward being membership in the EMU. This independence raised the possibility that some governments might engage in budgetary gimmickry simply in order to meet the targets, as they experienced intense political and economic pressure to join EMU and avoid further sanctions. As noted, the standard solutions for managing wayward actors in the principal-agency literature include monitoring the behavior of group members, imposing negative sanctions, and offering side-payments or incentives to induce cooperative behavior. To limit the excesses of what has been termed strategic budgeting, creative accounting, or just plain gimmickry, the Treaty's framers adopted several of these solutions.

One solution provided in Article 99 of the Treaty granted the ECOFIN Council the authority to monitor "broad guidelines" to "ensure coordination" of the economic policies of the member states. The European Commission's Directorate General II for Economic and Financial Affairs (DG ECFIN) would draft these guidelines, with the focus being whether the applicant nations moved towards compliance with the Treaty's budgetary goals. The Treaty and even the guidelines, nevertheless, proved to be silent about the specific policies the governments should follow. Furthermore, the rigor of these guidelines was tempered by a provision that permitted the member states themselves to determine which data to provide the Commission, as Article 99(3) declared

---

[7] Alexander Italianer. (1993). "Mastering Maastricht: EMU Issues and How They Were Settled," in Klaus Gretschmann (ed.), *Economic and Monetary Union: Implications for National Policy-Makers.* Dordrecht: Martinus Nijhoff, pp. 51–113; Edmund Stoiber (1997). "Defender of a Decimal Point," *Financial Times,* August 7, p. 13.

that the data provided to DG ECFIN would consist of "important measures" and "such information as [the member states] deem necessary." In any case, although the Commission produced endless analyses of the economic conditions of the member states, the guidelines proved to be expansive to the point of being essentially meaningless.

In July 1997, for instance, the Council's recommended set of guidelines provided paragraph-length directions for the member states, with instructions such as these: For France, "It is essential that budgetary consolidation should be put on a sustainable basis over the medium term by implementing its recently agreed convergence programme without fail. In particular, it is necessary to contain health spending and to balance the social security accounts and to ensure that any further tax reductions, in themselves supportive to growth and employment, will not slow down the pace of deficit reduction." For Spain, "It is important to continue the implementation of structural deficit-reducing measures, particularly to curb current expenditure and improve the efficiency in budgetary management." For Italy, "It is essential to fully implement the recently approved convergence programme. The objectives set out by the programme should be considered by the Italian government as ceilings, with a view to preventing shortfalls and to fostering faster decline in the government debt ratio." For Greece, "Sustained efforts on a wide range of fronts are required in order to meet the targets of the convergence programme, including reinforced efforts to widen the tax base, to increase the efficiency of the tax administration and of the tax collection system, to curb government spending and to pursue and extend privitisation plans."[8] The guidelines issued in July of 1996 proved to be even briefer and less directed. Thus, with this truly "broad" guidance, the possibility emerged during the convergence process that the EU member states might become budgetary free agents to the detriment of other EU governments, thereby posing a compliance problem for the fiscal integrity of the collective group of states. By granting such wide latitude in the Treaty's provisions, this rule-making stage ironically provided governments with incentives to engage in strategic budgeting, misrepresentation, and evasion.

Aside from the guidelines and from the outright denial of EMU membership, the Treaty included several forms of soft and hard sanctions. The soft sanctions remain largely advisory and of a private nature. Article 104 indicates that when

---

[8] The Council of the European Union (1997). "Council Recommendation on the Broad Guidelines of the Economic Policies of the Member States and of the Community," Brussels, July 3, 9669/97, pp. 10–13. See also, The Council of the European Union (1996). "Council Recommendation on the Broad Guidelines of the Economic Policies of Member States and of the Community," Brussels, July 1, 8577/96; Commission of the European Communities (1997). "Commission's Recommendation for the Broad Guidelines of the Economic Policies of the Member States and the Community," Brussels, March 23, COM(97)168. The Council's recommendations are identical to those of the Commission.

a member state engages in excessive deficit spending, the ECOFIN Council will offer recommendations on member state fiscal policy, and if no "effective action" is taken, these recommendations may be made public, presumably to impose reputational costs and shame the member state into compliance. The Council may also issue "notices" directing the member state to take action within a given time period to reduce the deficit, while requesting the government in question to produce reports on its progress. A failure to comply with these notices may result in the imposition of additional reporting requirements before a member state may issue bonds and securities. Moreover, the Council may apply hard sanctions, which consist of actual financial penalties, including the ECOFIN Council's "invitation" to the European Investment Bank to alter its lending policy with the noncompliant member state, and the imposition of unspecified fines and non-interest bearing financial penalties.

The Stability and Growth Pact contributed its own brand of sanctions by creating financial penalties that could be imposed on governments that violated the excessive deficit procedure once they became members of the EMU. In November 1995, Germany offered its plan for a stability pact to guarantee the fiscal credibility of the EMU by imposing fines for excessive deficits. In the first year of the violation, the fine would be composed of a fixed 0.2 percent of GDP and a variable portion of 0.1 percent for every percent above the 3 percent deficit target, with a maximum fine of 0.5 percent of GDP. The fine would take effect four months after a country's deficit was identified as excessive, and if that country failed to take action to bring the deficit down to at least 3 percent. Germany originally proposed that the fine be distributed among those EMU members that met the appropriate deficit level, but this provision was revised so that fines would be deposited in non-interest bearing accounts with the ECB, with the total returned to the offending country once it again complied with the Treaty. The deposit would be lost, however, if excessive deficits persisted for more than two years. Furthermore, a clause was added that permitted excusing the sanctions if exceptional conditions occurred, such as recession. Adopted by the European Council in 1997, the Stability and Growth Pact's financial penalties serve as an additional sanction against Treaty violators, with the ultimate sanction during the convergence process being the denial of EMU membership.

Before any of these sanctions could be imposed, whether they be based on the Treaty's original provisions or derived from the Stability and Growth Pact, the ECOFIN Council first required notice as to whether a member state actually exceeded the deficit and debt reference values. In other words, the Treaty's capacity to confront noncompliant member states and impose negative sanctions, depended upon a reliable, credible, and independent monitoring system to verify the member states' compliance.

2.3   The Maastricht Treaty's Surveillance Process

To create that monitoring system, the Treaty first delegated to the EC the responsibility for serving as the lead organization in the surveillance process. Article 104(2) declared that the Commission "shall monitor the development of the budgetary situation and of the stock of government debt in the Member States with a view to identifying gross errors . . . [and] examine compliance with budgetary discipline." The Commission's task was to pay specific attention to planned and actual deficits and debt as a proportion of GDP, and whether these ratios were either diminishing or approaching the two reference values.

The Treaty's "Protocol on the Excessive Deficit Procedure," shown in Table 2.2, provided more details. The budget deficit was identified as an applicant country's "net deficit" and the debt under consideration would be the country's gross debt "at nominal value outstanding at the end of the year and consolidated between and within the sectors of general government." The Protocol also referred to "investment" spending, in light of Germany's proposal that the proper measure of the deficit and debt should be measured by the "golden rule," where net borrowing should be less than the amount budgeted for investment purposes. The convergence criteria would be applied to the "general government," which meant that the treaty's reference values affected all levels of government and social security funds, not just those of the central government. The Protocol stated that the data used for treaty purposes would be supplied by the Commission. Equally important, the Protocol broadly outlined how these concepts should be measured and defined.

The drafters of the Treaty and the Protocol agreed that some standardized version of deficits and debt was needed as part of a system of multilateral surveillance due to the widely recognized variance in the measures of deficits and debt employed in the national budgets, which themselves varied widely in how they categorized expenditures and revenues. Consequently, to provide a unified system of measurement the Protocol declared that the European System of Integrated Economic Accounts (ESA), a centralized accounting system that covers a broad range of economic activities and government operations for a national economy, would set the standard for defining the technical scope of what constituted a deficit, debt, investment, and general government. The implementing regulations, or secondary legislation, called for by the Protocol came in the form of Council Regulation 3605/93, which was adopted by the Council of the European Union on November 22, 1993. This Regulation, shown in Table 2.3, provided more extensive definitions that ultimately relied on ESA as the authoritative document for enforcing the Treaty.

Table 2.2 Protocol on the excessive deficit procedure

THE HIGH CONTRACTING PARTIES,

Desiring to lay down the details of the excessive deficit procedure referred to in Article 104 of the Treaty establishing the European Community,

Have agreed upon the following provisions, which shall be annexed to the Treaty establishing the European Community:

ARTICLE 1

The reference values referred to in Article 104(2) of this Treaty are:

— 3% for the ratio of the planned or actual government deficit to gross domestic product at market prices;

— 60% for the ratio of government debt to gross domestic product at market prices.

ARTICLE 2

In Article 104 of this Treaty and in this Protocol:

— government means general government, that is to say central government, regional or local government and social security funds, to the exclusion of commercial operations, as defined in the European System of Integrated Economic Accounts;

— deficit means net borrowing as defined in the European System of Integrated Economic Accounts;

— investment means gross fixed capital formation as defined in the European System of Integrated Economic Accounts;

— debt means total gross debt at nominal value outstanding at the end of the year and consolidated between and within the sectors of general government as defined in the first indent.

ARTICLE 3

In order to ensure the effectiveness of the excessive deficit procedure, the governments of the Member States shall be responsible under this procedure for the deficits of general government as defined in the first indent of Article 2. The Member States shall ensure that national procedures in the budgetary area enable them to meet their obligations in this area deriving from this Treaty. The Member States shall report their planned and actual deficits and the levels of their debt promptly and regularly to the Commission.

ARTICLE 4

The statistical data to be used for the application of this Protocol shall be provided by the Commission.

Table 2.3 Council Regulation (EC) No 3605/93

On the application of the Protocol on the excessive deficit procedure annexed to the Treaty establishing the European Community

THE COUNCIL OF THE EUROPEAN UNION,

Having regard to the Treaty establishing the European Community, and in particular the third subparagraph of Article 104c (14) thereof,

Having regard to the proposal from the Commission (a),

Having regard to the opinion of the European Parliament (b),

Whereas the definitions of "government," "deficit" and "investment" are laid down in the Protocol on the excessive deficit procedure by reference to the European System of integrated Economic Accounts (ESA) (c); whereas precise definitions referring to the assification codes of ESA are required; whereas these definitions may be subject to revision in the context of the necessary harmonization of national statistics or for other reasons; whereas any revision of ESA will be decided by the Council in accordance with the rules on competence and procedure laid down in the Treaty;

Whereas the definition of "debt" laid down in the Protocol on the excessive deficit procedure needs to be amplified by a reference to the classification codes of ESA;

Whereas Council Directive 89/130/EEC, Euratom of 13 February 1989 on the harmonization of the compilation of gross national product at market prices (d) provides an adequate, detailed definition of gross domestic product at market prices;

Whereas, pursuant to the terms of the Protocol on the excessive deficit procedure, the Commission is required to provide the statistical data to be used in that procedure;

Whereas detailed rules are required to organize the prompt and regular reporting by the Member States to the Commission of their planned and actual deficits and of the levels of their debt;

Whereas, pursuant to Article 104c (2) and (3) of the Treaty, the Commission is to monitor the development of the budgetary situation and of the stock of government debt in the Member States and to examine compliance with budgetary discipline on the basis of criteria relating to government deficit and government debt; whereas, if a Member State does not fulfill the requirements under one or both criteria, the Commission must take into account all relevant factors; whereas the Commission has to examine whether there is a risk of an excessive deficit in a Member State,

HAS ADOPTED THIS REGULATION:

SECTION 1—RULES

ARTICLE 1

1. For the purposes of the Protocol on the excessive deficit procedure and of this Regulation, the terms given in the following paragraphs are defined according to

Table 2.3 *Continued*

the European System of Integrated Economic Accounts (ESA). The codes in brackets refer to ESA, second edition.

2. "Government" means the sector of general government (S60), that is central government (S61), local government (S62) and social security funds (S63), to the exclusion of commercial operations, as defined in ESA.

   The exclusion of commercial operations means that the sector of general government (S60) comprises only institutional units producing non-market services as their main activity.

3. "Government deficit (surplus)" means the net borrowing (net lending) (N5) of the sector of general government (S60), as defined in ESA. The interest comprised in the government deficit is the sum of interest (R41), as defined in ESA.

4. "Government investment" means the gross fixed capital formation (P41) of the sector of general government (S60), as defined in ESA.

5. "Government debt" means the total gross debt at nominal value outstanding at the end of the year of the sector of general government (S60), with the exception of those liabilities the corresponding financial assets of which are held by the sector of general government (S60).

   Government debt is constituted by the liabilities of general government in the following categories: currency and deposits (F20 and F30), bills and short-term bonds (F40), long-term bonds (F50), other short-term loans (F79) and other medium and long-term loans (F89), as defined in ESA.

   The nominal value of a liability outstanding at the end of the year is the face value.

   The nominal value of an index-linked liability corresponds to its face value adjusted by the index-related capital uplift accrued to the end of the year.

   Liabilities denominated in foreign currencies shall be converted into the national currency at the representative market exchange rate prevailing on the last working day of each year.

ARTICLE 2

Gross domestic product means gross domestic product at market prices (GDP mp), as defined in Article 2 of Directive 89/130/EEC, Euratom.

ARTICLE 3

1. Planned government deficit figures mean the figures established for the current year by the Member States consistent with the most recent decisions of their budgetary authorities.

2. Actual government deficit and government debt level figures mean estimated, provisional, half-finalized or final results for a past year.

Table 2.3 Council Regulation (EC) No 3605/93

SECTION 2—RULES AND COVERAGE OF REPORTING

ARTICLE 4

1. As from the beginning of 1994, Member States shall report to the Commission their planned and actual government deficits and levels of government debt twice a year, the first time before 1 March of the current year (year n) and the second time before 1 September of the year n.

2. Before 1 March of year n, Member States:

   — shall report to the Commission their planned government deficit for year n, an up-to-date estimate of their actual government deficit for year n-1 and their actual government deficits for years n-2, n-3 and n-4.

   — shall simultaneously provide the Commission for years n, n-1 and n-2 with their corresponding public accounts budget deficits according to the definition which is given most prominence nationally and with the figures which explain the transition between the public accounts budget deficit and their government deficit. The figures explaining this transition which are provided to the Commission shall include, in particular, the figures for net borrowing of the subsectors S61, S62, and S63,

   — shall report to the Commission their estimate of the level of actual government debt at the end of year n-1 and their levels of actual government debt for years n-2, n-3, and n-4,

   — shall simultaneously provide the Commission for years n-1 and n-2 with the figures which explain the contributions of their government deficit and other relevant factors contributing to the variation in the level of their government debt.

3. Before 1 September of year n, Member States shall report to the Commission:

   — their updated planned government deficit for year n and their actual government deficits for years n-1, n-2, n-3 and n-4 and shall comply with the requirements of the second indent of paragraph 2,

   — their actual level of government debt for years n-1, n-2, n-3 and n-4, and shall comply with the requirements of the fourth indent of paragraph 2.

4. The figures for the planned government deficit reported to the Commission in accordance with paragraphs 2 and 3 shall be expressed in national currency and in budget years.

   The figures for actual government deficit and actual government debt level reported to the Commission in accordance with paragraphs 2 and 3 shall be expressed in national currency and in calendar years, with the exception of the up-to-date estimates for year n-1, which may be expressed in budget years.

   Where the budget year differs fro the calendar year, Member States shall also report to the Commission their figures for actual government deficit and actual government debt level in budget years for the two budget years preceding the current budget year.

Table 2.3 *Continued*

ARTICLE 5

Member States shall, in accordance with the procedure laid down in Article 4 (1), (2) and (3), provide the Commission with the figures for their government investment expenditure and interest expenditure.

ARTICLE 6

Member States shall provide the Commission with a forecast of their gross domestic product for year n and the actual amount of their gross domestic product for years n-1, n-2, n-3 and n-4, under the same timing conditions as those indicated in Article 4 (1).

ARTICLE 7

In the event of a revision of ESA to be decided on by the Council in accordance with the rules in competence and procedure laid down in the Treaty, the Commission shall introduce the new references to ESA into Articles 1 and 4.

ARTICLE 8

This regulation shall enter into force on 1 January 1994.

This regulation shall be binding in its entirety and directly applicable in all Member States.

Done at Brussels, 22 November 1993.

For the Council

The President

Ph. MAYSTADT

(a) OJ No C 324, 1. 12. 1993, p 8; and

  OJ No C 340, 17. 12. 1993, p. 8.

(b) OJ No C 329, 6. 12. 1993.

(c) Statistical Office of the European Communities, *European System of Integrated Economic Accounts (ESA)*, 2nd.

(d) OJ No L 49, 21. 2. 1989. p 26.

For the first time in any of these Treaty-related documents, the Regulation employed accounting terminology to help define terms. For example, the Regulation in Section 1, Article 1, declared that " 'Government' means the sector of general government (S60), that is central government (S61), local government (S62) and social security funds (S63) to the exclusion of commercial operations, as defined in ESA." General government debt referred to government liabilities that included "currency and deposits (F20 and F30), bills and short-term bonds (F40), long-term bonds (F50), other short-term loans (F79), and other medium and long-term loans (F89), as defined in ESA." The letter "S" and the numbers 60, 61, and 62, correspond to sections in ESA, where S refers to the sector of the economy and F stands for financial accounts, and the numbers indicate respectively the subsector and subaccount. In addition to relying upon the ESA, Regulation 3605/93 did include one key surveillance provision. Section 2, "Rules and Coverage of Reporting," required all EU countries to submit biannual reports on their deficits and debt to the Commission. Due to the variation in national budgetary procedures, specifically regarding the timing of their fiscal years, the Regulation called for the reporting of deficit and debt figures in terms of calendar as well as fiscal years, except for the most current budgetary projections, which could be calculated in fiscal years.

The drafters of the Protocol turned to ESA's accounting rules at the urging of DG ECFIN. The ESA was well known to DG ECFIN. The ESA's rules had long been incorporated into the legal framework of the European Economic Community (EEC), and DG ECFIN itself employed ESA's accounting concepts for nearly two decades in the making of economic projections. ESA's established accounting framework appeared to be a readily available common measure that would offer some harmonized basis for resolving the differences among national budgets and finances. This lack of comparability among the various budgets, as explained by a DG ECFIN officer who helped staff the Monetary Committee, undermined any effort to achieve EU fiscal convergence:

What was clear in our analysis of budgetary policy was that each of the member states had very specific national budgetary procedures, and very specific national definitions of budget deficits, which were peculiar to each of the countries and depended upon the institutional framework of the country. They did not provide a useful basis for comparative analysis and for applying the same standards to each of the member states. We used to use those figures because that's what was available, and policy was set in those terms, but you always had to explain what the complex differences were.

So the idea of employing the ESA originated with DG ECFIN, not the finance ministers or the member states, and there seems to have been little discussion about the consequences of this decision. "The negotiators accepted it without necessarily being aware of all the implications of such a choice," another senior DG ECFIN official recalled. "It went through more on the basis of DG ECFIN initiation and more on the need for comparable data. The negotiators did not really discuss much the substance of this requirement." One significance of this decision was the drafters of the Maastricht Treaty activated a set of rules based on a technical accounting methodology that would come to guide, influence, and, in some instances, greatly constrain, member state fiscal policy. These rules, however, were never seriously examined for what affect they might have on member state behavior or for their enforceability. Significantly, those members of the European statistical community who employed ESA on a daily basis, especially those experts within the Commission other than DG ECFIN, were never called upon to comment on the suitability of ESA for the purposes designated in the Treaty. Nevertheless, aside from the comparability issue, DG ECFIN had an additional incentive to propose ESA's use. Because of its active familiarity with ESA, DG ECFIN fully expected that although the Treaty did not specify its role in the surveillance process, referring as it did to the "Commission," the agency's familiarity with ESA would lead it to play the central role, both politically and technically, and certainly within the Commission, in assessing whether an EMU candidate country complied with the Treaty. So, armed with ESA, the member states' reporting requirements, and the specifications of debt, deficits, and related financial information, the Commission undertook the task of monitoring the budgetary actions of the fifteen member states.

2.4   EU Bureaucratic Politics: DG ECFIN and the Missing European Court of Auditors

At this point it is useful to consider an alternative surveillance scenario, one relying upon the standard auditing of budgetary accounts by way of the European Court of Auditors, rather than one employing the ESA adjudicated by the Commission. Among the EU's administrative bodies, the Court's overarching function is auditing the EU budget, and in this role the Court's examiners, unlike any Commission personnel, were quite familiar with analyzing the details and probity of government budgets. Despite this expertise, it is a curiosity of the Treaty that the Court was never employed in the excessive deficit surveillance process. DG ECFIN officials claim that the Court was excluded from the monitoring process because the Court auditors had experience only in a cash basis of accounting, sometimes known as "public accounts" or cash budgeting, and not ESA's national accounts framework. The distinction between cash budgeting and national accounts is a crucial one. In a narrow, technical sense, a cash budget refers to the timing of when to count revenues and expenditures, where revenues are counted from the time they are physically received by the state's treasury, and expenditures are counted when checks are actually disbursed. The EU budget and the EU member states' budgets operate on a cash basis of accounting, which is highly idiosyncratic and varies tremendously among governments. Aside from the issue of when to count revenues and expenditures, in cash budgeting there are no set standards as to how programmatic budgets and units of spending may be categorized. Cash budgets are often highly fungible and porous among accounts, and they can vary significantly in such matters as what constitutes a fiscal year, how social services and pension contributions are collected and administered, and what indeed constitutes a public rather than a private entity. Cash budgets, in other words, may easily be gimmicked and subjected to creative accounting by the respective finance ministries. Because they exhibit these tendencies, the drafters of the Maastricht Treaty turned to the ESA and national accounts. In comparison to cash budgeting, the ESA through its national accounts methodology standardized economic and financial categories, and in that way harmonized the budgetary data of the EU nations.

Another, more compelling reason for the Court's exclusion from the surveillance process was political rather than technical. As DG ECFIN staff privately observed, the Court's aggressive auditing, based in part, as one Court senior official acknowledged as "the traditional conflict between auditor and auditee," would antagonize the national governments during this very delicate period in EU relations. Court auditors tended to be highly assertive in their duties, as they examined not only the whether, say, the various EU budget accounts added up and balanced accordingly, but also inquired into the effectiveness and administrative integrity of those programs funded in the budget. The last thing the drafters of Maastricht wanted, however, was for the Auditors to critique the honesty and efficiency of a member nation's budgets and programs. "It was never our intention to build up through these ESA figures an auditing dimension," a DG ECFIN officer recalled. Furthermore, the relationship between Commission and the Court was often adversarial in nature. The primary EU budgets audited by the Court belonged to the Commission, and this auditing process frequently resulted in publicly embarrassing revelations of administrative inefficiencies and wasted spending.

The Court has repeatedly criticized the Commission's internal control systems. . . . In the past, the Commission's responses to the Court's reports have often suggested that the Court is interfering in matters that are not its business, that it is bringing stale news, or that it is plain wrong. It is no secret that relations between former Commission President M. Delors, and the then President of the Court, M. Middlehoek, were less than harmonious.[9]

[9] Kathryn Hollingsworth and Fidelma White (1999). *Audit, Accountability, and Government.* New York: Oxford University Press, p. 184. Brigid Laffan offers the same interpretation of relations between the Court of Auditors and the Commission: "Relations between those carrying out expenditure programmes and external auditors are inevitably tense and sometimes hostile."

Indeed, it was the Court's highly critical analysis of financial management practices in the EU budget that eventually forced the mass resignation of the Commission's leadership in 1999, amid charges of corruption, fraud, and administrative malfeasance.[10] So, for reasons of preserving EU tranquility and long-standing internal EU bureaucratic politics, the most experienced budget analysts in the EU did not participate in the surveillance process.

2.5   Eurostat, DG ECFIN, and the European Statistical Profession

An examination of the Maastricht Treaty and its supporting Protocol and regulations reveals no mention of an organization named Eurostat, and certainly no reference is made to Eurostat having anything to do with surveillance or any other activities associated with the newly created EMU. In fact, through early 1994, Eurostat was at best an afterthought on the part of those EU officials responsible for the Treaty's enforcement. Slowly, however, almost to their surprise, EU and national government officials began to recognize that statistical measurements would soon determine the very fate of the EMU. When the Maastricht Treaty was drafted, virtually all participants believed that Germany and France, for example, would have little trouble fulfilling the treaty's budgetary requirements. Yet, by late 1996, observers became increasingly concerned about the fiscal performance of not only Germany and France, but much of the EU. As the 3.0 deficit figure became less a politically flexible reference value and more a hard numerical target, how would interested parties know if this requirement had been fulfilled in a consistent and legitimate fashion throughout the EU? More to the point, what entity in the EU would determine whether an applicant nation successfully complied with the treaty's budgetary provisions? Within the four years following the Treaty's ratification these questions were resolved. Article 104 of the Maastricht Treaty charges the EC with the duty of monitoring the deficit and debt levels of the EU member states. By 1995, Eurostat became the lead agency, certainly within the EC, responsible for ensuring that the Maastricht budgetary requirements were properly monitored and realized by the EMU applicant governments. How Eurostat came to be in this position, however, is best

Brigid Laffan (1997). *The Finances of the European Union*. New York: St. Martin's Press, p. 192. Also see Carol Harlow (2002). *Accountability in the European Union*. New York: Oxford University Press, esp. ch. 5, "Accountability Through Audit;" and E. L. Normanton (1966). *The Accountability and Audit of Governments: A Comparative Study*. Manchester: Manchester University Press.

[10] On the mass resignation of the Commission, see Neill Nugent (2001). *The European Commission*. New York: Palgrave, pp. 53–5; and Associated Press (1999). "All Commissioners of European Union Give Resignations," *New York Times*. March 17.

understood by examining its origins, its responsibilities within the EC, and its relationship to the epistemic community of statistics and national accounts professionals.

What exactly is Eurostat and what does it do that enables it to carry out such a significant task? Eurostat's role in the EU begins with the origins of the European Community. When Jean Monnet assumed the presidency of the European Coal and Steel Community in 1953, he immediately recognized the importance of national statistics for economic harmonization and planning. As Monnet recalled, among the "most urgent tasks" facing this infant organization was "drawing up a balance-sheet of the Community's coal and steel output. . . . the High Authority offered them a powerful means of action, in that it made public data which had previously been disguised or only patchily perceived. Our statistical inquiries at European level produced surprising revelations in the most obvious fields."[11] Monnet declared that statistical rules, harmonized data, and working parties for conducting cross-national consultations were necessary for policy and administration. He found this to be particularly true for this new and highly complex international organization, where making sense of conflicting national data bases and measures proved to be an invaluable aid to planning and decision-making. Monnet's concerns led to the establishment of the Statistics Division of the High Authority of the Community in 1953. As European integration progressed with the creation of the EEC in March 1957, so too did its increasingly reliance on compatible national statistics. Article 285 of the Treaty Establishing the EEC calls for the "production of statistics" that "shall conform to impartiality, reliability, objectivity, scientific independence, cost-effectiveness, and statistical confidentiality." The EEC's immediate statistical needs focused on foreign trade statistics for the purposes of tariff negotiations on behalf of the member states, agricultural statistics, and industrial statistics for the management of EEC industrial policies. The disparate statistical and national accounting systems of the initial six member countries forced the EEC to produce a more harmonized set of statistical methods and data bases. Subsequently, in 1959, the Statistical Division's status was raised to a directorate general in the European Commission and formally renamed the Statistical Office of the European Communities, more conventionally known as Eurostat.

Currently, Eurostat is staffed by approximately 650 professionals based at the EU's Kirchberg complex in Luxembourg, whose principal task is providing key statistical data for policy-making purposes to EU and Commission officials. The agency's most public responsibility is developing, collecting, and

---

[11] Jean Monnet (1978). *Memoirs*. New York: Doubleday & Company, p. 376, p. 391.

promulgating statistical data on virtually every significant facet of life in the EU. Eurostat, with the participation of the national statistical institutes (NSIs) of the EU governments, also manages the European Statistical System (ESS), which authorizes the methodologies employed in the gathering of statistical data. These data are collected by the NSIs and then submitted to Eurostat, which ensures they are compatible, harmonized, in compliance with the ESS's technical standards, and publicly disseminated. Much of Eurostat's data on such subjects as demographic and sociological trends, balance of trade, agricultural production, energy consumption, rates of unemployment, and economic and financial statistics are easily available on its web site (www.eurostat.eu.int), and a careful examination of most any newspaper story that includes statistical data on the EU attributes Eurostat as its source.

Yet, Eurostat is clearly one of the Commission's more obscure units and has been almost completely ignored by academic researchers. In one recent book-length study specifically on the EC, Eurostat received just half a sentence of attention.[12] Another study that explored the attitudes of Commission bureaucrats and officials towards European integration, explicitly exempted Eurostat and other EC units in Luxembourg for "practical reasons," despite Eurostat's central role in determining member state compliance with the Maastricht Treaty.[13] Unlike the Commission's nearly thirty numbered Directorate Generals, where DG II is the Directorate General for Economic and Financial Affairs (DG ECFIN), Eurostat is an unnumbered DG. Eurostat, in a technical sense, neither engages in economic forecasting nor economic planning as does DG ECFIN, and its use of the European System of Accounts is retrospective rather than prospective. Nevertheless, Eurostat's presence would surely be missed if it ceased to provide its statistical services, and its status as an independent, nonpolitical, technical entity, combined with its entrepreneurial leadership, enabled it to play a critically important, if publicly unsung, role in the Maastricht Treaty's convergence process.

Much of Eurostat's effectiveness stems from the professional status and self-identification its staff have as members of the "epistemic community" of statisticians. A defining characteristic of the EU is the presence of numerous epistemic communities, which consist of dense networks of transnational, interorganizational technical experts, policy analysts, and issue specialists in EU decision-making. These networks of experts form policy or technically based espistemic communities, each with its own shared set of beliefs, norms,

[12] Nugent (2001). *The European Commission*. New York: Palgrave, p. 165.
[13] Liesbet Hooghe (2001). *The European Commission and the Integration of Europe*. New York: Cambridge University Press, p. 40.

professional standards, and understanding of cause-and-effect relations.[14] In this regard, statisticians are well-socialized professionals, with their own technical standards, specialized knowledge, conferences, journals, national and international associations, workshops, and networks that extend throughout the world. The French government even operates two schools for its civil servant statisticians, the *Ecole Nationale de Statistique et de l'Administration Economique* and the *Ecole Nationale de la Statistique et de l'Analyse de l'Information*. As a somewhat envious senior ECFIN official observed, "These statisticians, they all come from the same schools, they all work together. I was fascinated by all the work of these international statistical associations... It's a very closed mafia. In fact, they all know each other. You can find the same people working on the UN [statistical] methodology, OECD methodology, and the European methodology." Particularly within the EU and the accession countries, statisticians are very well acquainted, connected, and networked. Former Eurostat personnel served in the European Monetary Institute (EMI), currently staff the statistical office of the European Central Bank, and provide statistical support throughout the directorate generals of the EC. Eurostat is, in fact, the most seconded directorate general within the Commission.[15] Seconded staff from the various national statistical institutes commonly serve in Eurostat for three years or longer, and are fully integrated into Eurostat's bureaucracy, though rarely at high policy-making, management levels, which are reserved for the core, full-time EC staff. Eurostat also provides extensive technical assistance not only to regular EU member states, but also to the Central European accession and candidate countries, and to the former Soviet republics through the Poland-Hungary Actions for

---

[14] There is an extensive literature on both policy networks and epistemic communities. On networks, see John Peterson and Elizabeth Bomberg (1999). *Decision-Making in the European Union*. New York: St. Martin's Press; Simon Hix (1999). *The Political System of the European Union*. New York: Palgrave; Jorg Raab (2002). "Where Do Policy Networks Come From?" *Journal of Public Administration Research and Theory*, 12(4), 581–622; Laurence J. O'Toole, Jr. (1997a). "Treating Networks Seriously: Practical and Research-Based Agendas in Public Administration," *Public Administration Review*, 57(1), 45–52; Laurence J. O'Toole, Jr. (1997b). "The Implications for Democracy in a Networked Bureaucratic World," *Journal of Public Administration Research and Theory*, 7(3), 443–59; Jeremy Richardson (1996). "Policy-Making in the EU: Interests, Ideas and Garbage Cans of Primeval Soup," in Jeremy J. Richardson (ed.), *European Union: Power and Policy-Making*. London: Routledge, 3–23. On epistemic communities, see the symposium in *International Organization*, 46(1), especially the first article, Peter M. Haas (1992). "Introduction: Epistemic Communities and International Policy Coordination," *International Organization*, 46(1), 1–36; Amy Verdun (1999). "The Role of the Delors Committee in the Creation of EMU: An Epistemic Community?" *Journal of European Public Policy*, 6(2), 308–28; Craig W. Thomas (1997). "Public Management as Interagency Cooperation: Testing Epistemic Community Theory at the Domestic Level," *Journal of Public Administration Research and Theory*, 7(2), 221–46.

[15] According to Nugent, a quarter of the Eurostat staff is seconded (2001). *The European Commission*. New York: Palgrave, p. 165.

Economic Reconstruction (PHARE) and the Technical Assistance for the Commonwealth of Independent States (TACIS) programs. Eurostat's employees and those of the NSIs, furthermore, typically identify themselves profession-ally as statisticians, who are generally university trained as statisticians, math-ematicians, and economists. Eurostat even publishes a quarterly magazine, *Sigma: The Bulletin of European Statistics*, a glossy, professional-looking journal of some fifty pages in each edition, which is distributed to statisticians throughout Europe. The magazine regularly covers Eurostat's activities, those of the member state and candidate country NSIs, details about new trends in statistical analysis, information regarding future conferences, and helpful reminders about the core professional values of statisticians.

Statisticians share a common set of professional norms or aspirations about the collection and dissemination of data. At Eurostat, the organization's announced "beliefs" about the appropriate collection and management of offi-cial statistics, include independence and impartiality. "For a democracy to flour-ish, statistics need to be objective and impartial—free of all political and economic interests. This principle is the cornerstone of our daily work." Statistics should be transparent and comparable, so that the methods and techniques employed in collecting and analyzing data are publicly accessible and can be held to "internationally-accepted standards."[16] According to Yves Franchet, who served as Eurostat's Director General during the Stage II convergence process through to 2003, these are the proper attributes of official statistics: "accuracy, rapidity, timeliness, comparability in time, comparability among countries, detail, consistency, coherence, reliability, adequacy, relevance, transparency, handiness, or openness." Underlying these norms and objectives is "our respect for colleagues throughout the statistical world."[17] "Statistics," declared Alberto de Michelis, Eurostat's chief of the directorate responsible for overseeing the excessive deficit procedure during the 1990s, "continue to be a fundamental tool in managing society and in managing the policies that govern society.... Without statistics we risk being faced with decisions taken purely on a political basis, in the true sense of the word.... The independence and development of statistics are good indicators of a country's democracy."[18]

Eurostat owes much of its professional creed, bureaucratic success, expand-ing role in European affairs, and especially its involvement in the Maastricht Treaty to the entrepreneurial leadership of Director General Franchet.

---

[16] Eurostat (1998). *Eurostat, Our Corporate Plan.* Luxembourg: Eurostat, p. 11.

[17] Yves Franchet (2000). "Eurostat and the Trade-Off Between Rapidity, Accuracy and Comparability: Past Objectives and Future Challenges," Luxembourg: Eurostat, p. 1/7.

[18] Steffen Schneider (2000). "A Man Still Brimming with Enthusiasm about His Job . . .," *Sigma: The Bulletin of European Statistics*, February, p. 45.

The term "entrepreneurial leader" characterizes political elites who are skilled at conceiving and articulating an organizational vision; identifying political and organizational opportunities; knowing when and how to exploit these opportunities given various types of constraints; mobilizing political, bureaucratic, and economic resources; and building supportive coalitions and networks inside and outside the organization.[19] Although this description best fits an ideal case, Franchet exhibited many of these qualities even before he joined the EC. Trained as a member of France's true administrative elite, Franchet graduated from the *Ecole Polytechnique de Paris*, received an advanced degree in economics from the *Université de Paris*, and a diploma in economics and statistics from the *Ecole Nationale de la Statistique et de l'Administration Economique de Paris*. He later served as director of both the *Ecole* and the *Centre Europeen de Formation des Statisticians et des Economistes des pays en Voie de Developpement*. Administratively well seasoned before becoming Eurostat's Director General in 1987, Franchet served in France's National Institute for Statistics and Economic Studies (INSEE), as Deputy Director of the European headquarters of the World Bank, and as Vice-President of the Inter-American Development Bank (IDB) in Washington, DC.

Scholars have noted that the service EC leaders experience prior to their assuming positions within the Commission can greatly influence how they view their responsibilities and the EC's role in the EU.[20] For Franchet, his experience in these various international organizations also colored his perspective of Eurostat's place in the surveillance process. They produced what Franchet described as a "world vision," where credible statistics and data enhance the

---

[19] On the role of policy and bureaucratic entrepreneurs, see, for example, Norman Forhlich, Joe A. Oppenheimer, and Oran R. Young (1971). *Political Leadership and Collective Goods*. Princeton: Princeton University Press; R. Douglas Arnold (1979). *Congress and the Bureaucracy: A Theory of Influence*. New Haven: Yale University Press; and John Kingdon (1995). *Agendas, Alternatives, and Public Policies*. New York: HarperCollins. On entrepreneurialship particularly within the Commission and the EU, see Christian Lequesne (2000). "The European Commission: A Balancing Act Between Autonomy and Dependence," in Karlheinz Neunreither and Antje Wiener (eds.), *European Integration After Amsterdam*. New York: Oxford University Press, pp. 37–51; Mitchell P. Smith (2000). "The European Commission: Diminishing Returns to Entrepreneurship," in Maria Green Cowles and Michael Smith (eds.), *State of the European Union: Risks, Reform, Resistance, and Revival*. New York: Oxford University Press. A dissent against entrepreneurial influence is Andrew Moravcsik (1999). "A New Statecraft? Supranational Entrepreneurs and International Cooperation," *International Organization*, 53(2), 267–306, and response, Oran R. Young (1999). "Comment on Andrew Moravcsik, 'A New Statecraft? Supranational Entrepreneurs and International Cooperation,'" *International Organization*, 53(4), 805–9.

[20] See, for example, Hooghe's interesting analysis of member state versus Commission socialization. Her data suggest that "state institutions appear to be more effective socializing agents than the Commission." Hooghe (2001). *The European Commission and the Integration of Europe*. New York: Cambridge, p. 108. One implication of these findings is that Franchet's experience in international organizations prior to joining Eurostat proved to be a more powerful socializing force than his service in the Commission.

quality of organizational decision-making. Consequently, upon "arriving in the Commission, I was convinced that given the issues at stake, that without a reliable data base, we'd be lost. What I learned in the World Bank and the IDB was that statistics were very important in policy making, but for that they had to be strong, reliable, and independent."[21] Franchet also learned valuable lessons from his observations of how Germany's Bundesbank gathered data for its policy-making purposes. Rather than relying solely upon government sources, the Bundesbank developed its own data collection system to ensure that it received prompt, accurate, reliable, and especially independent information. Franchet believed it was Eurostat's duty to bring these same qualities to the surveillance process.

Despite Eurostat's expertise in national accounts, however, its participation in the Maastricht process was at best an afterthought. EU officials never called upon Eurostat to offer its recommendations on the wording of the Treaty or the Protocol on the Excessive Deficit Procedure that specified the use of the ESA, and it played a relatively minor technical advising role in the development of Council Regulation 3605/93, which further delineated the definitions of excessive deficits and debt. In each of these cases, DG ECFIN assisted the Monetary Committee and the ECOFIN Council in drafting these provisions, with the firm expectation that it would play the lead role within the EC during the surveillance process. Given DG ECFIN's responsibilities in the Commission for charting the EU's economic and financial policies, these expectations were certainly reasonable, and this proved to be the case during the first two to three years following the treaty's adoption in 1992.

By 1995, however, for several reasons Eurostat surpassed DG ECFIN as the central agency in the surveillance process. First, though disarmingly charming and worldly, Franchet proved to be a tough-as-nails bureaucratic infighter who vigorously argued within the EC that since the ESA's creation in 1968, Eurostat formally served as its interpreter for statistical use by the member states. Since the Maastricht Treaty identified ESA for measuring national deficits and debt, then certainly Eurostat and not DG ECFIN should be the principal in interpreting national accounts for that purpose. Franchet's motivations for advancing Eurostat's interests in the surveillance process no doubt stemmed partly from his obvious desire to promote his agency's involvement in the most important European political activity since perhaps the signing of the Treaty of Rome. Yet, in addition to bureaucratic and personal self-interest, Franchet's experience in various international organizations convinced him that the surveillance process urgently required independent and reliable

---

[21] Interview with Yves Franchet, March 19, 2003.

statistical interpretations of member state budgetary data, and that this would not occur if DG ECFIN remained in control of the procedure. DG ECFIN demonstrated some knowledge of ESA, but Franchet countered, "It was doing policy monitoring" without paying attention to the technical integrity of the data. "DG II was never concerned about the quality of statistics."[22] Second, as the technical demands of the surveillance procedure quickly became evident to all participants, Eurostat's expertise in analyzing national accounts data enabled it to be more aggressive in asserting its authority at every step of the monitoring process. Despite DG ECFIN's active opposition to Eurostat's growing involvement, the reality was that it simply lacked the detailed technical expertise necessary to manage ESA. Third, EU officials and the member states considered Eurostat to be a more impartial organization than DG ECFIN. Eurostat's tasks within the EU were those of a data collecting and disseminating organization, whose reputation was one of independence and technical neutrality. DG ECFIN's standard Commission responsibilities were those of a politically oriented, policy-making directorate general, whose duties undermined its claim that it could serve as an impartial leader of the surveillance procedure. Consequently, the various EU governments as well as the EMI regarded Eurostat as a more attractive and reliable arbitrator for the surveillance process. As one senior Eurostat official diplomatically commented, "They saw we were more independent than DG II."

As tensions quickly flared between Eurostat and DG ECFIN, the Commissioner for Economic and Monetary Affairs, Yves-Thibault de Silguy, personally intervened. By way of at least two major rulings, De Silguy institutionalized Eurostat's bureaucratic triumph over DG ECFIN and legally enshrined its autonomous decision-making powers for all EU statistical matters. In Commission Decision 97/28EC, Article 5, labeled "Technical Autonomy," the regulation declares that "Eurostat is in charge" of developing, setting the standards, determining the methodologies, and interpreting European Community statistics. Another example of this legislation is Council Regulation 322/97, which states in Article 10: "In order to ensure the best possible quality in both deontological and professional aspects, Community statistics shall be governed by the principles of impartiality, reliability, relevance, cost-effectiveness, statistical confidentiality and transparency." The regulation goes on to define impartiality: " 'Impartiality' is an objective and independent manner of producing Community statistics, free from any pressure from political or other interest groups, particularly as regards the selection of techniques, definitions and methodologies best suited

---

[22] Interview with Yves Franchet, March 19, 2003.

to the attainment of the objectives as set out." On all technical matters regarding ESA, therefore, Eurostat's ruling would be the final word, legally determined in an independent and autonomous manner.

This decision, however, preserved for DG ECFIN the responsibility for determining the economic sustainability and policy implications of these national accounts data. DG ECFIN would continue to develop its annual "Recommendation for the Broad Guidelines of the Economic Policies of the Member States and the Community," in conformity with the Treaty's Article 99. These guidelines, based on the member states' deficits and debt status, regularly urged fiscal restraint and compliance with the Treaty and the Stability and Growth Pact. Important though this type of responsibility for DG ECFIN might be, de Silguy's decision nevertheless proved to be a great victory for Eurostat. At this stage of the EMU process, the whole dynamic regarding the budgetary aspects of the Maastricht Treaty was the technical one of certifying whether the EMU applicant nations complied with the 3.0 and 60 percent deficit and debt reference values according to ESA. Clearly, Eurostat's technical rulings as to how to calculate these deficits and debts meant more to the member states than DG ECFIN's broadly worded policy recommendations. Moreover, if a state failed for one reason or another to achieve these targets, then under the Maastricht Treaty the ECOFIN Council's finance ministers, not DG ECFIN bureaucrats, would make the key policy decisions regarding EMU membership.

Though Eurostat gained the upper bureaucratic hand for determining which nation complied with the convergence criteria for achieving EMU membership, DG ECFIN soon acted to regain for itself a position of unique and unchallenged responsibility in the excessive deficit procedure. DG ECFIN clearly disapproved of Eurostat's enhanced responsibilities. "I don't think that DG II was that anxious for that role to develop with Eurostat," a DG ECFIN officer carefully noted, "but progressively it was quite clear that we didn't either have the expertise or the authority for ourselves to manage that process, and to have Eurostat's more clearly recognized independent statistical rulings more and more was an advantage." Another senior DG ECFIN staffer complained of "infighting" between DG ECFIN and Eurostat, noting that "We felt in our unit a kind of competition with Eurostat. Eurostat found a role with the importance of these figures, while it was DG II that was responsible for the final convergence report and evaluation." DG ECFIN responded to Eurostat's recently won authority by seeking specific duties for itself in the Stability and Growth Pact. The Pact, as clarified in Council Regulation 1467/97, states in Article 2, Section 1, "In addition, the excess over the reference value shall be considered temporary if budgetary forecasts as provided by the Commission indicate that the deficit will fall below the reference value following the end of the unusual event or the severe economic downturn." The key word here is "forecasts," a word not mentioned in connection with the Commission's surveillance responsibilities in either the Maastricht Treaty, its Protocol, or Regulation 3065/93. These documents refer to "planned" and "actual" deficits, where planned deficits consist of simple extrapolated estimates for the current year and actual deficits are the final results of the past year. Although Eurostat's leadership proudly declared that was a statistical agency that collected and harmonized data, it did not engage in economic forecasting. DG ECFIN, however, prided itself on its forecasting activities, and while acting as staff to the ECOFIN Council during the drafting of the Stability and Growth Pact ensured that this new forecasting function was included in the clarified excessive deficit procedure. As one DG ECFIN senior staffer declared, "That's where we come in and where Eurostat does not do at all," because Eurostat only considers "historical" data. Furthermore, DG ECFIN's forecasting responsibilities worked to its advantage and authority in a way that Eurostat would never enjoy. Though Eurostat necessarily acted within the framework of ESA 79, as designated in the Treaty, no specified forecasting model was identified in the Stability Pact, which left DG ECFIN as the sole arbiter of the model's economic and statistical assumptions.

Commissioner de Silguy's decision nevertheless effectively marginalized DG ECFIN and elevated Eurostat into the politically precarious position of lead surveillance agency for the purposes of the Stage II convergence process, with the very fate of the EMU seemingly turning on its technical rulings. Even the Stability Pact's forecasting function may be viewed as only a precautionary device to warn of excessive deficits or to delay the imposition of sanctions, whereas the actual violation of the Pact turns on a member state exceeding the deficit and debt's reference values, and it would be Eurostat certifying this had truly occurred. Consequently, Eurostat's Yves Franchet faced the task of proving that his directorate general deserved de Silguy's confidence throughout this entire procedure.

The surveillance problem confronting the ECOFIN Council at Maastricht was how to ensure that EMU applicant countries' fiscal and economic figures would be calculated in a harmonized manner, so that member states could be evaluated equally and fairly for admission into the new EMU. The Treaty's solution to this problem called for the Commission to monitor the national budgets using the ESA as a standard measure. Because of its technical mastery with the ESA and due to the entrepreneurial efforts of its director general, Eurostat became the lead Commission agency in this process. By assuming this leadership role, however, Eurostat's reputation and standing, as well as

Franchet's career, might suffer grievously if it officially approved dubious budgetary statistics offered by desperate governments seeking entrance into the EMU.

Responding to his agency's new surveillance responsibilities, Franchet first reorganized one of Eurostat's directorates specifically to oversee the excessive deficit procedure. As Fig. 2.1, "Eurostat's Organization Plan" indicates, the agency is grouped into six directorates, A through F, reflecting its various responsibilities. Franchet assigned Eurostat's surveillance duties to Directorate B, which prior to Maastricht focused on such tasks as harmonizing price indexes and developing macroeconomic data and statistical methodologies for the single EU market. If this appeared to be a strange assignment for this directorate, it was one that confronted the entire Eurostat bureaucracy, for as Franchet freely acknowledged, "Our experience in public finance was limited. We had much more work on financial and national accounts."[23] Alberto de Michels, a career Eurostat civil servant, led Directorate B. An Italian who studied economics at the University of Florence, De Michels joined Eurostat in 1963 and rose through its ranks to direct agricultural statistics and later the unit responsible for coordinating Eurostat's relations with the European Community and international organizations, before heading Directorate B. Within the directorate, Dieter Glatzel directed the actual day-to-day analysis and surveillance conducted by unit B-4. Glatzel, a German educated as an economist in Cologne, worked as an investment banker in Geneva before joining Eurostat in 1973. Among the B-4 staff, Glatzel was well known for bringing his "banker's eyes" to examine statistical details. As it would be for the entire European statistical community, B-4's new responsibility for enforcing Maastricht proved to be a great learning experience. Prior to Maastricht, B-4's task focused on harmonizing data on money supply; the unit had never examined national budgets or employed ESA for that purpose. Rather small in size given its duties of monitoring the complex budgetary and public finance data of fifteen countries, B-4's staff numbered some ten professional and support personnel in total, including several statisticians seconded from member state NSIs.

2.6   Eurostat and the National Statistical Institutes

Fortunately for Eurostat, the pressure on its statisticians to become instant public accounts and cash budget experts to determine national deficit and debt levels was alleviated to a degree by role played in the surveillance process

---

[23] Interview with Yves Franchet, June 24, 2000.

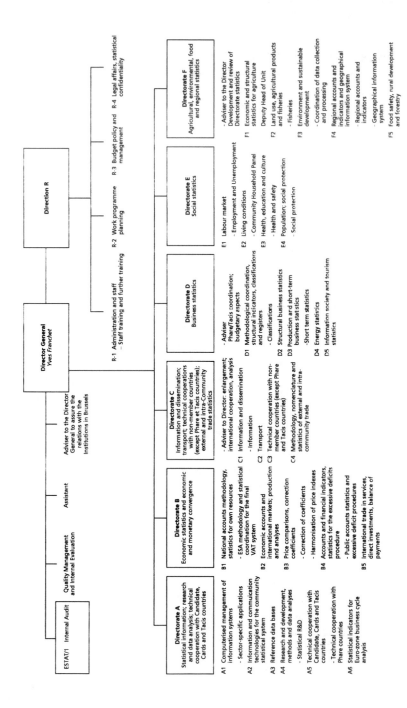

Fig. 2.1 Eurostat organization plan

by the European statistical community. The community's involvement in the surveillance process stemmed from the directives of Council Regulation 3605/93, which mandated that EU member governments should submit biannual budgetary and financial reports to the EC. Although they went unmentioned in the regulation, this stage of the process necessarily required the participation of three types of member state institutions: the national ministries of finance (MOFs); national central banks (NCBs); and national statistical institutes (NSIs).

Within virtually all EU governments there exists a division of labor in the collection, analysis, and dissemination of fiscal and economic data. First, the various MOFs generate data on their budget deficits, given their ongoing responsibilities for managing their respective national budgets. Second, the NCBs determine the size of their national debts by monitoring the quantity and types of government securities circulating in the various financial markets. The sole exception to this pattern is the case of Belgium, where its NCB provides both deficit and debt data. The third institutional member state player in the surveillance process, the NSIs, serve as the most important of the three for ensuring the integrity of these data. To the NSIs fall the critical task of transforming the general government cash budget figures gathered by the MOFs into national accounts data, and certifying that all national deficit and debt data submitted to the Commission by way of Eurostat are accurate. In this regard, the NSIs play the critical role of gatekeeper in the flow of national deficit and debt data to Eurostat. Because of their unique responsibilities and professional connections with Eurostat, the NSIs deserve special attention.

Eurostat's most regular contact with the governments of the EU is through the NSIs. Although Eurostat does collect statistical data it relies upon the NSIs as the primary source of EU member state information, which Eurostat ensures is harmonized and complies with the ESS. Consequently, Eurostat values its intimate working relationship with the NSIs, and it is in Eurostat's interest that the NSIs maintain high professional standards and independence in their decisions, are well-funded and well-staffed, and exercise political influence within their own governments.

Although often ignored by academics, many of these NSIs have long and colorful bureaucratic histories dating back to the eighteenth century, as suggested by Table 2.4.[24] The original function of most NSIs centered on collecting census and elementary economic data for royal governments.

[24] Like Eurostat, the member state national statisical institutes have generally been neglected by academics. Consider, for example, a recent study on Britain's public administration, which mentions that government's Office for National Statistics only in a footnote to a table. John Greenwood, Robert Pyper, and David Wilson (2002). *New Public Administration in Britain*, 3rd edn. London: Routledge, p. 26.

Their tasks grew more complex as the need for more detailed and diverse data bases supported their governments' economic and wartime activities. Despite these interesting histories, however, many of these statistical offices remain understaffed, subjected to budget reductions, and required to meet an ever growing demand for data by the EU and Eurostat. At gatherings of the NSIs, agency directors routinely express their concern that despite the EU's rapidly expanding statistical needs, their statistical institutes are underfunded and overworked. The Deputy Director General of Statistics Finland complained about the workload, saying, "We don't have many internal working groups on statistical development any more: they are at Eurostat in Luxembourg... Eurostat and EC directorates ... ask for something more than we expected."[25] Statistics Sweden, meanwhile, experienced a reduction of nearly a third of its budget in the years surrounding the signing of the Maastricht Treaty, and a loss of half of its staff from its peak 1977 level.[26] Germany's statistics institute reports "the number of tasks we have to fulfill for national and European purposes has further increased. Since 1993 a gap has opened between tasks and resources of about 500 full-time jobs."[27] The unit in France's INSEE that oversees the collection and analysis of financial data for the convergence process has received no additional staff in spite of its new responsibilities and workload. "In my organization, nothing has changed on paper, but the time spent by the people in public finance data has been multiplied by five times or more," reports that unit's director. "I spend sixty percent of my time on public finance, but I should spend more of my time on corporate accounts, which are as important for economists using national accounts. But, inevitably, the Maastricht Treaty has rendered public finance data high priority."

Regardless of their staffing and budgetary problems, Eurostat relies not only upon the technical expertise of the NSIs, but also upon whatever political autonomy they enjoy within their various governments. Eurostat's historical relations with the NSIs, their personal ties and professional affiliations, and their shared loyalty to professional statistical standards, are counterbalanced by the reality that the NSIs are agents of their national governments. As such, they are obligated to represent their national interests, and that may often mean presenting statistical data that best reflect their governments' fiscal conditions, as well as arguing for an interpretation of the ESA that will provide their governments with an advantage in the calculation of national accounts. Some of these

[25] John Wright (1995). "Big Job to Finish," *Sigma: The Bulletin of European Statistics*, Summer, p. 31.

[26] John Wright (1996). "Wind of Change at Statistics Sweden," *Sigma: The Bulletin of European Statistics*, Winter, pp. 38–46.

[27] Barbara Jakob (1998). "Making the Most of Diminishing Resources," *Sigma: The Bulletin of European Statistics*, March, p. 38.

Table 2.4 Brief histories of selected national statistical institutes

- Sweden's Central Bureau of Statistics was established in 1858, with the responsibility for collecting population, economic, and financial data. A newly named Statistics Sweden with a staff of 1,300 was created in 1992. Nearly half of the agency's budget is derived from contract work with the private sector. When Finland later became part of Russia, Statistics Finland was formed in 1865, and its tasks focused on collecting trade and navigation data. With a staff of 800, it now functions as a separate institute under the Ministry of Finance.

- In 1899, a royal decree created the Central Bureau of Statistics and the Central Commission of Statistics of the Netherlands. The Central Commission was given oversight authority of the Central Bureau, which had to gain Commission permission to conduct its statistical studies. In 1917, the Bureau assumed responsibility for trade statistics, which until that time were ineffectively compiled by the Ministry of Finance. Remarkably, the Dutch government made the Bureau's tasks more difficult by splitting the agency into two geographically distant offices. The relationship between the Bureau and the Commission was reaffirmed in 1996, with the Central Bureau renamed Statistics Netherlands. The Bureau is divided into two offices, with a total staff of 2,400.

- The United Kingdom's Office for National Statistics with its staff of 1,500 dates its founding to the darkest days of the Second World War, when Winston Churchill created the Central Statistical Office to aid him in directing Britain's wartime economy. As a result, Britain, where causal statistics developed in the seventeenth century, became the first country to incorporate national accounts in the form of national income and expenditure measures developed by John Meynard Keynes in its budgetary process. The Office served as a part of the Cabinet until 1989, when it absorbed the responsibilities for inflation, trade, and later employment data from other agencies, and in 1996 became a separate agency in its own right.

- Belgium possess an unusual combination of statistical offices, beginning with the Office of General Statistics established in 1831. That organization was renamed and transferred around the Belgian bureaucracy until in 1946 it became the National Statistical Institute. Upon the advent of the Maastricht Treaty, the government recognized that the Institute lacked the capability to produce high quality and reliable budgetary, debt, and GDP statistics for the excessive deficit procedure. Consequently, in 1994 the management of national accounts was transferred to a new organization, the Institute of National Accounts. The Institute serves as a management committee, chaired by the Secretary-General of the Ministry of Economic Affairs. The ministry, in turn, is the home agency for both the National Statistical Institute with its staff of 850 and the Federal Planning Office, which actually produces the national accounts budgetary data in cooperation with Belgium's central bank, the Belgium National Bank.

- Germany's organized statistical efforts emerged first in Prussia in 1805, Bavaria in 1808, and Wurttemberg in 1820. Eventually an Imperial Statistical Office was formed

Table 2.4 *Continued*

in 1872, and statistical services were further centralized by the Nazi government, though individual offices existed in the various *Länder*. After the Second World War, statistical offices were set up in the various occupied zones, with those of the American and British sectors joined together as the Statistical Office of the Unified Economic Area. This unit evolved into the statistical office of the Federal Republic of Germany. Upon the unification of Germany in 1990, all *Länder* offices had to comply with the Federal Statistical Act, and were required to coordinate their efforts with the German Federal Statistical Office and its staff of 700. The Statistical Office, in turn, reports to the Ministry of the Interior.

- France's National Institute for Statistics and Economic Studies (INSEE) provides perhaps the most extensive statistical service among EU nations. France's statistical efforts date from the 1801 census, with the modern history of INSEE stemming from its founding in 1946. INSEE, a directorate general which reports to the Ministry of Finance, employs 6,500 staff located at twenty-four regional directorates, with its headquarters in Paris, and five data-processing centers. To train its future staff, the Institute established several elite training schools, which enroll more than 600 students in the fields of mathematical statistics, economics, public finance, and information processing.

NSIs, despite their declared autonomy, report directly to or are organizationally a part of their MOFs. Statistical officers throughout the EU privately indicate there clearly is a range in the degree of political independence exercised by the NSIs, although this is such a sensitive topic that no one is willing to identify where individual NSIs may be registered on that continuum.

Not surprisingly, NSI directors publicly claim their units enjoy political independence. Johann Hahlen, president of Germany's statistical office, announced, "I am very proud of the fact that our technical autonomy is respected. The Maastricht criteria, for example, were of enormous political importance, but there was no hint of an attempt to influence our work in any way whatsoever. The former Federal Chancellor, Helmut Kohl, himself stated that there must be no question marks over the integrity of the Statistical Office. This was simply not a topic for discussion."[28] "There is," Portugal's president of the National Institute of Statistics, Carlos Correa Gago, proclaimed, "no political control or influence over the content of our output whatsoever. We are an adult democracy! . . . What certainly happened in the old days, before the revolution, is that some information could not be disseminated. But to issue manipulated figures, I think, was never the case, except at the time of election, and this didn't involve the

---

[28] Barbara Jakob (1998). "Making the Most of Diminishing Resources," *Sigma: The Bulletin of European Statistics*, March, p. 36.

[NSI]."[29] A senior official at France's INSEE claims that its independence is actually enhanced by its being an institute within France's MOF.

I must say that some people say that you are not independent because you are working and get the data from the Ministry of Finance. . . . What I can say is that compared to other countries we have inside the house information because of the contacts we have, and we have a common [organizational] culture, and we know more [about the Parliament's budgetary tricks] than the other countries. So I don't think we have perfect accounts, but that we master more than in the other countries. Independence is not a question of status, it is a question of smartness.

A concrete example of NSI independence occurred in Finland during the critical summer of 1997, when EU member states were preparing their budget deficit numbers for the EC. The Finnish NSI forced the government to reestimate its deficit upwards from 2.6 percent of GDP to 3.1 percent, because the Finnish MOF overlooked liabilities associated with public housing loans. As reported by the *Financial Times*, the revision greatly embarrassed Finland's finance minister, Sauli Niinisto, who "stressed that the government's official statistical agency operated independently from the government."[30] In any case, some NSIs clearly do have greater ability than others in challenging their MOFs and NCBs in their statistical decisions.

Eurostat has three ways of politically strengthening the NSIs through the surveillance process. First, by 1997, as part of its efforts to ensure its own responsibilities in the surveillance process, Eurostat won the right to certify the status of the member states' compliance with deficit and debt reference values, and in this arrangement the NSIs were authorized to do the same at the national level. This right to certify data is an important political and administrative weapon for Eurostat, because if a member state's data are refused certification, this immediately becomes known throughout the Commission, the ECOFIN Council, and the press. Questions about faulty and unreliable data arise, as well as political pressure to remedy the problem. In 2002, for example, Eurostat refused to certify the biannual reports submitted by Austria and Greece, which embarrassed both governments.[31] This certification power, therefore, may be used to support the NSIs in their negotiations with their

---

[29] John Wright (1999a). "EU Support for Portuguese Statistics Has Been 'Decisive,'" *Sigma: The Bulletin of European Statistics*, February, p. 39.

[30] Lionel Barber (1997e). "Budget Deficit Error Deals Blow to Finns," *Financial Times*, July 28, p. 2.

[31] See Eurostat news release (2002). "Government Deficit at 1.3% of GDP and public debt at 69.1% of GDP," N. 35/2002, March 21; Bart Maganck to Heinrich Traumuller, Kabinettchef, Bundesministerium der Finanzen (2002). "Government Real Estate in Austria," Eurostat, July 2; Dieter Glatzel to Reinhold Schwarzl, Statiskik Osterreich (2002). "EDP Notification—Austria," Eurostat, September 12. In the case of Austria, that government was embarrassed by Eurostat's decision because it had publicly pledged to

respective MOFs and NCBs to improve their data collection and analysis capabilities. Second, during its missions to the various EU countries, which take place at least on an annual basis, Eurostat can require that the MOFs and NCBs clarify the nature of budgetary and financial decisions. When the interpretation of these decisions in terms of the ESA run counter to NSI findings, Eurostat can rule in favor of the NSIs. Third, although Eurostat is the final arbiter in interpreting the ESA, it relies upon an advisory committee structure to assist it in developing its interpretations and rulings, a structure that favors the NSIs rather than the MOFs. These advisory committees play a critical role in the surveillance process, for the Maastricht Treaty itself identifies the ESA as the standard for measuring deficits and debt, and because Eurostat and this community in the ESS are the interpreters of ESA, their technical rulings on ESA cannot be overridden even by the ECOFIN Council.

2.7   The Committee on Monetary, Financial, and Balance of Payment Statistics (CMFB)

The ESS refers to the formal consulting and decision-making process by which the recommendations of Eurostat and the individual NSIs can be proposed, analyzed, and approved on the full range of EU statistical issues. This structure revolves around three principal committees and allied working groups and task forces, each of which is staffed by Eurostat. The Statistical Program Committee serves as the ESS steering committee, consists of the directors of the NSIs, and is chaired by Eurostat. The European Committee on Economic

balance its budget at the same time Eurostat refused to certify it had accomplished this goal. As Yves Franchet recalled,

We were informed by the media, by the opposition parties, by the national statistics office, by the central bank, and come in the middle and say, 'We are sorry minister, but you said zero deficit, but the deficit is 0.5.' At a given point, the minister said, 'That's enough. Who are these [sic] Eurostat who is preventing us from what we think we should be doing? We are elected officials, we are reporting to parliament, and here are some Eurocrats coming in.' I was called upon by the prime minister of Austria on the topic, 'Why are you against our policy?' And I had to go to Vienna and explain to him and the minister of finance that I was not against their policy. 'I have no influence upon your policy. But you have to be comparable with the others. You are committed to the eurozone, to a number of principles and a consultative process.' And in the end I think he understood that.

Interview with Yves Franchet, March 19, 2003. Regarding Greece, Eurostat reported that

There seems to be a persistent gap between the variation of debt and deficit. This phenomenon is not new but instead of disappearing over time still persists. . . . In the past, Eurostat has asked the statistical services of Greece to supply the necessary information for the elabortation of the excessive deficit statistics. However these information proved to be unsatisfactory, incomplete and sometimes even contradictory. It could be there is a serious problem of quality in the Greek statistical system.

Among EU statisticians, Greece's data were widely agreed to be the worst in Europe (2002). "Report on the Greek EDP Notification of September 2002," September 20, p. 1 and p. 15.

and Social Information offers an opportunity for statistical users in the EU, such as private sector enterprises, universities, and trade unions, to converse with Eurostat about the broad statistical needs of the EU. Last, the Committee on Monetary, Financial, and Balance of Payments Statistics (CMFB) is the premier body within the statistical community for setting policy on the requirements and methodologies in providing statistical services to the EU, the EMU, and the EMI/ECB. CMFB's authority is broad-ranging, and it is the most important of the three committees for developing statistical policies related to the excessive deficit procedure.

Because of its relationship to the surveillance process, the creation of CMFB deserves particular attention. Council Regulation 91/115/EEC established CMFB in 1991 at Eurostat's request, to ensure that the NCIs and NCBs cooperated in the development of the statistical data bases and methodologies that might be needed by the new EMU in the areas of monetary, financial, and balance of payments statistics. Significantly, in a decision that enhanced Eurostat's authority and independence over statistical rulings, the Council did not charge CMFB with comitological powers. This means that by itself CMFB cannot overturn Eurostat decisions or serve as part of the Council's system of committees that oversee Commission behavior.[32] After Maastricht, the Council directed that the EMI also belongs to CMFB. Some of the member state organizations initially opposed this effort at coordination, and the CMFB "was rather coolly received by some independently-minded parties."[33] Nevertheless, during the next few years, the CMFB and its two subordinate working parties, the National Accounts Working Party and the Financial Accounts Working Party, became the locus of formal policy-making and discussion for the excessive deficit procedure for the EU's statistical community.

As events unfolded, the significance of CMFB for the convergence process became so apparent that conflict erupted within the member states as to which bureaucracy would hold CMFB membership. Prior to 1992, Eurostat and the various MOFs experienced only limited contact, and what little that took place focused on the collection of national GDP data by Eurostat for the calculation of member state contributions to the European Communities budget. Later, in 1993 and 1994, as they realized the importance of national accounts for the determination of member state deficits and debt for

---

[32] Comitological power refers to the authority exercised by the extensive system of some 380 committees that aid in the governing and administration of the EU. Although these "powers" vary depending upon the committee, generally speaking they require the Commission to consult with the national experts on the committees on the implementation of EU legislation. Simon Hix (1999). *The Political System of the European Union*. New York: Palgrave, pp. 41–5; Thomas Christiansen and Emil Kirchner (eds.) (2000). *Committee Governance in the European Union*, Manchester: Manchester University Press, esp. ch. 2.

[33] John Wright (1999*b*). "Crucial Role of CMFB," *Sigma: The Bulletin of European Statistics*, March, p. 13.

Maastricht, many of the MOFs claimed that they had the right to take over their member state's NSI seat on CMFB. Eurostat, together with the NSIs, fended off these demands, thereby enhancing the NSIs' authority for the surveillance process.

Council Regulation 96/174/EC outlines the makeup of the CMFB's membership. The committee is chaired by an elected representative from one of the member states, who chairs both the CMFB and its Executive Body. Voting on all matters is on a majority-rule basis. The national delegations may be represented by as many as three delegates to CMFB, who often are the chief or very senior statistician of the NSI and senior NCBs officials. EU accession and candidate countries may also send up to three observers to CMFB. Additional attendees at CMFB meetings are officers representing DG ECFIN, the EMI/ECB, and guests from the Organization for Economic Cooperation and Development (OECD) and the International Monetary Fund (IMF). DG ECFIN is most typically represented by staff from the units ECFIN-A, "Economic Studies and Research," ECFIN-B, "Economics of the Member States," and ECFIN-C, "Economy of the Euro Zone and the Union." Eurostat, of course, staffs CMFB and is present at all meetings. Altogether, committee meetings of the CMFB and its two working parties consist of some 100 participants. These groups conduct their meetings at Eurostat's headquarters in a large, elaborate conference hall equipped with translation booths accommodating as many as six languages and video camera coverage. The task forces, by comparison, are the smallest gathering of statisticians, with approximately ten members each, depending upon the usually very technical matter at hand. A CMFB decision, which constitutes a recommendation to Eurostat, represents the culmination of a long deliberative process that often involves a great deal of staff work and many other meetings at the task force and working group level.

Suppose, however, that a member state NSI objects to a majority vote ruling on a statistical matter. What are its alternatives? Could it simply ignore the CMFB's decision, or perhaps submit questionable data to Eurostat? Clearly, this problem could become acute if the member states' NSIs avoided compliance, where noncompliance includes the failure to change statistical methodologies and gathering procedures, or simply by an NSI providing what statisticians describe as "camouflaged" data.

Compliance, however, is encouraged in several ways. First, in cases where a member state submits incomplete or inaccurate data, Eurostat's most draconian response is simply to withhold its certification of the member state's biannual report, which is required by the Maastricht Treaty to be statistically acceptable. In these instances, the Commission reports to the ECOFIN Council that a member state stands in violation of the Treaty, which would produce a host of political and reputational costs for the member state. In addition to the demand that the member states comply with the explicit demands of the Treaty, the existence of CMFB itself helps to stiffen the NSIs' resolve to provide requisite data, to assert their rights in negotiations with their national MOFs to provide accurate and properly interpreted data, and to comply with the majority-vote rulings of their peer NSIs and Eurostat. Rather than opposing just Eurostat, noncompliant member states also must confront their member state counterparts, where peer group pressure by the other statisticians can become quite intense and costly to ignore. "Even if there is an interest for one member state to have a ruling in its favor," Eurostat's Dieter Glatzel noted, "all the others which are more strict, who have reduced their deficits, they say, 'We don't see why there should be exceptions made for someone else. We want to keep a strict ruling.' In these cases, we see a good consensus."[34] Similarly, member state statisticians who present poorly reasoned national accounts arguments to justify their claims, or who fail to comply with legitimate data requests, often suffer reputational costs with their fellow professional statisticians. In an iterative decision-making process, the loss of reputation and credibility can undermine their ability to influence the outcome of future CMFB and Eurostat rulings.

2.8   Conclusion

The Maastricht Treaty's delegation of surveillance duties to the EC produced the unexpected outcome of Eurostat, rather than DG ECFIN, taking the lead in the critical monitoring process. Though unforeseen, the scope of the delegation and its reliance upon the ESA allowed for Eurostat's ascendency into this role, once the agency's entrepreneurial leader successful bested DG ECFIN in Commission bureaucratic politics. Nevertheless, it is important to recall that although the Treaty designated the Commission to act as a monitor, thereby delegating it some of the characteristics of the "guardian of the Treaty," in fact, the Treaty never granted the Commission autonomy in this role. There is no provision in the Treaty that explicitly insulates the Commission from EU or member state interference in the surveillance procedure. Instead, Eurostat asserted its autonomy, first within the Commission, and then within the EU, as a matter of European treaty-based law and secondary legislation. Beginning with the Treaty Establishing the European Economic Community and continuing on at least through Commission Decision 97/28/EC and Council Regulation

---

[34] Interview with Dieter Glatzel, March 19, 2003.

322/97, Eurostat could invoke any number of EU rules to defend the principles of impartiality, objectivity, scientific independence, and transparency in protecting the autonomy of its rulings. Article 285 of the Treaty declared that the "production of statistics shall conform to impartiality, reliability, objectivity, scientific independence, cost-effectiveness, and statistical confidentiality." Employing almost precisely the same language, the Commission Decision, which stemmed from Eurostat's bureaucratic conflict with DG ECFIN, announced that in addition to being "in charge," "Eurostat shall execute its task in accordance with the principles of impartiality, reliability, relevance, cost-effectiveness, statistical confidentiality and transparency." Yet, even with this supportive legislation, Eurostat still faced the practical matters of managing the surveillance process and interpreting the ESA in specific cases, within the context of the ESS and the CMFB.

The following three chapters analyze how Eurostat attempted to fulfill its responsibilities. Chapter Three examines how the EC confronted the task of creating a compliance information system to monitor the fiscal policy decisions of the member states, as well as collect, analyze, and evaluate their budgetary data. In this regard, the academic literature on treaty monitoring offers insight into the many of the surveillance techniques employed to build this capacity. Meanwhile, the dynamics of bureaucratic politics between Eurostat and DG ECFIN continued to play out in the creation of this information system. As a result, Eurostat added to the relative autonomy it enjoyed within the EC through its technical expertise in the surveillance procedure.

Chapters 4 and 5 explore the evolution of the national accounts rule-making process and the critical decisions it produced. Principal-agency theory provides a framework for understanding the politically sensitive task of rule-making and the relationship between Eurostat and the member states' CMFB representatives. Eurostat possessed the formal authority and independence to make these rulings. The dynamics of the rule-making process, however, resulted in Eurostat's growing reliance upon the CMFB for its own political autonomy and the legitimacy of its decisions. Meanwhile, though the individual NSIs served as agents for their respective governments, their epistemic relations with Eurostat and their peer institutions proved to be a complex one, made so particularly by the CMFB's majoritarian voting rules and its lack of comitological authority. The critical rulings that stemmed from this process, which continue to promote EU institutionalization and Europeanization, eventually resulted in three member states gaining entry into the EMU.

3

Designing a Compliance Information System: ESA and the Techniques of Surveillance

Effective international treaty monitoring relies upon the successful collection and analysis of data through a compliance information system. To be politically and publicly credible within the European Union (EU), a system of this type requires rules that clearly define what data need to be collected and how frequently; a transparent information processing and analysis procedure; bureaucratic and administrative capacity on the part of data producers, collectors, and analyzers alike; an independent central agency to oversee and monitor this process; on-site inspections and other means of data verification; and a dispute resolution mechanism that resolves differences in interpreting the data in a manner agreeable to all parties. This surveillance regime, furthermore, might combine elements of both "police patrol" and "fire alarm" approaches to monitoring. A police patrol system refers to a centralized, proactive, routinized surveillance process, whereas a fire alarm system relies upon reactive and informal procedures, especially the involvement of interested and aggrieved third-parties. The actual collection of data, moreover, often depends upon some combination of self-reporting by treaty participants and data gathered from various parallel and independent third-party sources. Self-reporting, which is a basic element of virtually all international treaty compliance information systems, including the one developed for Maastricht, presents its own set of challenges. Problems in self-reporting stem from imprecise rules for data collection and analyses; confusing or vague reporting forms; questionable data reliability and validity; deliberate misrepresentation and the submission of irrelevant or ambiguous data; non-, or incomplete, or late reporting; and administrative incapacity, all of which impede the gathering of meaningful and usable data. To overcome these problems, incentives can be offered to data collectors and providers to build capacity and generate timely, credible, and employable data. These incentives include making the successful reporting of data essential in the allocation of treaty rewards and sanctions, requiring data that actually may be of value to the provider, and offering technical assistance to help build the data collector's administrative capacity.[1]

The Maastricht Treaty and its Protocol, as we have seen, initiated the development of a compliance information system to determine whether the EU member states fulfilled the Economic and Monetary Union's (EMU's) fiscal convergence requirements. In particular, these rules delegated to the Commission the responsibility for administering the surveillance procedure, and they specified that ESA 79 would serve as the standard for measuring member state deficits and debt. This formal delegation to the European Commission (EC) and the identification of ESA 79 as the harmonized standard, however, led to the unforeseen outcome of Eurostat emerging as the lead agency in determining whether the EMU applicant countries complied with the Treaty's deficit and debt reference values. Eurostat's prominence in this regard stemmed from the agency's supranational bureaucratic entrepreneurship, successful mobilization of political support within the Commission, technical knowledge over national accounts, and its historical role as the primary interpreter of the European System of Integrated Accounts (ESA), all of which enabled it to supersede Directorate General II for Economic and Financial Affairs (DG ECFIN) in the surveillance process. Related to Eurostat's rise was the fact that the Treaty's data gathering requirements necessarily mobilized the entire EU statistical community in an unique effort of data collection and harmonization. This endeavor required the services of the member states' national statistical institutes, the statistical offices of their national central banks, and the statistical experts in the European Monetary Institute (EMI), each of which, to a significant extent, looked to Eurostat for direction.

---

[1] The idea of a compliance information system comes from Ronald B. Mitchell (1993). "Compliance Theory: A Synthesis," *Review of European Community and Insitituional Environmental Law*, 2(4), 327–34; Ronald B. Mitchell (1994a). *International Oil Pollution at Sea: Environmental Policy and Treaty Compliance*. Cambridge, MA: MIT Press; Ronald B. Mitchell (1998). "Sources of Transparency: Informaton Systems in International Regimes," *International Studies Quarterly*, 1(42), 109–30; Ronald B. Mitchell (1994b). "Regime Design Matters: Intentional Oil Pollution and Treaty Compliance," *International Organization*, 48(3), 425–58. On the elements of a successful surveillance system, in addition to the above, see Abram Chayes and Antonia Handler Chayes (1991). "Compliance Without Enforcement: State Behavior Under Regulatory Treaties," *Negotiation Journal*, 7(3), 311–30; Abram Chayes and Antonia Handler Chayes (1993). "On Compliance," *International Organization*, 47(2), 175–201; Abram Chayes and Antonia Handler Chayes (1995). *The New Sovereignty: Compliance with International Regulatory Agreements*. Cambridge, MA: Harvard University Press; Petros C. Mavroidis (1992). "Surveillance Schemes: The GATT's New Trade Policy Review Mechanism," *Michigan Journal of International Law*, 13(2), 374–414; Nancy W. Gallagher (1999). *The Politics of Verification*. Baltimore: Johns Hopkins University Press. On self-reporting, see ch. 4 in Mitchell's *International Oil Pollution at Sea*, ch. 7 in Chayes and Chayes' *The New Sovereignty*, and Mavroidis.

Eurostat, in turn, incorporated this networked, epistemic community into an advisory committee system, which aided in the interpretation of ESA while strengthening the autonomy of Eurostat's decision-making process.

Eurostat and the European statistical community confronted the challenge of creating a compliance information system to provide budgetary data for the Maastricht Treaty's surveillance procedure. Fortunately, the Treaty and its accompanying directives provided the Commission and Eurostat with what any bureaucratic organization would envy: a designated time period of six years from the date of the Treaty's approval to prepare for the crucial moment in March 1998 when applicant countries would be evaluated for EMU membership. Rarely is any organization granted such advanced notice to prepare to meet a clearly defined task, although Eurostat's participation in the surveillance process came completely unexpected and it was only several years after the Treaty took effect that its role became preeminent. Nonetheless, the Treaty granted Eurostat the time urgently required to make internal organizational adjustments to meet its new responsibilities, sort out unresolved organizational roles within the Commission, and establish the needed oversight and reporting relations with other national and international statistical organizations. Equally if not more important, these six years allowed Eurostat the time to make and learn from its mistakes in the creation of the surveillance procedure.

Yet, though the broadly worded Treaty and Protocol initiated this procedure, neither document provided the Commission with instructions on how to manage or conduct the surveillance itself. These more complex details were outlined soon after the treaty's ratification in Council Regulation 3605/93. This regulation, for instance, more carefully defined key terms that had been employed in the Treaty and specified the nature of the data the member states were required to submit to the Commission. Equally important, the regulation reiterated that the European System of Accounts would serve as the basis for calculating the member states' deficits and debts. Consequently, before examining the mechanics of the Treaty's compliance information system, a brief introduction to the logic underlying ESA and its creation by the world's statistical epistemic community greatly adds to an understanding of how the surveillance procedure works.

3.1   The ESA and the Harmonization of National Accounts

When the drafters of the Maastricht Treaty turned to statistical accounting techniques for its budgetary surveillance process, they drew upon the decades-old labor of statisticians and national accounts experts who struggled to produce a common set of statistical rules to measure the world's economic activities.[2] The European System of Accounts is the product of years of effort at statistical harmonization by numerous international institutions worldwide, an effort that long predated the political and economic integration of Europe. The drive for increased compatibility among national economic standards can be traced as early as the 1928 International Conference Relating to National Statistics sponsored by the League of Nations. The participants' agreement on the necessity for comparable statistics led to the publishing of the League's *World Economic Survey* in 1939, which provided national income data for twenty-six countries. At this point, the national statistical offices of the various countries, when they even existed, were so primitive and poorly developed that half of the national statistics were derived from private rather than government sources.

The Great Depression and the Second World War highlighted the need for improved data bases at both the national and international level for the purposes of economic policy-making and war mobilization. During the war, representatives from Canada, the United Kingdom, and the United States reached the first international agreement on the standardization of the display and conceptualization of national estimates. In 1945, a subcommittee of the League's Committee on National Income Statistics began work on outlining rules for defining and measuring national income. The subcommittee report published in 1947 identified how to develop and display national income and gross domestic product (GDP) measures by analyzing the fundamental transactions of economic systems, rather than simply building a single total figure. This procedure was labeled the "social accounting approach." The critical appendix to the report delineated the twenty-four accounts that mirrored an advanced industrial economy's savings, income, expenditure, and capital formation aggregates.

This study led to two major sets of national accounting rules, *A Standardized System of National Accounts*, published by the Organization for Economic Cooperation and Development (OECD) in 1952, and *A System of National Accounts and Supporting Tables* (SNA) published by the Statistical Commission of the United Nations (UN) in 1953. The SNA's conceptually path-breaking

---

[2] On the history of international statistics, see Inter-Secretariat Working Group on National Accounts (1993). *System of National Accounts, 1993.* Brussels: United Nations Publications, especially pp. xxxvi–xiv; John W. Kendrick (1972). *Economic Accounts and Their Uses.* New York: McGraw-Hill; R. G. D. Allen (1980). *An Introduction to National Statistical Accounts.* London: Macmillan Press; G. Stuvel (1986). *National Accounts Analysis.* London: Macmillian; Nancy D. Ruggles and Richard Ruggles (1999). *National Accounting and Economic Policy: The United States and UN Systems.* Cheltenham: Edward Elgar; Carleen O'Loughlin (1971). *National Economic Accounting.* New York: Pergamon Press.

system produced a model based on six standard accounts that reflected the transactions of three basic economic sectors: enterprises; households and non-profit entities; and government. The UN's national accounting system could be applied to developing as well as advanced industrial countries, and, indeed, it was designed to assist public policy-makers understand the relationship between government policies, planning, and economic development. Although other statistical systems for national accounts were later developed by such organizations as the OECD, the International Monetary Fund (IMF), and the World Bank, the UN's SNA and its various revised editions continue to serve as the leader for international accounting rules. As a result, in a true effort at statistical harmonization, the 1993 version of the SNA was cooperatively produced by the Inter-Secretariat Working Group on National Accounts, composed of the UN, OECD, IMF, the World Bank, and Eurostat. More recently, in 2003, the Bureau of Economic Analysis in the United States Department of Commerce announced that it would begin incorporating SNA concepts into its calculation of its National Income and Product Accounts, furthering the harmonization of the world's accounting formats.[3] As these events unfolded, so too did the European Statistical System (ESS) of what was to become the European Economic Community (EEC) and later the EU. To meet the needs for harmonized economic data in the EEC, Eurostat in the early 1960s began to develop the Community's own accounting rules in the ESA. First published in 1968, the ESA was largely based on the SNA's model of the economy.

Briefly, the ESA attempts to "provide a systematic, comparable and, as far as possible, complete picture of the economic activity within each member country of the European Communities."[4] ESA assumes that a national economy is comprised of four institutional units: producers and enterprises; consumers and households; financial institutions; and government. Between and among these economic units are flows of financial and capital transactions, as shown in Fig. 3.1. Every transaction involves two parties, which are grouped into sectors, and each party is assumed to value the same transaction at the same time and at the same value. Between the government and consumer–households sectors, for example, social benefits flow from the government and it, in turn, receives taxes and social contributions, such as social security taxes. Between financial institutions and producer–enterprises, loans flow from the financial institutions and they receive interest payments on the loans.

<hr/>

[3] Brent R. Moulton and Eugene P. Seskin (2003). "Preview of the 2003 Comprehensive Revision of the National Income and Product Accounts," *Survey of Current Business*, June, 17–34. The adoption of SNA concepts includes the use of the term "net lending or net borrowing" to describe the US government's fiscal position, the same term that is employed by the Maastricht Treaty to describe EU member states' budgetary status.

[4] Eurostat (1979). *European System of Integrated Economic Accounts, ESA*. Luxembourg: Eurostat, p. 9.

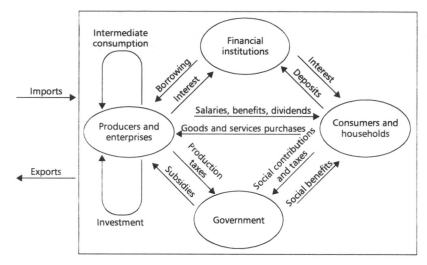

Fig. 3.1 The ESA's understanding of the national economy

Altogether, the ESA examines the relationships of seven economic sectors, of which government is one. General government is classified as S60, and it is defined as one that "includes all institutional units which are principally engaged in the production of non-market services intended for collective consumption and/or in the redistribution of national income and wealth. The principal resources of these units are derived directly or indirectly from compulsory payments made by units belonging to other sectors."[5] Institutional units of government include general government agencies; nonprofit institutions that are legally independent entities that conduct non-market services and that receive government payments; and autonomous pension funds. Excluded are public enterprises or public corporations that are legally independent or are classified as quasi-corporate enterprises. The general government sector is further disaggregated into central government (S61), local government (S62), and social security funds (S63). For Germany, ESA 79 offered a special interpretation specifying that the *Länder* were to be counted as part of the central rather than the local governments.

The advantages of ESA were explained by a DG ECFIN officer who helped staff the drafting of the Protocol and supporting Regulation 3605/93:

You needed a common standard, one that in the end could only be provided within a standardized, national account framework, which had both the advantage of a clear

---

[5] Eurostat (1979). *European System of Integrated Economic Accounts, ESA.* Luxembourg: Eurostat, p. 31.

conceptual treatment of a number of flows, and, even more important in the early stages, a common broad-ranging definition of government, that is, general government, not just central government or the state, but a full range of government activities defined in a comparable way between member states. From our point of view, it was very important that those data fit in with an overall view of the economy. Because they are national accounting data they relate to one sector of the economy [government], so you see how developments in the household sector impact on tax payments and government receipts. Whereas the more traditional government budget analyst who went into great complexities and detail about government finances, did not really have a good overview of the rest of the economy.

This simplified outline of national accounts masks the great complexity of interactions delineated and categorized in the ESA, which was later revised in 1970, 1979, and 1995. ESA 79 was the version identified in the Maastricht Treaty for evaluating the EMU applicant countries' deficit and debt levels, all under the direction of Eurostat and the ESS. Finally, it should be noted that the Maastricht Treaty set out a number of economic requirements for EMU membership aside from its deficit and debt provisions, including exchange rate controls, managing inflation, and limiting interest rate growth. The ESA is a set of accounting rules that measures economic and financial transactions, and does nothing intrinsically to further these Treaty goals.

3.2   The Beginning of the Excessive Deficit Surveillance Procedure: The Treaty's Biannual Reports

3.2.1   Treaty Requirements for the Biannual Reports

The surveillance process that finally emerged, in both its formal and informal aspects, evolved between 1993 and 1997. The process begins with the technical consideration of the Commission's biannual reports. In Article 104(2), the Maastricht Treaty empowered the Commission to monitor the "budgetary situations" of the EU member states, and the Protocol specified in Article 4 that "The statistical data to be used for the application of this Protocol shall be produced by the Commission." Section 2 of Council Regulation 3605/93, furthermore, required member states to submit biannual deficit and debt data to the Commission, according to the following timetable.

Prior to March 1, these data needed to include:

(1) the member state's planned deficit for the current year, an updated estimate of the immediate past deficit, and the actual deficits for the three preceding years;

(2) the government's "public accounts" or cash basis budget deficit, and the data that are used to transform these figures into the net borrowing total for all levels of the general government;

(3) the actual level of debt for the immediate past four years;

(4) the level of investment and interest expenditure;

(5) the GDP forecast for the current year and the actual GDP data for the preceding four years.

Prior to September 1, these data needed to include:

(1) the update planned deficit for the current year, and the actual deficits for the preceding four years;

(2) the actual level of debt for the immediate past four years;

(3) the level of investment and interest expenditure;

(4) the GDP forecast for the current and the actual GDP data for the preceding four years.

These figures had to be expressed in national currencies and in calendar years, except in the case of the March 1 estimates of the immediate past year's deficit, which could be expressed in national fiscal years. Moreover, when the fiscal year differed from the calendar year, the member state had to submit the actual deficit and debt figures for the two years preceding the current fiscal year. Finally, this reporting requirement would take effect in 1994, which enabled the Commission to establish a baseline of budgetary and economic data, while it perfected the data collection and analyzing process.

The necessity for multiple reporting dates was based on the clearly established practice of making estimates of budgetary expenditures, revenues, and deficits periodically throughout the fiscal year. In the United States, for example, the Office of Management and Budget is charged with taking a number of "snapshots," or budgetary estimates, during the fiscal year in order to determine whether sequesters, or across-the-board spending cuts, should be made in various budgetary accounts if certain expenditure caps are breached. Turning to the EU, in the case of France, for instance, French budgetary accounts are also refined throughout the fiscal year. An early "provisional" version of the data are first published in the spring, which are then revised twice more in a "semi-definitive" form, before a final or "definitive" form is published at the end of the fiscal year.[6] These revisions in France and throughout the various EU member state budgets reflect the ebb and flow of expenditure

[6] National Council on Statistical Information (1994). "Report of Working Group, Calculation of the Criteria of Convergence," Paris, September; National Institute for Statistics and Economic Studies (1998). "Level of Cooperation with Maastricht Criteria," Paris, February 5.

and revenue patterns at all levels of government; seasonal changes in regional, national, and international economies; and variations in data collection, analyses, and reporting systems. Hence, Regulation 3605/93's reference to the "planned deficit for the current year," and "updated estimate of the immediate past deficit" for the March 1 reports. Even in the case of a completed fiscal year, where the "immediate past deficit" is calculated and officially reported, it is not uncommon for governments to revise their deficit figures later on the basis of newly interpreted budgetary data. Thus, the Regulation calls upon the member states to submit "actual deficits for the preceding four years" to accommodate those changes in the September 1 reports.

3.2.2 The Biannual Report Form

Following the drafting of the Treaty, DG ECFIN quickly assumed the task of collecting the member states' economic data, given its traditional role as economic policy-maker for the Commission, and because DG ECFIN staff believed that its working knowledge of ESA would permit it to assess the reports. One task facing the Commission was developing a format for the member states' data. Whatever the format, the data submitted by the member states obviously required harmonization and standardization for use by the Council of Economic and Finance Ministers (ECOFIN) if they were to provide any coherent understanding of where the countries' budgetary conditions stood in a comparative sense. The figures submitted to the Commission needed to include not only the deficit, debt, and GDP information required by the Treaty, but also some level of transparent calculations that demonstrated how the countries arrived at their conclusions. The later step was necessary to ensure consistency and integrity in the data gathering and analysis process within the various governments. Consequently, DG ECFIN and Eurostat developed a four-page reporting form, which has been modified somewhat to reflect interpretations of ESA that have occurred since 1993–4.

An example of the reporting form is shown in the set of figures that comprise Figs 3.2 through 3.5, "Reporting of Government Deficits and Debt Levels for France, 1994–1998," dated February 27, 1998, submitted in compliance with the March 1 reporting date. Figure 3.2 is largely a summary of data collected from the remaining three figures. This figure indicates the fiscal years involved, and it includes the estimated and planned deficits for 1997 and 1998, which were the critical data required for EMU membership. The "codes" refer to the various national accounting categories of the ESA. The budgetary and economic data reported here comply with the most explicit provisions of Regulation 3605/93 regarding the calculation of "net borrowing or net

Country: France
Data are in......
Date: 27/02/1998

	ESA CODES	1994 half-finalized	1995 half-finalized	Year 1996 half-finalized	1997 estimated	1998 planned
Net borrowing (–) net lending (+)	N5					
General government	S60	-423,6	-372,2	-323,4	-244,5	-253,1
- Central government	S61	-352,3	-304,0	-282,6	-214,1	-248,5
- Local government	S62	-15,0	-17,2	3,4	17,4	5,6
- Social security funds	S63	-56,3	-51,0	-44,2	-47,8	-10,1
						forecast (3)
General government consolidated gross debt level at nominal value outstanding at end of year		3572,4	4020,9	4359,4	4698,9	4893,3
By category:						
Currency and deposits	F20 & F30	290,8	295,4	298,2	278,7	
Bills and short-term bonds	F40	238,7	294,8	346,9	375,4	
Long-term bonds	F50	2268,6	2554,4	2924,2	3211,7	
Other short-term loans	F79	107,7	190,9	96,8	142,2	
Other medium- and long-term loans	F89	666,6	685,6	693,3	690,9	
Gross fixed capital formation	P41	234,7	234,0	209,1	226,6	249,1
Interest expenditure	R41	262,6	284,8	296,3	294,5	301,9
Gross domestic product at market prices	N1	7364,3	7624,8	7830,4	8096,5	8436,6

(1) Please indicate status of data: estimated, half-finalized, final
(2) Data for subsectors S61 and S63, to be provided in accordance with an agreement reached in the Expert Group "Comparison of Budgets" are to be provided by the Member States in accordance with statement n°7 to the Council Minutes
(3) Forecast of level of government debt to be provided by the Member States in accordance with statement n°7 to the Council Minutes

Fig. 3.2 Reporting of government deficits and debt levels and provision of associated date in accordance with the definitions and rules laid in Council Regulations (EC) No 3605/93, France, 1994–8

lending," which is the national accounts conceptual equivalent of the deficit or surplus as understood in public accounts, as well as the calculation of the consolidated gross debt and the GDP.

One item that deserves mention in Fig. 3.2 is the "Gross Domestic Product at Market Prices," which is located at the bottom of the figure. The calculation of the GDP is an immense undertaking. The technical aspects of this set of equations run into the hundreds of variables, most of which are direct data sources, and quite literally thousands of pages have been written about how the GDP should properly be determined. As with the deficit and debt calculations, the GDP figures must also be updated and revised through the fiscal year. Finally, the matter of comparable data and methodologies among the member states applies to GDP as well as the other data required by Maastricht. Whereas the Treaty required the harmonization of national deficit and debt figures, the economic and statistical community's efforts to harmonize GDP predated Maastricht. The most recent effort in this regard began in 1989, with the creation of the "GDP Committee," whose task has been the verification and harmonization of GDP methodologies across national boundaries, and to reconcile differences between GDP and Gross National Product (GNP). Hence, the biannual report simply provides a single line for entering GDP data, without further elaboration as to its calculation.

The remaining figures provide the basis for transforming public accounts into national accounts, with Fig. 3.3 of the set of figures focusing on the deficit and Fig. 3.4 on the debt. In Fig. 3.3, under "Net Balance to be Financed by the State," the cash or public accounts are subjected to national accounts requirements. In national accounts, a vital distinction is made between financial and nonfinancial transactions, where all financial transactions must be counted "below the line" and excluded from determining the size of government net borrowing, and all nonfinancial transactions must be counted "above the line" and included. These key categories of exclusions and inclusions are subsequently provided for in Fig. 3.3. For example, under ESA, the disbursement and repayment of loans and the acquisition and sale of equities are excluded from the deficit calculation. If a country, say, is in the position of running a budget surplus and decides to repay its debts by purchasing its outstanding securities, under cash budget accounting these expenditures would normally reduce the size of the surplus, perhaps even pushing the government into deficit spending. According to ESA, however, expenditures used to repay loans are excluded from the net borrowing net lending calculation. This ruling, consequently, would enhance a country's budget surplus, thereby improving its deficit position. Also excluded from the calculation would be the sale of equities, as for instance the sale of shares of stock in public enterprises as would occur in an

Country: France
Data are in......
Date: 27/02/1998

Designation * in national language	Designation in English (t)	Operator (3)	1996 half-finalized	Year 1997 estimated	1998 planned
Net balance to be financed by the state (public accounts)	Solde budgétairs hors FSC et hors FMI	=	−295,4	−267,7	−257,9
Exclude disbursement (−) and repayment (+) of loans	Solde du compte de prêts	−	−3,8	−1,2	−1,6
Exclude acquisition (−) and sale (+) of equities	Recettes de privatisation	−	17,7	−58,3	−28,0
Exclude other net financial transactions included in the budget	Dotations en capital	−	−17,9	−58,3	−27,5
	Désendettement de l'Etat		0,0	0,0	0,0
Include accounts receivable (+) and payable (−)	Solde des autres opérations financières	−	−3,3	0,0	−1,6
Include net borrowing or net lending of other central government bodies	Soldes des opérations non financiéres non budgétaires	+	−4,2	−0,4	−0,0
Exclude net borrowing or net tending of state entities not part of central government				−265,6	−259,6
Other adjustments	Capacité de financement des ODAC	+	9,8	51,5	11,0
Net borrowing of central government (ESA national accounts)	Capacité de financement des APUC	−	−282,6	−214,1	−248,5
Include net lending (+) or net borrowing (−) of : Local government	Capacité de financement des APU	+	3,4	17,4	5,6
Social security	Capacité de financement des ASS	+	−44,2	−47,8	−10,1
Net borrowing of general government (ESA national accounts)	Capacité de financement des APU	=	−323,4	−244,5	−253,1

* Please specify the transition items taking of institutional characteristics in your country whilst the broad classification of transition categories,

(1) Please provide a translation of all specified items in English.
(2) Please indicate status of data: estimated, half-finalized, final.
(3) The operator denotes whether the transaction is included (+) or excluded (−).
(4) Net receipts are entered with a +, net expenditure with a −, The overall sign of operation by the combination of the operator and the item sign.

Fig. 3.3 Provisions of the data which explain the transition between the public accounts budget deficit and the government deficit in accordance with article 4(2), second indent, of Council Regulations (EC) N° 360/93, France, 1994–8

Country: France
Data are in......
Date: 27/02/1998

Designation* in national language	Designation in English (1)	Operator (3)	1996 half-finalized	Year 1997 estimated	1998 planned
Net borrowing of general government	Besoin de Fianancement des APU	=	323,4	244,5	253,1
(ESA national accounts)					
Include disbursement (–) and repayment (+) of loans (F79 + F89)	Crédits à court et long terme hors refinancements	+	64,5	–24,9	
Include acquisition (–) and sale (+) of equities (F60)	Acquisition ou ventes d'actions, OPCUM	+	13,7	–17,8	
Include net accumulation (–) of other financial assets (F20 + F30 + F40 + F50 + F90)	Variations du solde-du Trésor à la Bdf + créances sur prises en pension	+	–6,1	27,0	
Exclude increase (–) or decrease (+) of general government liabilities held as assets within general government (consolidation)	Flux net d'autres actifs financiers	+	13,7	109,7	
	Opérations de consolidation	–	57,7	–3,4	
Exclude accounts receivable (+) and payable (–) and short-, medium-, and long-term trade credit (–) (F72 + F71 + F81)	Decalages comptables et crédits commerciaux	–	19,3	7,6	
Adjustments					
Include capital uplift (–) of index-linked liabilities					
Include appreciation (–) or depreciation (+) of foreign currency debt					
Include correction from market to nominal value when applicable					
Other	Remboursement dette TVA	+	6,4	5,2	
Change in government debt(5)**	Variation de la dette brute des APU	=	338,5	339,5	194,4

* Please specify the transition items taking of institutional characteristics in your country whilst respecting the broad classification of transition categories,
** Government debt of general government consolidated gross debt at nominal value as defined in Council Regulation (EC) IV 3605'89

(1) Please provide a translation of all specified items in English.
(2) Please indicate status of data : estimated, half-finalized, final.
(3) The operator denotes whether the transaction is included (+) or excluded (–).
(4) Net receipts are entered with a +, net expenditure with a –, The overall sihn of operation by the combination of the operator and the item sign.
(5) A negative entry in this row means that debt increases, a positive entry tat debt decreases.
(6) Forecast change in government debt to be provided in accordance with statement Nº 7 by the Member States to the Council minutes.

Fig. 3.4 Provisions of the data which explains the distribution of the government deficit and the other relevant factors to the variation in the government debt in accordance with article 4(2), fourth indent, of Council Regulations (EC) nº 36o5/93, and the Statement nº 7 to the Council Minutes, France, 1994–8.

Country: France
Data are in......
Date: 27/02/1998

Statement number		Year				
		1994	1995	1996	1997	1998
2	**Trade credit (F71 and F81)**	377,3	375,3	413,7	420,4	n.d.

3 **Amount outstanding in the government debt from the financing of public undertakings**

Data:

Institutional characteristics

4 **In case of substantial differences between the face value and the present value of government debt, please provide information on**
i) the extent of these differences

La valeur de marché de la dette publique au 31 décembre 1997 était supérieur de 283,3 milliards de Francs à sa valeur nominale

ii) the reasons for these differences:

10 **Gross national product at market prices (1)**

(1) Data to be provided in particular when GNP is substantially greater than GDP.

Fig. 3.5 Provisions of either data in accordance with the statements contained in the Council Minutes, France, 1994–8

act of privatization, thereby excluding these revenues derived from privatization from the deficit calculation. This ruling leaves the deficit unchanged.

By comparison, turn to Fig. 3.4, which addresses the calculation of the national debt. Council Regulation 3605/93 requires that a member state's debt must be valued in nominal terms or at face value, which may differ from the world market value of such debt instruments. The Regulation also states that the debt under consideration is a member state's consolidated debt, which means that government debt held by the government is excluded from the net borrowing calculation. Furthermore, "outstanding payables," such as trade credits and other accounts payable, as well as receivables are also excluded. What is included in the calculation is the expenditure of funds used in the repayment of loans and the sale of publicly held equities and equities in public enterprises, which improves a nation's debt position. These various exclusions and inclusions are shown in Fig. 3.4 under the section, "Net Borrowing of General Government." The notation F79 refers to the ESA accounting code for short-term loans, F89 for medium- and long-term loans, and F60 refers to shares and equities. Meanwhile, the net accumulation of these other financial assets would be included in the debt calculation: F20, currency and sight deposits; F30, various time and savings deposits; F40, bills and short-term bonds; F50, long-term bonds; and F90, certain insurance reserves. What all of these calculations essentially mean is that a member state's debt equals liabilities minus payables, minus trade credits, valued at nominal value.

Finally, Fig. 3.5 makes some data requests, but its most interesting element is the section "Amount Outstanding in the Government Debt from the Financing of Government Undertakings." This inquiry responds to the argument that the size of national debts varies due to domestic institutional arrangements, where some member states incur greater levels of debt due to their larger number of public enterprises and other semi-public entities that benefit from government financing and public borrowing. This question essentially asks how much of a government's debt stems from borrowing in support of these enterprises, as compared to the more standard operations of government. This section, in any case, is informational and has no effect on the calculation of a member state's debt for purposes of the convergence criteria.

3.3   Applying ESA: The Case of Privatization

At this point, it is worthwhile to consider one particular application of ESA as specified in the reporting tables, the case of how to account for the receipts stemming from privatization, as requested in Fig. 3.3. The value of examining this matter is threefold. First, the EU, and especially the Commission's Competition Directorate General, views privatization as a means of enhancing economic liberalization and the future economic well-being of Europe. Clearly, a ruling that encourages privatization furthers these goals. Second, the classification of government privatization efforts stands as one of the earliest and fiscally most significant of Eurostat's rulings affecting the fiscal policies of the member states. These governments anticipated they would be able to count revenues derived from privatization as a source of receipts that could be applied to their deficit calculations. Third, though the reader may wish to bypass the technical aspects of these examples, working through these cases of privatization illustrates the accounting issues and complexities facing Eurostat and the ESS when employing ESA's national accounts framework. As will be seen, in all of its rulings the key question confronting Eurostat was whether in terms of national accounts to classify items as either financial or nonfinancial transactions. The matter of privatization highlights that distinction.

A common method of raising public revenues is the selling of government owned or controlled assets. Privatization, however, means more than simply revenue raising to reduce deficits. Since the late 1970s, privatization has been associated with concerted ideological efforts at reducing the size of the state as a proportion of the economy, and restricting the government's presence and intervention in the economy.[7] The ESA, however, indicates that certain types of asset sales must be classified as financial transactions, they must be counted below the line that separates the calculation of an equation from its sum, and thus they have no effect on a government's net lending or net borrowing position. Broadly speaking, the ESA distinguishes between two types of assets, financial and nonfinancial. Financial assets include stocks and bonds and other equity and liquid holdings, while nonfinancial assets include land, building, and inventories. On the one hand, when nonfinancial asset sales are directly sold by the government, the sale is recorded in what is known as the capital account, it is counted above the line of the calculation, and it affects the size of the government's deficit. On the other hand, the sale of financial assets, such as the sale of stocks in a publicly owned enterprise for cash, is recorded in the financial account. This type of transaction is regarded as simply the exchange of one type of financial asset for another, therefore must be counted below the line, and does not affect the net lending, net borrowing calculation.

[7] Kathleen R. McNamara (1998). *The Currency of Ideas: Monetary Politics in the European Union*. Ithaca: Cornell University Press; Paul Pierson (1996). *Dismantling the Welfare State?: Reagan, Thatcher, and the Politics of Retrenchment*. New York: Cambridge University Press; Harvey Feigenbaum, Jeffrey Henig, and Chris Hamnett (1999). *Shrinking the State: The Political Underpinnings of Privatization*. New York: Cambridge University Press.

Simply stated, financial transactions are registered below the line, while non-financial transactions are counted above the line, and only activities counted above the line influence the size of the deficit and debt.

From a statistical and accounting perspective, the following four examples demonstrate the logic of how the sale of financial and nonfinancial assets are classified by ESA and Eurostat, as shown in the accompanying tables, where standard national accounting concepts are indicated in capital letters. These examples help clarify one very important set of ESA rules, and they offer some insight into the reasoning that underlies national accounts statistics, as expressed especially in tables 2 and 3 of the biannual reporting statement. In each case, the flow of sales is a transaction in currency and deposits, identified as AF.2 in national accounts. The term "public enterprise" in each case refers to a fully or partially owned government entity.

3.3.1   The Direct Sale of Nonfinancial Assets

In the first example, the government directly sells and collects the receipts from the nonfinancial assets in a public enterprise. The direct sale of these nonfinancial assets, also called gross fixed capital formation, such as buildings, land, and other fixed assets by the government is included in the government's deficit calculation because it changes the balance of assets and liabilities in the government's capital account, and it is the only one of the four examples of privatization to do so. Thus, the revenues from these direct sales can be used to reduce the size of the deficit.

As shown in Table 3.1, the general government's Opening Balance Sheet begins with $100 in nonfinancial assets (AN), as for instance two buildings each worth $50 each. The sale of one of the buildings must be recorded in the government's capital account as a $-$50 change in assets (AN), with a remaining balance (B.9) of +$50. The cash proceeds from the sale (F.2) are recorded in the Financial Account as +$50, with a balance (B.9) in liabilities of +$50. In accounting terms, the balance of the Capital Account must equal the balance of the Financial Account. The Closing Balance Sheet shows the government's nonfinancial assets (AN) are $100 - 50 = +$50. Thus, the change in the balance (ΔB.90) is zero, as the government still holds $100 in assets, though now half are in cash.

3.3.2   The Direct Sale of Financial Assets

In this case, the government directly sells and collects the receipts from the financial assets in a public enterprise. The direct sale of financial assets,

Table 3.1 Direct sale of nonfinancial assets

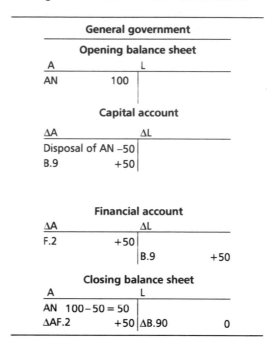

General government	
Opening balance sheet	
A	L
AN 100	

Capital account	
ΔA	ΔL
Disposal of AN −50	
B.9 +50	

Financial account	
ΔA	ΔL
F.2 +50	
	B.9 +50

Closing balance sheet	
A	L
AN 100−50 = 50	
ΔAF.2 +50	ΔB.90 0

particularly stocks and equities, must be recorded in the government's Financial Accounts and in those of the enterprise involved. Privatization in this case is the withdrawal or direct sale of financial assets in a partially or totally owned public enterprise, where there is an exchange of one type of financial asset in the form of equities for another, cash. Consequently, there is no effect on the deficit or the net borrowing net lending calculation, which means these types of sales do not improve a government's deficit position.

In this simple example, as shown in Table 3.2, the general government is selling half of its equity holdings in a public enterprise. In the Opening Balance Sheet, the general government holds $100 in financial assets (AF.5). The sale of $50 worth of these assets to a third party (not shown in the illustration) is recorded in the government's Financial Account as a −$50 loss of equity (F.5) and the +$50 gain of cash (F.2) by the general government. The balance (B.9) is zero, as there is no change in the value of the assets, just their composition. Therefore, there is no change in the government's deficit. In the Closing Balance Sheet, the government's assets in equities (AF.5) is $100−50 = $50, and its assets in cash (AF.2) is +$50, so the change in the total balance of assets as compared to its opening asset position (delta B.90) is 0, as the total remains $100. For the enterprise, its liabilities in equities (AF.5) remains $100,

Table 3.2 Direct sale of financial assets

General government				Public enterprise		
			Opening balance sheet			
A		L		A		L
AF.5	100				AF.5	100
			Financial account			
ΔA		ΔL		ΔA		ΔL
F.5	−50					
F.2	+50					
		B.9	0			
			Closing balance sheet			
A		L		A		L
AF.5 100−50 = 50					AF.5	100
AF.2	+50					
		ΔB.90	0		ΔB.90	0

as its stock is still owned by other entities, and its change in liabilities (ΔB.90) is zero.

3.3.3 The Indirect Sale of Financial Assets

The ESA's rules indicated that certain types of privatization, the sale of stocks and equities, have no effect on a government's ability to reduce its deficit, while the sale of nonfinancial assets will indeed aid a government in this effort. During the years immediately following the signing of the Maastricht Treaty, some governments contended that although direct government financial asset sales did not count as revenue, these revenues could be gained indirectly, through sales conducted by public enterprises under government control. These enterprises would then simply transfer the revenues from their asset sales directly to the government. In other words, a publicly controlled intermediary would sell the asset rather than the government itself, with at least part of the revenues reverting to the government. Eurostat, however, declared that as with the direct sale of financial assets, indirect sales also have no effect on a government's deficit calculation.

In this case there are four actors, the first two of which are shown in Table 3.3: general government; public enterprise A, which is controlled by the government; enterprise B, which is partially controlled by A; and enterprise C, which is the purchaser of B's equities from A. The Opening Balance Sheet of the general government shows financial assets (AF.5) in equities worth $100.

Table 3.3 Indirect sale of financial assets

General government			Public enterprise A		
			Opening balance sheet		
A	L		A	L	
AF.5	100		AF.5	70	AF.5	100
			Financial account		
ΔA	ΔL		ΔA	ΔL	
F.5	−50		F.5	−50	F.5	−50
F.2	+50					
	B.9	0		B.9		0
			Closing balance sheet		
A	L		A	L	
AF.5 100−50 = 50			AF.5 70−50 = 20	AF.5 100−50 = 50	
AF.2	+50					
	ΔB.90	0		ΔB.90		0

Public enterprise A holds assets (AF.5) worth $70 in enterprise B, and it has $100 worth of liabilities (AF.5) in equities, which are owned by the government, with the unseen balance being +$30. The enterprise then sells for cash $50 worth of its assets in B to C, with the intention of forwarding these cash assets to the government. The government's Financial Accounts records the lost equity assets (F.5) in B as −$50, as well as the forwarded cash assets (F.2) as +$50. The subsequent balance is 0, as there is no change in the government's asset worth. Hence, there is no effect from this sale on the net lending, net borrowing calculation. For public enterprise A, it records its change in assets due to the sale of its B holdings to C as a −$50 reduction in equities (F.5), but its equity liabilities (F.5) to the government are also reduced by −$50. Here again, the balance (B.9) is 0, as the loss in equities are balanced by the reduction in liabilities. Finally, the Closing Balance Sheet for the government shows its financial assets (AF.5) to be $100 − 50 = $50, and its cash assets (AF.2) from the sale of A's equities in B to be +$50. As the government's total assets remain $100 when compared to its initial asset position (AF.5), its change in balance (ΔB.90) is 0. Public enterprise A shows remaining financial assets (AF.5) of $70−50 = $20 after its sales of equities in B, and its financial liabilities (AF.5) of $100−50 = $50 to the government. The change in balance (ΔB.90) is 0, as the difference or balance between the enterprise's assets and liabilities is +$30, both in its Opening and Closing Balance Sheets.

3.3.4   The Indirect Sale of Nonfinancial Assets

This transaction is similar to the indirect sale illustrated above, with the difference being that the assets from the public enterprise being sold are nonfinancial in nature, yet here again the receipts from the sale are paid indirectly to the government by the enterprise. As with the indirect sale of financial assets, this transaction has no effect on the government's deficit calculation.

As in the indirect sale of financial assets, there are the same four actors present, but with only general government and public enterprise A pictured in Table 3.4. In the Opening Balance Sheet, government holds as financial assets (AF.5) $100 worth of equities in A. The enterprise holds $70 in nonfinancial assets, such as land (AN), in B, and $100 of financial liabilities (AF.5) owed to the government, with the unseen balance being +$30. A sale of $50 of A's assets in B to C takes place, and is recorded in the Capital Account. Public enterprise A's nonfinancial assets (AN) fall by −$50, and its balance (B.9) is +$50, because in accounting terms the sale reduces the need for capital formation, maintenance, and financing. In the Financial Account, the government records the sale of assets (F.5) in B as −$50, as they are ultimately owned by the government, and +$50 in cash assets (F.2) as a result of the funds forwarded from A derived from the sale of these assets. As there is no change in the holding of assets, just their composition, the balance (B.90) is 0. What is

Table 3.4 Indirect sale of nonfinancial assets

General government		Public enterprise A	
Opening balance sheet			
A	L	A	L
AF.5	100	AN	70 AF.5 100
Capital account			
ΔA	ΔL	ΔA	ΔL
		AN	−50
		B.9	+50
Financial account			
ΔA	ΔL	ΔA	ΔL
F.5	−50		F.5 −50
F.2	+50 B.9 0		B.9 +50
Closing balance sheet			
A	L	A	L
AF.5 100−50 = 50		AN 70−50 = 20 AF.5 100−50 = 50	
ΔAF.2	+50 ΔB.90 0		ΔB.90 0

significant here, is that for the government this transaction must be viewed simply as a financial transaction. Consequently, there is no recording of it in the government's Capital Account, and thus there is no effect on its net lending net borrowing deficit calculation. For enterprise A, its financial liabilities (F.5) fall by $-$50$, and its balance (B.90) from the sale is $+$50$. Because, again, accounting principles hold that the balance in the Capital Account must equal the balance in the Financial Account, both are $+$50$. The government's Closing Balance Sheet shows its holdings of financial assets (AF.5) in A at $100-50 = 50, and its change in cash assets (ΔAF.2) is $+$50$, for a total of $100, leaving its change in balance from its Opening Balance Sheet (ΔB.90) at 0. The enterprise's nonfinancial assets (AN), or in this case landholding, in B fall to $70 - 50 = 20. Meanwhile, A's financial liabilities (AF.5) owed to the government fall to $100-50 = 50, and its change in balance (ΔB.90) is 0, as the difference or balance between the enterprise's assets and liabilities is $+$30$ in both its Opening and Closing Balance Sheets.

These four examples apply to the calculation of a government's deficit position, and they indicate that certain types of privatization in the form of financial asset sales are excluded and may not be counted above the line. All the same, however, recall that when determining its debt figure, a government may indeed include these equity sales in its calculations. One example of using privatization for this purpose is Germany's selling of Deutsche Telekom shares in 1997. As an analysis by the *Financial Times* pointed out, "The sale of the Telekom stake would not help directly with the deficit criteria as Maastricht does not allow the use of privatization proceeds to offset a deficit. But funds raised could be used to retire debt, reducing interest payments and bringing Germany closer to meeting the benchmark on overall debt."[8] Thus, ESA produces an interesting disincentive for privatizing public enterprises for purposes of deficit reduction, but a counterpart incentive to privatize for debt reduction. Certainly, there are compelling economic and even budgetary reasons for governments to sell off public enterprises, as encouraged by the Commission, but reducing their deficits to comply with the Maastricht Treaty and Stability and Growth Pact are not among them. Nevertheless, if a government's national debt level jeopardized either its status for gaining EMU membership or complying with the Stability and Growth Pact, asset sales would clearly be one important method of generating revenues.

Finally, it should be noted that the process of drafting this reporting form offered Eurostat its first significant opportunity to influence the surveillance procedure. Although DG ECFIN initiated the crafting of the form, it quickly became obvious that it lacked the technical skill necessary to interpret how

---

[8] Ralph Atkins (1997a). "Budget Concerns May Spur Telekom Sell-Off," *Financial Times*, May 15, p. 2.

ESA would be used to develop the various data required of the member states. Consequently, DG ECFIN came to rely increasingly upon Eurostat's assistance and expertise, which resulted in Eurostat authoring virtually all of the reporting form's tables. Eurostat's technical competence in interpreting ESA during the drafting of the form clearly foreshadowed the critical role the agency would play throughout the rest of the surveillance process. By the end of 1995, Economic and Monetary Affairs Commissioner de Silguy ruled that Eurostat would take the lead role over DG ECFIN in arbitrating the technical interpretation of ESA. Later, in November 1997 the ECOFIN Council determined that Eurostat should manage the biannual notification procedure in time for the decisive March 1998 determination of which countries would be admitted into the EMU. "Because," as one senior Eurostat official observed, "they liked the independence of the situation in the compilation [of the data]."

3.4   The Challenge of Collecting Budgetary and Economic Data

Following the creation of the Commission's reporting form, the initial efforts at gathering member state data revealed a great many organizational, technical, and political obstacles that needed to be overcome before the completed tables could be presented to the EMI and the ECOFIN Council. First, serious problems existed in the comparability, accuracy, and promptness in the economic and budgetary data collected and submitted by the national statistical institutes (NSIs) and national central banks (NCBs). Like Eurostat, none of these organizations were experienced in transforming public or cash accounts into national accounts, while using the specific methodology of the ESA. Consequently, Eurostat's personnel would not only have to educate themselves in the application of ESA to cash budgets, they would also be involved in training and helping to clarify ESA's subtleties to the national statistical experts. Second, the limitations of ESA 79 surfaced even during the drafting of the biannual report. Many "gray areas," as the statisticians characterized them, of how to interpret ESA 79 emerged in such matters as defining exactly what constituted a public versus private entity, how to apply accrual concepts in order to determine when receipts should be counted, or how to value certain financial instruments, such as derivatives, for which there were no nominal values, but where the Treaty called for debt to be valued at nominal rather than marketplace value. All of these questions and many more had yet to be resolved.

Simply put, a great deal of confusion existed throughout the EU as to how to use the reporting form and make sense of ESA 79. "In the beginning we were lost," Dieter Glatzel, Eurostat's chief of unit B-4, candidly recalled. "The member states were lost."[9] The initial set of biannual reports submitted to the Commission by the various EU governments were replete with misclassification of transactions and the misinterpretation of ESA, leading to numerous queries by confused NSI, NCB, and ministry of finance (MOF) officials. To assess the situation, Eurostat conducted a survey in 1994 of the NSIs to determine their ability to decipher ESA 79 for the excessive deficit procedure. The results proved to be disheartening, as Eurostat found extensive institutional incapacity among the member states, with many of the NSIs woefully inadequate and unprepared to undertake their new responsibilities. Particularly deficient were the "Club Med" member states of Greece, Italy, Portugal, and Spain, with Greece's data perhaps the most unreliable in the EU. Noncompliance in submitting appropriate data could be explained primarily in terms of incapacity rather than noncompliance as a preference. Furthermore, although Eurostat personnel were quite familiar with their counterparts in the NSIs and the NCB statistical offices, new working relationships needed to be established between B-4 and the MOFs. Prior to 1992, Eurostat maintained minimal contact with the MOFs, where their discussions were primarily focused on measuring the national GDPs, which was the key component in assessing a member state's contribution to the EU. Moreover, newly designated as Eurostat's point unit for the excessive deficit procedure, B-4's small staff lacked any working experience employing national accounts to interpret member state budgets organized on a cash or public accounts basis. The learning curve throughout the EU proved to be extraordinarily steep, particularly as the member states began to compile the economic and budgetary data demanded by the Maastricht Treaty.

Data collection may appear to be no more than a prosaic bureaucratic chore, yet it is one potentially fraught with intense politics that reflects its own principal-agency problem. The fundamental data collection problem facing Eurostat for the surveillance process is its dependence upon economic and financial information submitted from a highly segmented chain of data producers that extends all the way down to the lowest levels of government. The chain is segmented in the sense that data producers consist of data compilers and gatherers, who are not always data analyzers, who may be different from data suppliers. At each link along this chain, there may be opposition to what statisticians call the "burden of change." Every time there is a new or additional requirement, such as a change in coding or the requirement of creating new and unique data, there is a burden or cost of that change that must be absorbed somewhere along the chain. Certainly the pressures, benefits, and

---

[9] Interview with Dieter Glatzel, February 10, 2000.

costs of these burdens vary among data users, suppliers, and gatherers, and when the burden is too great for technical, administrative, financial, or political reasons, this encourages the evasion of these new data requirements. Without adequate positive and negative sanctions to discourage this evasion, data compilers, analyzers, and suppliers may simply not comply, they may produce what is known as "camouflaged statistics," or they could engage in a "blame game" by claiming that some other link in the chain, supposedly beyond their reach or authority to control, is breaking the chain when they, in fact, are responsible.

As the Maastricht Treaty's budgetary reference values apply to "general government," financial data need to be collected from all the levels of government within a member state, not simply from the central government. So, for example, the French Ministry of Finance gathers data from more than fifty prefects, which in turn obtain budgetary data from hundreds of local governments within their jurisdictions. Altogether, this data gathering, processing, and analysis involves thousands of units of government and public enterprises. In the case of Spain, the local government level comprises some 9,000 institutional units, including 6,000 towns with less than 5,000 inhabitants, all of which produce budgetary data. After the member state MOFs gathers these data, they are translated into national accounts statistics by the NSIs, each of which have their own unique organizational structure consisting of data gathers, compilers, and analysts, who submit the required convergence information to Eurostat.

3.5   The Assumption of Trust in the Surveillance Process

Reflecting the Maastricht Treaty's explicit surveillance delegation, the political reality of the relationship between the EU and the member states, and its own workload capacity, the Commission and the member states based the surveillance process on the assumption of trust. This notion of trust reflected the way in which DG ECFIN and Eurostat interpreted their responsibilities: the Commission's function is not to evaluate the accuracy or the integrity of national budgetary data, in the way that, say, the European Court of Auditors might. Rather, its task is to ensure that cash based, public accounts budget and financial figures are properly translated into national accounts data, are correctly entered in the biannual reports, and are submitted to the proper EU authorities. This interpretation of the Commission's task also complied with the direct charge it received in the Maastricht Treaty. The Treaty states in Article 104(2) that "the Commission shall monitor the development of the budgetary situation . . . in the Member States with a view to identifying gross errors." Thus, the Treaty itself declared that what mattered was not that every single budgetary transaction be reviewed, but only gross transgressions or significant attempts to evade the requirements of the convergence process. As Dieter Glatzel put it, "We are only looking for the big things."[10] The Commission's assumption of trust also reduced what at first appeared to be an overwhelming and unmanageable bureaucratic task for ensuring the accuracy of these budgetary data. Neither Eurostat nor the NSIs maintain sufficient staff in terms of numbers or expertise to analyze the national budgets in great detail. Instead, these statistical agencies depend upon the normal auditing and accounting checks on national budgets conducted by executive, legislative, and independent oversight.

The assumption of trust, it should be pointed out, is not unique to Eurostat, but is a common assumption throughout the Commission. As Neill Nugent reveals, "The Commission is faced with many difficulties in attempting to carry out its supervisory and monitory tasks . . . . The first is that the Commission has very limited resources. It just does not have enough staff to watch over the activities of national administrative agencies as closely as ideally desirable. The Commission therefore depends heavily on the good faith and willing cooperation of the agencies."[11] Consequently, the Commission's presumption is that if budgetary data are misleading or inaccurate, intentionally or not, these errors will be detected at the national level because interested domestic and international parties have a stake in reliable and precise cash budget figures. "The problem [with trying to cheat]," observed a Eurostat official,

is that you have a lot of other kinds of information; the sector 'general government' is only one [level of government that submits budgetary data]. So, if you try to cheat on this one you have to cheat on the whole system, and this, I think, we would have detected. If you try to manipulate in one sector you have to manipulate in another, and [for example, if you try to alter the deficit to GDP ratio] you may end up with higher contributions to the EU budget because of sudden GDP increases!

Hence, the MOFs are presumed to deliver to the NSIs honest budgetary data that will then be transformed by the NSIs into national accounts, which will be presented to Eurostat.

[10] Interview with Dieter Glatzel, March 19, 2003.
[11] Neill Nugent (2001). *The European Commission*. New York: Palgrave, p. 276.

Similarly, the NCBs presumably report honest debt figures to their national NSIs, which have their own sources of external validation. One factor encouraging the integrity of the debt figures submitted by the member states is the clear definition of what constitutes government debt as offered by the Protocol on the Excessive Deficit Procedure and Council Regulation 3605/93. The Regulation defines debt as the "liabilities of general government in the following categories: currency and deposits (F20 and F30), bills and short-term bonds (F40), long-term bonds (F50), other short-term loans (F79), and other medium and long-term loans (F89) as defined in ESA." The notations F20, F30, and so on, refer to the financial sector of the economy and types of financial instruments in that sector. Consequently, this comparatively detailed definition offers more clarity and less flexibility in the interpretation of national accounts data reported by the NCBs to their NSIs. Moreover, as compared to the national deficit figures compiled by the MOFs, the national debt figures produced by the NCBs are more publicly transparent, as the financial markets subject government securities to far greater scrutiny than is commonly given to regular budgetary statistics. Finally, as the politics of Maastricht evolved in 1997 and 1998, it became increasingly clear that the focus of political attention was on national deficits rather than debt as the determining factor in gaining EMU membership. For this reason, and because the debt data were less subject to creative accounting and gimmickry due to the stricter definitions and external scrutiny, Eurostat and Committee on Monetary, Financial, and Balance of Payment Statistics (CMFB) rulings on member state data concentrated on deficit rather than debt figures. So, for the surveillance process, the member states presumably supply honest deficit and debt figures, leaving Eurostat to focus its attention on how these data are translated into national accounts, while monitoring the member states' "gross errors."

This assumption of trust, therefore, narrows the scope of Eurostat's charge, lessening both its administrative and political monitoring burden. In a broader sense, the assumption of trust reduces the scale of the principal-agency problem facing both Eurostat and the EU's leadership. Rather than being forced to challenge the integrity of member state budgets themselves, Eurostat more simply monitors the integrity of national accounts' interpretation of the deficit and debt data. As the agency's administrative burden is reduced, so too is its political exposure. This helps to minimize Eurostat's political vulnerabilities while strengthening its capacity to make independent decisions for the surveillance procedure. As events unfolded, this responsibility fully tested Eurostat's bureaucratic and political abilities, particularly in 1996 and 1997.

3.6   The Techniques of Surveillance: Asking the Right Questions, Mission Visits, the Press and External Sources of Information, and Training and Secondment

3.6.1   Asking the Right Questions

Despite the assumption of trust, Eurostat maintained an active surveillance of member state fiscal activity. This monitoring reflected Eurostat's responsibility to ensure that the proper application of ESA national accounts occurs in the categorization of member state cash budgets, all while operating under the assumption that the budgets themselves were accurate and honest. "The whole system," a Eurostat official declared, "depends on member states supplying numbers [where] you can't question the correctness of the figures. The question was whether they conformed to ESA or not. You take for granted that the member states will not cheat on the figures." Thus, ironically, at the same time as the Commission's staff presupposed honest national budgets, they remained highly skeptical about how these budgets were translated into national accounts data for use on the biannual reports. At the same time, however, by analyzing and sometimes challenging the member states' national accounts interpretations of their budgetary data, Eurostat discovered questionable calculations of the cash based figures. One DG ECFIN official expressed the underlying wariness felt throughout the Commission staff during the convergence process as a result of the member states' willingness to press their interpretations of ESA and manipulate its gray areas: "All the countries are guilty, they all exploited ESA to the full of its ambiguities. Talk about fudging! [They] used every margin in the national accounting system, and exploited all, I would not say loopholes, but lacuna, in the balance sheets, that's clear."

The member states certainly were motivated to fulfill the Maastricht criteria and gain entrance into the EMU, and, later, to avoid potential sanctions imposed under the Stability and Growth Pact. As *The Economist* observed, "Countries collect their own numbers and report them to the European Union. Given the penalties for transgression, there is a clear incentive to cheat."[12] The NSI, NCB, and MOF representatives of these states fully understood this, and they were prepared to present their data in the best possible light to aid their governments. Moreover, their governments pressured them in this direction. As one NSI director reflected:

There were four of us [NSI directors]. We were talking about the Maastricht process, and I said the process was good now because we didn't get any political pressure to change

---

[12] "Roll Over, Enron," (2002). *The Economist*. August 3, p. 42.

the [ESA] definitions to manipulate the numbers through to change the deficit, and that I can make a professional decision and will have the strength of Eurostat behind me. All the other members from the other countries sat back and roared with laughter and said, "Come on now, you're not serious." The point was there was clear admission by those three countries that they had been under pressure to present numbers in a most favorable way.

The Commission's personnel, in turn, were keenly aware that the NSIs and the other national organizations were agents of their governments, with the shared interest of presenting their data to the best possible advantage of their respective member states. Moreover, the ESA 79's limitations and uncertainties as to whether a particular budgetary activity should be counted as a nonfinancial or financial transaction, simply encouraged and offered a degree of legitimacy to the member states' efforts at submitting self-promoting data.

Eurostat, therefore, necessarily approached its task of adjudicating and interpreting ESA as more than just a passive agent, and it adopted many of the monitoring techniques that are typically employed by the Commission in its role as guardian of EU treaties.[13] While being politically sensitive, Eurostat pressed the NSIs, NCBs, and MOFs to discover the background and details of perplexing and unusual, if not suspicious, member state interpretations of ESA. Questions needed to be asked, data gathered, and new information sources developed. Particularly as Eurostat began to take on the lead role in the surveillance process, the agency issued one request for information after another to the member states, surveying them on such matters as the structure of their public debts, the treatment of interest paid on bonds used in fungible tranches, and the standardization of privatization revenues. These questions were required to understand the unique budgetary practices of the various member states, while they in turn formed the basis for asking additional, more probing and accurate questions. "Our problem," one Commission official noted, "was to ask the right questions."

The information we got from the excessive deficit procedure [biannual reports] was basically an overall figure, and then you have additional information from the budget. Then you got some hint that something looked strange, and then you started asking questions. Or, sometimes member states asked questions directly. Of course, the weakness is that a member state that wouldn't supply the figures and wouldn't ask the questions, you could not see whether they are cheating with the figures, because we couldn't

---

[13] For the Commission's standard monitoring techniques, see Neill Nugent (2001). *The European Commission*, ch. 1. New york: Palgrave. Also see E. L. Normanton (1996). *The Accountability and Audit of Governments: A Comparative Study*, chs. 8–11. Oxford: Manchester University Press, for comparative monitoring techniques employed by national audit agencies.

control them, and it was not really our task. It worked on trust and you had to take for granted that no crimes are committed.

Eurostat personnel learned to ask the right questions by employing a variety of monitoring techniques throughout the surveillance procedure, including unobtrusively scrutinizing media sources, accessing websites, and occasionally receiving inside information from within the member states. More overtly, the Commission instituted mission visits to each of the member states to serve the twin purposes of surveillance and building technical capacity among the NSIs.

3.6.2 Mission Visits

Soon after the Commission received the first set of biannual reports in 1994, Eurostat initiated a series of mission visits to the member states to help remedy the information sharing and mass organizational learning problems experienced by the national governments. These missions also served the purpose of supplementing in a more formal manner the extensive correspondence, telephone, Internet, and CMFB-related meetings that occurred between EU officials and the member states following Maastricht. Unlike the CMFB meetings and their associated working parties and task forces, these visits focused solely on the country in question, rather than EU-wide considerations. Furthermore, these country visits symbolized the Commission's willingness to work cooperatively with their member state partners in the surveillance process. A few "fact finding" mission visits to three member states occurred in 1995, followed by regular annual missions to the member states beginning in 1996. Given B-4's tremendous workload, second visits would take place only in unusual circumstances.

Typically, a mission consisted of representatives from Eurostat, DG ECFIN, and the EMI meeting with representatives from a member state's NSI, NCB, and MOF. Eurostat developed an agenda submitted in advance that usually required clarification of a broad range of budgetary, economic, public finance, and macroeconomic matters. While responding to these inquiries, the member states routinely posed questions of their own. As one Eurostat participant recalled, "Usually the countries came with difficult cases and asked for clarification. There was no ruling, just a discussion." The uncertainties surrounding the application of ESA 79 enhanced the need for discussion and clarification. "There were cases where there was no rule from ESA. We have to discuss the case, the economic justification, keeping in mind all the principles of sound accounting." Moreover, as the years passed, the implications of misusing ESA and thus miscategorizing budgetary activity provoked more inquiries from the member states. "Countries tended to raise questions," observed a DG ECFIN staffer, "because increasingly there was an awareness that a problem identified at the last minute could have very important political costs."

Although the missions provided an opportunity for open discussion and the clarification of national accounts questions, they clearly supported the Commission's monitoring and surveillance activities. The Eurostat, DG ECFIN, and EMI personnel serving on the mission teams learned how to ask the right questions through trial and error. They noticed inconsistencies in interpretation. They looked at the economic meaning of the public balance sheet, at the sale of assets, at the participation of the state in providing capital injections into public and private enterprises, and at the correspondence between the public accounts and their transformation into national accounts. Over a period of time, as the number of visits increased, the mission teams learned by comparison to identify differences in how the member states classified similar transactions. "We discovered something in one country," remembered B-4's Dieter Glatzel, "and then started asking the same questions in other countries."[14] Then, once a member state was forced to reclassify its transactions and revise its data, not uncommonly it quietly began to provide Eurostat with information about other states that employed the older classification.

3.6.3   The 1996 Missions

The 1996 missions offer an instructive account of how they served to assist the member states in developing their national accounts capacity, while providing Eurostat with important information about member state fiscal activity. Mission visits were conducted in each of the fifteen EU member states in 1996. The discussions that took place during these visits provide some indication of the condition of the surveillance at that time, the efforts Eurostat made to develop harmonized economic data, and the challenges it faced in doing so. By asking the same questions to each of the countries, Eurostat could detect variations and potential problems arising in particular member states. At the same time, these questions were targeted to a few key topics that had emerged and proved troublesome during the past two years. What neither the missions nor indeed the entire surveillance process intended to do was conduct a thorough, synoptic examination of the various national budgets. Eurostat's unit B-4 simply lacked the staff, the time, and the competency to examine these budgets and their translations into national accounts with any depth. Instead,

---

[14] Interview with Dieter Glatzel, March 22, 2000.

as an "aid to calculation," the staff sampled what they called the "big issues" that were brought to their attention by way of their formal and informal sources of information.[15]

The 1996 mission visits were largely fact-finding in nature, and they tended to ask big issue types of questions. The agenda for these visits generally focused on recent developments in the member state's ability to generate national accounts data; the distinction between insurance and pension funds; the restructuring and privatization of public enterprises; cases of debt assumption and cancellation; issues related to the issuance of nonconventional debt instruments; and matters more specific to the individual country. The matter of debt assumption and cancellation, for instance, could have significant repercussions, as many of the EU governments engaged in activities of this nature. Denmark canceled student loans and loans made to developing countries. Belgium canceled housing debts in Brussels. Spain's central government assumed agricultural and industrial debt. The dynamics of the meetings were largely of an informative nature, as suggested by the discussions summarized in Table 3.5, with the member states looking for advice and advising the Commission staff as to the status of their abilities to comply with ESA.

One defining characteristic of the 1996 missions was the sense of uncertainty and organizational learning taking place throughout the European statistical community. As these very brief examples from the missions suggest, in a number of cases Eurostat was not prepared to rule or provide a final interpretation of ESA 79. By 1996, some of the ESA's very important gray areas remained unresolved. To a degree, Eurostat and the ESS could afford this additional year of learning, but 1997 would be far different. The political and economic context surrounding the creation of the EMU, the European Central Bank (ECB), and the euro became increasingly tense, and the margin for error and mismanagement of the surveillance process quickly diminished. The obvious urgency of the matter and the rapidly approaching March 1998 evaluation date meant that Eurostat needed to produce a set of rulings that would finally clarify ESA 79's "big issues." The member states would have just three more opportunities to submit their biannual reports, with the deficit and debt data taking on increasingly more important political significance. Consequently, beginning in 1997, Eurostat began issuing a series of sometimes highly controversial rulings on the proper national accounts interpretation of the member

---

[15] The idea of "aids to calculation" was originiated by Aaron Wildavsky, as a way to understand how budget makers rely upon experience, satisficing, and incrementalism to reduce the complexity and enormous amount of calculations and choices that are associated with producing budgets, usually by understaffed personnel who lack the resources to engage in synoptic decision-making. Aaron Wildavsky (1984). *The Politics of the Budgetary Process*. Boston: Little, Brown, esp. chs. 2 and 3.

Table 3.5 1996 mission discussions

- Belgian authorities stated that revenues received from privatization were being calculated as financial transactions from 1995 onwards, thus not aiding the country's deficit position; this was not true for 1993 and 1994. The authorities explained this was a "very delicate matter," since these revenues were formally adopted into the budgets and it was too late to change them.

- In discussions with the Irish representatives, Eurostat indicated that ESA 79 provided little guidance on sale–leaseback agreements, where governments sold public assets and then leased these same assets from the private owner. The sale's revenues could reduce the government's borrowing requirement, and might be used as a form of collateralized loan to aid the government's budgetary position. Eurostat would develop some guidelines on this matter.

- The Irish and the Danish meetings raised the matter of how to record the retroactive time distribution of benefits determined by legal rulings. In the Irish case, as it came to be known, an Irish court ruled in 1995 that an EU directive mandating the equal treatment of men and women's welfare benefits superseded Irish law. This meant these women would receive a delayed payment of 262 million pounds, but the question was deciding in which fiscal year these expenditures should be recorded. An initial attempt to employ ESA 79 called for distributing the arrears over the years during which they were accruing due. Discussion within the ESS and the Financial Accounts Working Party, however, suggested that the full liability should be counted when the court determined the liability had been established, which meant recording the full amount in 1995. A not completely dissimilar case emerged in Denmark, where a 1992 EU court ruling abolished the Labor Market Contribution. This led to Danish taxpayers filing suit requesting a tax refund for the years 1988–91. Because the court had not yet ruled, a change in accounting was not yet required.

- The German delegation stated that in an effort to reclassify governmental and quasi-governmental units appropriately, public-sector hospitals were being transferred from the S60, the general government sector, to S10, the nonfinancial corporations and quasi-corporations sector in ESA. This would change the classification of the investments in such hospitals, thereby reducing the government's deficit by 2–4 billion marks.

- The Greek government informed Eurostat that among the debts assumed and canceled were a series of bonds issued to the Bank of Greece, where the amount was included in the central government's debt, but not as it should have in the government's deficit totals. The Greeks awaited further guidance from Eurostat, which noted that ESA 79 was "silent" on the matter of debt assumption and cancellation. Consequently, relying upon ESA 95, when a government assumes or cancels debt of a unit in another classification of the economy, this must be counted in both the government's deficit and debt figures.

- The Finish MOF asked for clarification on the proper classification of swap revenues. Governments engage in currency (and sometimes interest rate) swap agreements so

Table 3.5 *Continued*

that their basket of currency holdings include important foreign currencies, primarily borrowed dollars and yen in exchange for national currencies. Thus, the domestic debt may be measured in part in the exchange rate value of the borrowed currency, where the difference in value between the domestic and foreign currency may produce revenue gains. Foreign currency debt accounted for about half of Finland's total public debt in 1996. Eurostat responded that given uncertainties associated with ESA it was not prepared to recommend the appropriate accounting categorization, but it would provide that information as soon as possible.

states' deficits and debt calculations. As a result, though the 1996 mission visit agenda began with the broad informational topic of "recent developments in the member state national accounts system," the 1997 agenda focused on the compliance matter of the "implementation of recent Eurostat decisions," which are analyzed in the next chapter.

3.6.4   The Press and External Sources of Information

In addition to the mission visits, the world and national press provide vitally important sources of independent information for the surveillance process. Commission staff frequently rely upon the press for its coverage of critical budgetary and economic news to learn the details of member state fiscal and economic transactions. Eurostat's Unit B-4 assigns staff to create a weekly clipping packet distributed to all personnel on government finance issues, with stories collected from the EU's major newspapers and numerous Internet web sites. Time and again, Eurostat's Glatzel noted, "the press pointed us in the right direction."[16] "Because we had to detect things ourselves," a DG ECFIN official observed, "we looked to the press for assistance. It could be a newspaper, like the *Financial Times*, that could have written something and then we ask questions from what we see." In one case, for example, *The European* identified apparently dubious accounting practices conducted by the Spanish government: "In the privatization of petrochemical company Repsol last year, a significant amount of the income the government raised from selling part of its stake went to reducing the budget deficit, even though this is against the rules of Eurostat, the Commission's statistics arm"[17] The press's contacts are far more diverse than Eurostat's. Whereas Eurostat must seek information primarily through formal channels, reporters from the major newspapers may

---

[16] Interview with Dieter Glatzel, March 22, 2000.
[17] Parry, John N. (1997). "Spanish Reputation Falls In Hole," *The European*. May 29–June 4, p. 4.

search for more informal sources or even disaffected government employees. "They had people on the inside," recalled Eurostat's Alberto De Michelis, "there was somebody inside [the MOF] telling the press something was going on."[18] Newspaper and television stories alerted Eurostat to two of the most important cases upon which it and the CMFB would rule, that of France Telecom and the sale of Italian gold reserves, both of which will be discussed in the next chapter. In the case of France Telecom, MOF officials appeared on television and announced that France's deficit problems were solved due to France Telecom's partial privatization. The newspapers *Le Monde* and *Les Echos* then immediately picked up the story. As a result, said De Michelis, "the case was [made known to us] because the press raised it."[19] In addition to identifying government fiscal activities, the presence of the press soon acted as its own form of restraint on member state behavior. Not only did Commission staff pay attention to the press, so too did officials throughout the EU, making member states aware of the budgetary practices of their peers, thus adding to the pressure on the states to conform with Eurostat and ESA. "Countries would watch each other very strongly," Eurostat's Yves Franchet noted, "and call us and say 'we are worried about this case, and the press will say we're trying to cheat.' Each time we would have a new review process [to consider the member state's behavior]."[20]

Eurostat's staff rely heavily on electronic communications for surveillance and the transmission of information. The Internet offers Eurostat ready access to budgetary information from the various MOF and other government web sites. Though they vary in quality, the web sites permit Eurostat personnel to review for themselves the status of budgets and economic transactions. These budget figures may be cross-checked against information gathered from such sources as the mission visits, press reports, and data submitted by the member states. E-mail and fax machines also provide Eurostat with rapid forms of communication that transmit large quantities of information, and that immediately enable parties to ask questions and clarify national accounts interpretation of data.

International financial credit ratings also serve Eurostat's surveillance efforts. These ratings services evaluate the financial status of government bonds and securities for investors, with low grades often boosting the interest rates governments must offer to induce the purchase of their debt instruments. "Something which helped me very much," Franchet recalled,

was the following situation: In one country which had been reporting data that was very unreliable for years, and the markets had been reacting to that, the Moody Index

---

[18] Interview with Alberto De Michelis, February 13, 2000.   [19] Ibid.
[20] Interview with Yves Franchet, May 24, 2000.

[rating for that country's fiscal status] was quite low. We went to this country and we went to the minister of finance, and we put pressure on them that we had to have access to their books. As a consequence, [of their providing all the data, the calculation of their] deficit and debt went up. But at the same time, their Moody Index went up because the new data are now credible. So now I tell everybody that credibility is as much at stake as the level of deficit and debt.[21]

Eurostat is able to access many of these investor rating services, such as Moody's and Standard & Poor's, on the Internet, and then connect the information derived from these sources to press and media reports, other public and private Internet web sites, and alerts offered by the various member states.

3.6.5   Training and Secondment

To remedy the need for technical training in the member states, Eurostat inaugurated training sessions for the various NSI staff. These sessions later were expanded to include representatives from the EU accession and candidate countries, who generally speaking had little experience with national accounts and whose NSIs tended to be woefully understaffed and underfunded. These training sessions supplement the regular working parties and task forces in the sharing of information and developing potential solutions to national accounts problems. Secondment of NSI staff with Eurostat offers an additional way to train personnel and explore national accounts issues. Eurostat, however, is aware of potential conflicts of interest with seconded staff who might favor their member state's position. "Sometimes what we do," Eurostat's Dieter Glatzel commented, "is to the people who are too new on secondment, we don't give them their country's portfolio, we don't want to play the game like that."[22] Seconded staff often, however, accompany Eurostat on country mission visits, and, with their insider knowledge, clarify the fiscal and economic activities of their home states. In this way, training and secondment serve the dual functions of building member state institutional capacity and aiding the surveillance process.

3.7   Conclusion

Soon after the signing of the Maastricht Treaty, the EC developed a variety of formal and informal processes to begin the surveillance of the EU member

---

[21] Interview with Yves Franchet, March 19, 2003.
[22] Interview with Dieter Glatzel, March 19, 2003.

country budgets. The initial surveillance procedure mandated by the Treaty consisted of biannual reporting of member state economic and budgetary data beginning in 1994. To supplement the existing formal committee structure of the ESS, Eurostat followed up on the collection of these data by way of country missions that enabled the Commission to conduct one-on-one discussions with representatives of the individual member states. Eurostat, moreover, turned to a variety of obtrusive and unobtrusive methods for monitoring member state budgetary and economic activity, all in an effort to ensure that the member states properly employed ESA when they translated their cash budgets into national accounts data.[23] Furthermore, the Commission limited the scope of the surveillance through the idea of trust, where the reliability of member state budgetary data was accepted as a fact; but this notion of trust did not, however, extend to the member states' translation of these data into national accounts. This idea of trust reflected what were viewed as the political realities of the day, where it would be unacceptable for the Commission to challenge the veracity of the member states' budgets, as well as the limited institutional capacities of the both the Commission and the member states' NSIs to monitor these budgets in intricate detail. Nevertheless, the idea of trust still required extensive surveillance and monitoring by Eurostat of member state fiscal and economic activity. Consequently, determining the success of Eurostat's surveillance depended not on the quality of these data in terms of the accuracy of member state budgets, but upon whether Eurostat could assure the ECOFIN Council and the EMI that the biannual reports reflected a proper national accounts interpretation of deficits and debt. Still, to some degree the two notions were obviously linked and demanded Eurostat's attention.

Finally, the entire period from 1993 through 1997 was marked by significant organizational learning by all parties involved in the surveillance, and a growing need to resolve the uncertainties of ESA as early as possible in 1997. EU authorities quickly discovered through their early surveillance activities and from the first submissions of the biannual reports that ESA 79 proved to be notably lacking as a complete guide for interpreting the budgetary data required by the Treaty. The European statistical community recognized even before the Maastricht deliberations began that ESA 79 required revising, and at the very time the Treaty was signed, Eurostat and the NSIs were in the process of developing the next generation of national accounts in what would be become ESA 95. The fundamental problem with ESA 79 stemmed from the fact that by 1992 the very nature of the world economy and its financial activities

---

[23] Eugene J. Webb, Donald T. Campbell, Richard D. Schwartz, and Lee Sechrest (1966). *Unobtrusive Measures: Nonreactive Research in the Social Sciences*. Chicago: Rand McNally.

had changed in often dramatic ways. A host of new forms of financial instruments and types of public enterprises complicated the definition of what constituted a governmental unit, for example, with the result that ESA 79 simply failed to incorporate these innovations into its methodology. Although ESA 79 suffered from such limitations, the drafters of the Treaty on European Union were unaware of these problems because neither the professional statisticians of Eurostat nor those of the NSIs were ever consulted during the treaty-making process. As a result, despite its various limitations, the Treaty mandated that ESA 79 be regarded as the official set of rules that the Commission was obligated to employ during Stage II of the Maastricht process. Following the Treaty's approval, the gaps between ESA 79's accounting standards and the actual nature of national economies and public finance became increasingly apparent, which meant that the Commission's surveillance responsibilities became far less a simple cook book application of ESA 79 and more an interpretive role in adjudicating the gray areas of national accounts. Eurostat's rulings on these gray areas, reached by way of the CMFB advisory process, effectively constituted administrative case law that ultimately determined how member state cash budgets would be interpreted through national accounts.

4

European Statistical Case Law for Stage II Convergence, 1994–7

Rule-making is a central function of the European Commission (EC). These rules articulate, clarify, and implement the grand bargains that constitute European Union (EU) treaties. These rules take many forms, including secondary legislation such as regulations, decisions, and directives, as well as clarifying memoranda, notifications, and reports. Yet another type of rule-making comes in the form of administrative case law, which is the form of rule-making employed by Eurostat in its efforts to interpret European System of Integrated Economic Accounts (ESA). Eurostat's authority to issue case law rulings stemmed, first, from the Maastricht Treaty, which designated ESA as the basis for measuring the member states' deficits and debts, and second, from various Council regulations that delegated to Eurostat the responsibility for acting as ESA's interpreter. Thus, Eurostat proceeded to exercise its case law making authority in a highly independent fashion, but one that gained legitimacy only with the support and approval of the member states in Eurostat's statistical advisory committee, the Committee for Monetary, Financial, and Balance of Payment Statistics (CMFB).

Beginning in 1994, Eurostat issued a number of case law rulings that determined how certain financial and budgetary transactions would be recorded according to ESA's national accounts methodology. These rulings produced marginal, though sometimes decisive changes in budgetary outcomes from what the member states intended. Consequently, the presumption that the Economic and Monetary Union (EMU) fiscal convergence process permitted the member states to undertake whatever actions they regarded as necessary, such that the Maastricht Treaty "simply forced member-state governments to fund expenditure through taxation (or other forms of revenue generation, such as privatization)," is unfounded, as is the assertion that "EMU involved neither programmatic intervention, regulatory reform, nor the reshaping of rights."[1] The Maastricht Treaty, in fact, imposed a regulatory structure and regulatory reform on member states' fiscal policies by way of the surveillance procedure, and reshaped rights by declaring ESA to be the measure of government fiscal behavior with the Commission serving as ESA's interpreter. Although EU governments retained their programmatic choice of fiscal policies, their policy selections could be significantly influenced by the determination of whether these policies furthered their goals of deficit and debt reduction, according to ESA.

As the March 1998 deadline for determining EMU membership grew nearer, ESA's importance increased dramatically. Although in 1992 a number of Maastricht signatories appeared able to comply with the treaty's fiscal provisions with little effort, by the end of 1996, only Luxembourg completely fulfilled the fiscal convergence criteria: Ireland, Luxembourg, and the Netherlands achieved compliance with the 3.0 percent of Gross Domestic Product (GDP) deficit requirement, while Finland, France, and Luxembourg reached the 60 percent debt target. Though during the first few years of the Treaty's existence the various ministries of finance paid scant attention to Eurostat, as the political significance of a few tenths of a percent loomed larger, they necessarily were forced to consider much more seriously the ramifications of ESA for their budgetary decisions.

Between 1994 and March 1998, Eurostat issued seven major rulings and a number of lesser rulings, the latter of which are considered in the Appendix to this book. Most of these decisions proved to be highly technical and relatively uncontroversial. Others, however, were reached under the most tense of political circumstances, for quite literally the fate of the EMU lay in the balance. Of the seven major areas of case law considered here, the France Telecom decision deserves special attention. This case, ruled upon in 1996, proved to be decisive in directing the statistical community's decision-making process, moving it from one characterized by unilateral, centralized decision-making on the part of Eurostat, to one that witnessed a more collective, transparent, deliberative procedure, where institutions and consultation were significantly enhanced. The France Telecom decision, in fact, marked the low point in Eurostat's credibility and standing during the convergence process. Yet, it also promoted the role of the member states in this process, and thereby, in the long run, actually strengthened Eurostat's independence and autonomy in exercising its surveillance responsibilities.

---

[1] Alberta Sbragia (2001). "Italy Pays for Europe: Political Leadership, Political Choice, and Institutional Adaptation," in Maria Green Cowles, James Caporaso, and Thomas Risse (eds.), *Transforming Europe: Europeanization and Domestic Change*. Ithaca: Cornell University Press, p. 79.

4.1   Belgium and the Treatment of Indirect Privatization (1994)

In one of its earliest cases, Eurostat confronted the issue of how to classify indirect privatization. In 1993 and 1994, Belgium reorganized the financial institution *Caisse General d'Epargne et de Retraite* (CGER). A public holding company, the *Societe Financiere de Participation*, sold 50 percent of its interest in CGER's bank and insurance companies, and then transferred the income from this equities sale to the Belgian government, 32.2 Mrd BFR in 1993 and 12.7 Mrd BFR in 1994.

Belgium's Ministry of Finance (MOF) attempted to count this income as revenue that could be applied to the country's deficit. Moreover, this effort at indirect privatization, where one public enterprise sold equity in another public equity while transferring the proceeds to the government, sidestepped the widely agreed upon principal that under ESA the proceeds from sales of equities by way of direct privatization, as described in Chapter 3, had no effect on the calculation of the deficit, as this was classified as a financial transaction. "It was very difficult for us to convince politicians, in Belgium for instance," recalled Alberto De Michelis, Eurostat's director of the surveillance process,

that when you sell something, this did not give you a capital transfer in terms of national accounts, which makes you richer. But it is just a financial transfer, because you sell something and you receive money for that, but there is no enrichment of the state. But the politicians say 'We receive money, we reduce the deficit.' In the beginning it was difficult, but in the end they agreed to comply.[2]

In the instance of the CGER, the intervening use of the two subsidiaries to funnel money back to the state from a national accounts basis did not affect the economic standing of the state. Consequently, Eurostat ruled this to be a financial transfer, with no influence on the calculation of Belgium's deficit. This decision in 1994, therefore, established a precedent for evaluating all future efforts at indirect privatization.

4.2   Ireland and Retroactive Accounting (1995)

The Irish case essentially determined whether certain transactions would be recorded according to the principles of accrual accounting, the system

---

[2] Interview with Alberto De Michelis, February 23, 2000.

preferred by national accounts statisticians found in the ESA and in the United Nations' System of National Accounts and Supporting Tables (SNA), or in line with cash accounting employed by virtually all the EU member states in the development their public budgets. The outcome of this decision, in addition to the specific effect it would have on Ireland's deficit position, would establish the supremacy of the statisticians over the member states' ministries of finance in this critical question of which format would be used in calculating member states' deficits and debt.

In 1995, the Irish supreme court ruled in favor of a women's association, which claimed that since 1985 the Irish government failed to implement an EU directive, the Directive on Equal Rights adopted in 1978, regarding equal rights between men and women. The court ordered the government to pay 183 million punts, the accumulated unpaid amount due over the ten-year period, plus a 60 million punt penalty.

The national accounts question was how to record this government payment. A cash basis records transactions when public funds are actually collected or disbursed. An accruals basis of recording follows the accounting principles of "prudent bookkeeping" and "established right," which means that rights and claims are recorded when they are acquired, and liabilities or debts are recorded when they are certain. The Irish national statistical institute (NSI) recommended the following treatment, and requested guidance and approval from Eurostat: The unpaid 183 million punts would be recorded on an accrual basis, based on the principle of established right, where the benefits would be recorded retroactively over the ten years when they were due. These payments, furthermore, would be recorded in the household and government sector balances. The 60 million penalty, because this right was established by the Irish court, would be recorded only in 1995.

After consulting its advisory CMFB, Eurostat accepted the accruals basis proposed by the Irish, but relied on the model's "certainty principle," which means that transactions are recorded when both parties have established the certainty of the transaction. Consequently, Eurostat ruled that Ireland had to record the benefits due payment as well as the penalty in its 1995 fiscal year accounts, the year in which the transaction was a certainty for both the women's association and the government. Moreover, Eurostat found this transaction to be a capital transfer, thereby adding 0.5 percent of GDP to Ireland's 1995 deficit. This ruling became the precedent for evaluating other cases of retroactive benefits, as in an Italian supreme court case where pensioners were granted additional, retroactive pensions.

4.3   The Assumption of Germany's *Treuhandanstalt* Debt (1995)

Aside from the matter of how to classify the assumption and cancellation of debt, the *Treuhandanstalt* case demonstrated the difficulty of employing ESA 79 when its methodological framework simply proved to be inadequate. The German government established the *Treuhandanstalt* in the early 1990s to oversee the privatization of public enterprises in the former East Germany, with the expectation that the funds derived from this privatization would help finance Germany's reunification. Instead, as one EC official observed, the privatization process proved to be a "disaster," and the *Treuhandanstalt* accumulated a debt of 204 billion DM, or 5.9 percent of GDP, in a four-year period. At that point, in 1995 the German federal government absorbed the *Treuhandanstalt* with its debt assumed by a federal agency, the *Eblastentilgungsfond*. The national accounts issue was whether the state's debt also grew by the same amount. Germany's NSI initially classified the debt assumption as a capital transfer, which did indeed raise Germany's public debt level and, according to a senior Eurostat official, increase the budget deficit to some 10 percent of GDP. The German MOF, however, in the biannual economic reports submitted to Eurostat, indicated the assumption constituted an "extraordinary transaction" that should indeed have no effect on the country's fiscal position.

When considering the national accounts application of whether the MOF or NSI were correct in its interpretation, Eurostat first looked to ESA 79. Although ESA 79 largely fulfilled its task of indicating how to record transactions, it proved unable to describe how to record nontransactional flows or stocks, including the appearance and disappearance of assets, such as debt. The earliest versions of ESA 95, however, integrated these types of transactional and nontransactional activities into a more complete national accounting system, and for that reason, with the assent of the CMFB, Eurostat turned to the newer ESA for guidance.

ESA 95 provides a rule for the recording of an assumption of debt by general government, which states in section 5.16, "the counterpart transaction of debt assumption and debt cancellation is classified in the category capital transfers and is recorded in the capital account." Consequently, the debt would be counted towards a government's net borrowing position. Nevertheless, there are three exceptions to this rule: First, "if the owner of a quasi-corporation assumes liabilities from or cancels financial claims against the quasi-corporation, the counterpart transaction of debt assumption or debt cancellation is a transaction in shares and other equity." Second, "If government cancels or assumes debt from a public corporation which disappears as an institutional unit in the system, no transaction is recorded in the capital account or the financial account. In this case a flow is recorded in the other changes in the volume of assets account." Third,

> If government cancels or assumes debt from a public corporation as part of an ongoing process of privatization to be achieved in a short term perspective, the counterpart transaction is a transaction in shares and other equity. Privatization means the giving up of control over that public corporation by the disposal of shares and other equity.[3]

The first and third of these provisions make reference to transactions in shares and other equities, which indicates the transaction is financial in nature, and thus has no effect on the deficit and debt. In addition, Eurostat's interpretation focused on the second proviso, which addressed the case where the assumption of debt from a "disappearing institutional unit" is considered as a change in volume or quantity. A disappearing unit is one where it no longer contains financial and economic purpose. Because the *Treuhandanstalt* disappeared both as an organizational and economic entity, in that the state absorbed its functions and purpose, Eurostat ruled that the economic flow associated with its debt should be treated as an "other change in volume" rather than as a capital transfer. As a Eurostat official rhetorically inquired, "There was one company which had a economic amount of debt, but this [company] disappeared. So, if you do a capital transfer, to whom do you do a capital transfer? So we prefer to say this was a change in volume, not a sound budget process. This was an exceptional case. " Eurostat, therefore, overturned the decision of Germany's NSI to count the *Treuhandanstalt* debt absorption as a capital transfer, which meant that Germany avoided incurring significant fiscal encumbrances that could have severely affected its budgetary position in 1996 and 1997.

4.4   France Telecom (1996)

Clearly, the case of France Telecom proved to be the most important, if not infamous, test of Eurostat's credibility throughout the Stage II convergence process. France Telecom bloodied Eurostat, toughened it, matured it politically, and forced Eurostat to strengthen its decision-making processes. The lessons of

---

[3] Eurostat (1996). *European System of Accounts, ESA 1995*. Luxembourg: Office for Official Publications of the European Communities, p. 95.

France Telecom enabled Eurostat to avoid future political pitfalls and manage successfully the difficult decisions that it confronted in 1997. Where Eurostat had become rather brash and aggressive in late 1994 and increasingly through 1996, as it found its technical expertise offered it a leading role in the Treaty process, France Telecom instilled Eurostat's leadership with a healthy dose of humility, caution, and political savvy. Significantly, Eurostat learned from France Telecom, and successfully transformed its institutional arrangements, decision-making procedures, and relationship with the press.

The France Telecom case focused on how to calculate or record the enterprise's retirement funds in terms of national accounts. France Telecom, the state-owned telecommunications giant, emerged from the first of two major reforms of France's Postal Telephone and Telegraph (PTT) utilities service. The first reform occurred in 1990, when PTT was divided into two autonomous public organizations, France Telecom and *la Poste*, which permitted their employees to maintain their civil service designation. As such, the employees' retirement plans were based on a pay-as-you-go financing, the same as for other civil servants. France Telecom, however, provided contributions to offset the retirement deficit for that portion generated while its employees remained in service. In this scheme, under national accounts, these entities were classified under the sector S10, nonfinancial corporate and quasi-corporate enterprises. PTT was regarded as a quasi-corporation, with its two break-off entities considered corporations. Retirement flows were also viewed as being internal to the organizations, with nothing recorded in the central government to affect the deficit or debt.

In July 1996, the second reform transformed France Telecom into a national corporation, leaving the state with a majority owning share of the enterprise's capital. The enterprise's employees retained their civil service status as *fonctionnaire* and their benefits under the unfunded civil service pension plan. Doing so, however, changed France Telecom's pension status, from one where pensions paid by the state were reimbursed by the enterprise, to one where France Telecom was obligated to make an employer's regular social contribution to the state. This standard rate of 38 percent, comparable to other enterprises in the communications industry, lowered the level of retirement payments France Telecom contributed for its employees. To make up the difference, which would result in a loss of revenue for the state, the law required France Telecom to make a huge lump-sum payment to the national government of 37.5 billion francs ($7.32 billion). These funds were deposited in a special account at the Treasury that would be distributed in annual payments of 1 billion francs per year until the sum expired, a rate that would prevent an artificial one-year balloon in state revenues. This annual benefit would remain as long as France Telecom's special account lasted with the Treasury, though France would claim the lump-sum payment as revenues and apply it towards its deficit in 1996. When it was extinguished, the French government would absorb the retirement liability and the subsequent reduction in its revenue stream. The state would meanwhile enhance its revenues by privatizing a third of France Telecom in 1997 for 42 billion francs.

All this, the French government claimed, would aid its fiscal condition. "The Ministry of Finance of France went on television one day," recalled Eurostat's De Michelis, "and said, 'We have solved the problem, we now have [revenues of] minus 1 percent of GDP because of this question of France Telecom.'"[4] Nevertheless, by 1997 it had well been established that a direct privatization was considered a financial transaction, as in the case of the state selling equity shares in France Telecom, and therefore any revenues derived from the sale would not count towards the deficit or debt. What proved quite troubling for the murky national accounts framework of ESA 79 was how to classify the 37.5 billion payment to the French government, a staggering amount of money totaling some 0.5 percent of GDP.

How Eurostat resolved this question in the face of a very skeptical world press would directly affect both its credibility and the legitimacy of the convergence process itself. As Eurostat's De Michelis noted, even the French newspapers *Le Monde* and *Les Echos* "said there is something wrong, how can this be?" According to the *Financial Times*,

The French government has fully exploited the magic of Maastrichtian mathematics to convert a projected 1997 state budget deficit of 3.45 percent of GDP into an overall public deficit of 3 percent. . . . Some unkind spirits might conclude that the 1997 budget had been concocted in Versailles' Hall of Mirrors than the finance ministry's dour fortress at Bercy. . . . Next year's big windfall, however, comes in the form of the special FFr37.5bn payment by France Telecom to the government to cover future pensions liabilities for its employees—part of a deal with the unions on the company's privatization. This imposes a new liability on the state, but one that is difficult to calculate and is not, according to Bercy, calculated in the national accounts of any EU state running similar pay-as-you-go pension schemes. Paris consulted Brussels on the France Telecom payment and the European Commission said this week that "at first sight" it sees no problem.[5]

The English press proved to be particularly hostile to France's attempt to claim the France Telecom largesse as revenues, viewing this as just one more reason

[4] Interview with Alberto De Michelis, February 23, 2000.

[5] David Buchan (1996). "The Magic of Maastrichtian Mathematics," *Financial Times*. September 19, p. 3.

for the United Kingdom to avoid EMU membership, as suggested by coverage of the story in *The Times*:

Last week, France announced an astonishing deal with France Telecom. Before it is privatised, the state-owned company will make a one-off payment to the Government of Fr37.5 billion, the equivalent of £4.7 billion or 0.5 percent of gross domestic product. In return, the Government has promised to keep in the public purse the future cost of telecom workers' pension payments. Put baldly, France gives itself a fighting chance of meeting the Maastricht deficit criteria but also burdens future taxpayers with huge unfunded pension liabilities. Yves-Thibault de Silguy, spokesman for Europe's Monetary Affairs Commissioner, has said that the Commission has not yet taken a definite position on the transfer, but it is inconceivable that France will be stopped. The Commission is so desperate for the single currency to go ahead, whatever the economic arguments, that is reputed to boast a team devoted to exploiting the vague language of Maastricht and dreaming up accounting wheezes to ensure that enough countries make the EMU grade. . . . For the Bundesbank, this is a nightmare. For British Euro-sceptics, it is ample reason to remain deeply suspicious about the single currency. . . . If France is allowed to get away with outrageous interpretations of Maastricht's deficit rules, why can't Greece or Portugal?[6]

So, how would the Commission's accounting "team" address France Telecom? Eurostat's solution to France Telecom called for treating this payment as a capital transfer, thus counting towards France's deficit, which in 1996 stood at 4.1 percent of GDP. Eurostat officials based their interpretation of ESA on the civil service status of France Telecom's employees. Under conditions where a public enterprise's pay-as-you-go unfunded pension burden exceeds its workers' contributions, the state may provide the unsupported amount. This state payment then would be regarded as a "miscellaneous current transfer," and the state may elect to be compensated in the form of a one-time payment. When the pension system is unfunded, in other words where there are no reserves supporting the scheme, ESA does not consider pension rights as either an household asset or a liability on the system. What this means is that transactions and flows of funds in this system are not financial transactions. Consequently, France Telecom's one-time exceptional payment to the state should be regarded as a capital transfer, or R70 in national account terms, and not a financial transaction.

Eurostat presented this interpretation to two of the European Statistical System's (ESS's) technical working groups, the National Accounts Working Party and Financial Accounts Working Party (FAWP) in October 1996. These

---

[6] Janet Bush (1996). "Why Further Euro-Fudge Will Sweeten Path to EMU," *The Times*, September 10, p. 31.

meetings proved to be exceedingly contentious, with many of the NSI representatives challenging Eurostat's interpretation with those of their own. At least four other analyses were offered by FAWP: First, the one-time payment constituted a future benefit stream; second, this was the beginning of a funded, as opposed to unfunded, pension program; third, this payment simply was the outgrowth of the 1990 reform and represented the sale of a government asset; and, fourth, this was no more than a capital withdrawal of funds by the state from France Telecom. Each of these alternatives viewed the payment as a financial transaction rather than a capital transfer. After some very tense discussion, neither of the two working groups reached consensus on how to classify the transaction. This stalemate left Eurostat seeking approval for its ruling with the CMFB, the highest policy-making body in the ESS.

How Eurostat went about gaining this approval, however, set off a firestorm of controversy within the ESS, the media, and the EU member states. Following the disagreement within the working parties, a CMFB meeting was called for October 23, with the agenda item "Transactions between the state and public enterprises related to the financing of retirement pensions in the framework of the ESA 2nd edition." The ensuing discussion failed to produce a solution, so FAWP was ordered to reexamine the issue, develop further alternatives, and identify its preferred classification. A questionnaire for this purpose would be distributed to CMFB members, with its Executive Body using this information to arrive at an agreed upon classification. Eurostat would then receive this decision in the form of a recommendation, leaving it to make the final ruling. All this would be completed by November 6, the date of European Commissioner Yves-Thibault de Silguy's press conference on the matter. What occurred instead was that the survey issued by Eurostat, acting as the secretary for FAWP, contained only two options, one supporting Eurostat's capital transaction interpretation, the other subsuming the FAWP's earlier four alternatives into a single option that interpreted France Telecom as a financial transaction. Furthermore, the consultation process was "fore-shortened," as responses had to be submitted by noon on October 31, 1996. At that time, Eurostat Director General Yves Franchet announced that by an 11 to 4 vote, CMFB endorsed Eurostat's solution, with both representatives from Germany, Finland, the United Kingdom, and one representative each from Austria and the Netherlands voting in the minority.

Many CMFB members, including its chairman, Austria's Wolfgang Duchatczek, were deeply angered by what they regarded as a distinct lack of consultation and a "shortcutting" of the process. In a statement to CMFB, Duchatczek declared that he had never been consulted about the survey's changed deadline, he learned of the decision only by way of the press, and no written statement had yet been provided to CMFB members explaining either the logic or the scope of this ruling.[7] This last point was particularly crucial, Duchatczek argued. Did the ruling apply to all similar transactions, or only to France Telecom? If only to the single case, then the implication was that for all such incidents the individual countries would have to "ask for approval by Yves Franchet." Franchet, moreover, failed to explain to the press the extent of the division within CMFB, where ten member state delegations believed the alternative financial transactions interpretation was equally consistent with ESA as Eurostat's capital transfer version.

Franchet's brief explanation to Duchatczek was that an intervening holiday reduced the number of days for the surveying process, that much information and discussion had been shared orally as well as in writing, and that because CMFB was not a committee with comitological authority with formal voting procedures, its decisions were more consensual and advisory to Eurostat. So, the results from the survey were sufficient for making the decision. Duchatczek's "statement is in my opinion," Franchet continued, "the expression of a minority of participants with strong views against the proposed solution, and the Executive Body should be careful in forewarding [sic] such a biased view."[8]

Despite Franchet's warning, a deep rupture occurred within the EU statistical community, with Eurostat heavily criticized both on grounds of substance and procedure. To begin with, Eurostat's decision appeared to many to be a French conspiracy, made up of a French commissioner, a French director of Eurostat, and French staff in Eurostat's unit B-4, aimed at aiding France's efforts at deficit reduction. "I think first that it was a French issue," observed one NSI director, "with a French commissioner [de Silguy], and a French official in Eurostat [Franchet], which was very damaging. There was a lot of shock when the France Telecom issue happened because it was handled very badly, they got it wrong." A senior Director General II for Economic and Financial Affairs (DG ECFIN) official described France Telecom as a "fireworks case," while a chief statistician serving with the European Monetary Institute (EMI) recalled that "It's burned on the minds of everyone who was involved in it." Even a French statistical official in the MOF agreed that "I probably don't think that it was the best decision in the context of national accounts, but it's one of those gray areas." Participants to the decision aired their disagreements in the press, as German National Central Bank (NCB) and NSI representatives openly voiced their opposition to Eurostat's ruling, while a Spanish CMFB

---

[7] Wolfgang Duchatczek (1996). "Statement Wolfgang Duchatczek (Chairman of CMFB), Delivered by John Kidgell (Vice Chairman), on the 'France Telecom' Case," November 27/28, p. 2.

[8] Yves Franchet (1996). "Note for the Attention of the Chairman of CMFB," November 5, 1996.

delegate astonishingly admitted he voted for France because President Jacques Chirac announced he endorsed Spain's efforts to join the EMU. By voting for Eurostat's solution, the official reasoned that this would "make it easier for Spain to qualify." Franchet, meanwhile, defended his position, declaring, "I think 11 of 15 [votes on CMFB] is a good consensus. It's not for me to judge the budget policy of France." All of this deeply embarrassed the European statistical community. As one senior French official concluded, France Telecom "has evidently affected the credibility of our system of accounting in the eyes of international observers."[9]

The call for clarifying the CMFB's role and standardizing the process for makings national accounting statistical decisions was widespread among the EU member states. The director of the Italian NSI, who actually voted in favor of Eurostat's ruling, declared in a letter to Yves Franchet:

These events have a negative influence on the credibility of statistics in this delicate phase of development of the Economic and Monetary Union. It is absolutely necessary therefore to ensure that similar events will not take place in the future. To this end I believe we should define a work plan and a calendar of actions aimed at increasing the transparency of the decision making process and allowing the experts to undertake the in depth analysis with the necessary delays. I therefore propose that Eurostat defines well in advance the work plans of the committees that are called upon to express their views on such issues, and comply rigorously with actions and deadlines envisaged in the plan, resisting any possible pressure being put forward from various sources (national authorities, the media, other services of the Commission).[10]

Following this letter, CMFB chair Duchatczek charged the incoming chair, John Kidgell of the United Kingdom, with developing a new set of procedures for CMFB, warning that "of greatest concern must be the damage done to the public perception of our economic statistics. There has been much discussion in the press. It has been highly critical."[11]

Kidgell's proposal, in turn, contained little in terms of formal procedure, other than to request that Eurostat submit its proposed rulings to the FAWP, which would pass its comments on to CMFB for its opinion. Eurostat would then make its final ruling based on this consultation. As Kidgell noted, "There is already some precedent for this (e.g. the Irish case, indirect privatization,

---

[9] The NSI officials' comments as well as Franchet's statement appeared in Tom Buerkle (1996). "Germany Grows 'Suspicious' Over EMU," *International Herald Tribune*, November 11, p. 5.

[10] Paolo Garonna (1996). Letter to Yves Franchet, Rome, November 13.

[11] Duchatczek (1996). "Statement Wolfgang Duchatczek (Chairman of CMFB), Delivered by John Kidgell (Vice Chairman), on the 'France Telecom' Case," November 27/28, p. 3.

etc.), but past cases have been handled in different ways, and the procedures have been established as required, rather than being planned in advance."[12] This reformed procedure emphasized transparency, in part by requiring that if questionnaires were to be used again in the future the data would be collected by the chair of the CMFB and then turned over to Eurostat, rather than Eurostat gathering the data and announcing the results. Eurostat would also be required to provide the CMFB with a written statement that completely explained the logic underlying its final rulings. This process of consultation with CMFB, Kidgell reminded, was just that, for according to the Maastricht Treaty it was the Commission, with Eurostat acting as the Commission's lead agency, which determined how ESA would be interpreted. Unless the CMFB itself were granted comitological powers, which would enable it to exercise oversight over Eurostat and gain direct access to the European Council, then "the alternative is to strengthen the consultative machinery by voluntary means—'a gentleman's agreement.' "[13]

Eurostat, in fact, had every reason to accept most eagerly this gentleman's agreement. The France Telecom decision took a terrible toll on Eurostat's, and Yves Franchet's, credibility, undermining the agency's norms of statistical neutrality, impartiality, and independence.[14] France Telecom, as Franchet openly admitted, was "a mistake," and if the agency were successfully to fulfill its Maastricht Treaty responsibilities, this trust needed to be regained as quickly as possible.[15] What is significant about Franchet's reaction to France Telecom is that he both learned from the experience and made it work to Eurostat's advantage.

Franchet readily adopted Kidgell's reform procedures. Although he recognized that his authority permitted him to override these recommendations, "we learned that unless we built a completely transparent and known-by-everybody system, we would go from crisis to crisis." If this were to occur, clearly Franchet and Eurostat would be blamed for compromising the entire Maastricht Treaty surveillance process. Moreover, by making his ruling on France Telecom without full consultation, Franchet found his personal reputation stained by the charge that he made what should have been a technical decision solely on the basis of his nationality. If the integrity of both Eurostat and the Maastricht process were to be ensured, then any future national accounting decisions necessarily had to be transparent and embedded in a consultative framework. "I have learned," Franchet concluded, "and the

---

[12] John Kidgell (1996). "Procedures for Handling Transactions That are Not Clearly Defined in ESA," December.   [13] Ibid., p. 3.

[14] On these norms, see Neill Nugent (2001). *The European Commission*. New York: Palgrave, pp. 210–11.   [15] Interview with Yves Franchet, March 19, 2003.

countries and the actors have learned that hiding things was much more risky than consulting."[16]

Franchet also realized that France Telecom severely damaged Eurostat's credibility with the press, and this critical relationship urgently needed attention. Franchet freely acknowledged that when it came to the press, "we were not professional. When you are a statistician touching areas which are very sensitive politically you have to be communicative. I communicated to the Commission but not to those involved in the decision process. You must have a process that can be presented [to the public] without shame. You have to be able to stand up and answer all the questions addressed to you. [Credibility with the press] takes years to build and minutes to lose."[17]

Drawing upon his own observations on how the World Bank managed its public relations program, Franchet immediately began holding extensive press conferences and issuing detailed press releases on any significant national accounts decisions affecting the surveillance process. Starting in the early spring, Eurostat released six press releases between February 1997 and January 1998 clarifying the substance of its rulings.[18] Each of these press releases contain a section titled "A Long Process of Prior Consultation," which outline the CMFB's role in the process, the function of the working parties, and the threefold basis of the CMFB's "opinions": First, conformity with ESA 79; second, reliance upon ESA 95 when ESA 79 fails to provide a solution to the problem; and, third, if there are two or more satisfactory interpretations, that the committee turn to generally recognized accounting principles, such as those offered by the United Nations' SNA 93. These releases, however, clearly stated that although the CMFB opinions provided a valuable source of information, Eurostat exercised the final decision on classifying deficit and debt statistics.

---

[16] Interview with Yves Franchet, May 24, 2000.

[17] Interview with Yves Franchet, February 10, 2000.

[18] These press releases help significantly to illuminate Eurostat and CMFB's rulings. "Deficit and Debt: Eurostat Rules on Accounting Issues," N. 10/97, February 3, 1997a; "Accounting Rules: Eurostat Takes Further Decisions on Deficit and Debt," N. 16/97, February 21, 1997b; "Accounting Rules: Complementary Decisions of Eurostat on Deficit and Debt," N. 24/97, March 26, 1997c; "New Decisions of Eurostat on Deficit and Debt: Payments from Central Bank to the State, Changes in the Due for Payment Dates for Taxes, Salaries, Social Contributions and Benefits," N. 88.97, December 17, 1997d; and "New Decision of Eurostat on Deficit and Debt: Payment to the State Following the Sale of Monetary Gold by Ufficio Italiano dei Cambi (UIC) to Banca d'Italia," N. 5/98, January 27, 1998. Also enormously helpful are two presentations by Eurostat's B-4 staff: Jean-Pierre Dupuis (1998). "The Reliability of the National Accounts in the Context of the Excessive Deficit Procedure," Seventh National Accounts Seminar, National Accounts Association, Paris, January; and Dieter Glatzel (1998). "The Excessive Deficit Procedure: Statistical Measurement of Debt and Deficit," December 31. Also see Wolfgang Duchatczek (1997). "Report on Statistical Work Concerning the Excessive Deficit Procedure," November 2.

In this way, Eurostat attempted to make the logic and procedures underlying its rulings understandable and transparent to the press and the various stakeholders in the EMU convergence process. What the press releases made clear was that the entire EU was vested and participated in these accounting decisions. Eurostat's rulings, and by implication those of the full Commission, were authoritative and final, but they were neither autocratic nor made in isolation. They were open and transparent, trustworthy, and held to some publicly accessible standard, those of ESA. Consequently, with some degree of confidence an outsider could believe the process was accountable and reasonably insulated from political influence.

Significantly, Franchet's effort proved to have some success, as the press incorporated Eurostat's news releases into their own stories, employing them as a guide to identify the political and economic importance of Eurostat's decisions for the convergence process, as suggested by this report that appeared in the *Financial Times* in 1997:

The European Commission will publish guidelines on Monday attempting to clarify when governments can use creative accounting to reduce their public deficits in order to qualify for economic and monetary union. Statisticians from the 15 EU member states were finalizing a draft of the report at a meeting in Luxembourg yesterday. Their recommendations will be passed to Eurostat, the agency which handles statistics for the European Commission. National statisticians are said to be unhappy about political pressures to influence their conclusions. Commission officials stressed again yesterday that Eurostat is an independent professional body whose work conforms with internationally accepted accounting procedures. . . . Financial markets will scrutinize the Commission report to see if the argument over creative accounting is moving in favor of more leniency. A restrictive interpretation would damp what many believe is excessive confidence in a "broad EMU" embracing the southern countries.[19]

The newspaper made reference to the embarrassing France Telecom incident, Belgian gold, and the Italian eurotax. For the first time, Eurostat's CMFB consultation process received at least some description, where the CMFB's recommendations were passed on to Eurostat for a final ruling. The story also noted the political pressures felt by the statisticians, particularly due to the weak fiscal condition of the "southern countries," Italy, Spain, and Greece, and especially Italy's "creative accounting" efforts to gain entry into the EMU with the aid of the eurotax and its classification of its railroad public enterprise debt. The article certainly suggested that if the statisticians were to carry out their tasks correctly, they needed to be insulated from such pressure.

[19] Lionel Barber (1997a). "Brussels to Clarify Stance on Deficits," *Financial Times*, February 1–2, p. 2.

Thus, ironically, the France Telecom debacle worked in important ways to Eurostat's advantage. Franchet called it the "birth certificate of Eurostat." For until France Telecom, Franchet's agency and its connection to the Maastricht Treaty was simply unknown and unreported by the press. Even negative press coverage raised Eurostat to prominence and gave it a public identity. This public recognition actually insulated Eurostat and the CMFB to a degree from outside political interference and pressure. As Franchet noted with some amusement, the France Telecom press stories "frightened everyone at the Commission, so nobody dares to even think about intervening."[20] "In all this process, the most important decision [stemming from France Telecom]," Alberto De Michelis stated,

was to give a role to the CMFB. Because we used to trust the NSIs, but in Europe, sometimes the statistical offices are under the influence of political authority. Giving a role to the CMFB, this strengthened the independence of the NSIs, because they could say to their ministries, 'Oh look, I take this position, and I know you don't like this decision, but I take this decision because it has been taken by the group, and you can not reject this decision.' This process strengthened the relation between NSI and NCBs, and gave a real role to the statisticians. Because when a decision was taken by Eurostat, following the consultation of the CMFB, no one could oppose it, otherwise immediately the press would be informed.[21]

A senior ECFIN officer concurred, noting with some admiration that "Eurostat has responded to political pressure by building up some kind of institutional consultation system to sort out the contentious issues. So they are always backed by very, very thorough consultation of the member states before taking their decision. They have always systematically decided along the lines of the dominant position in the CMFB." Indeed, one of Eurostat's most vigorous critics among the NSI directors agreed that "since we introduced that process in early 1997, it is clear that every decision that Eurostat made was supported by the CMFB majority." Yet, he also shrewdly observed that the press and the new process also constrained Eurostat's independence. "Eurostat was sufficiently frightened by the publicity that would be thrown at them because of the transparency . . . there were enough strong spoken people [at CMFB] to embarrass Eurostat if they had made a ruling against a majority of statisticians, even if there was political pressure within the Commission."

The France Telecom case, therefore, produced several outcomes. First, it greatly enhanced the transparency of the Maastricht Treaty's surveillance

---

[20] Interview with Yves Franchet, February 10, 2000.
[21] Interview with Alberto De Michelis, February 23, 2000.

process, as it applied to the determination of the EU member states' deficits and debt levels. Eurostat press releases, for example, identified both Eurostat's ruling and CMFB's position and its vote. Second, the France Telecom case of 1996 provided invaluable lessons about what procedural flaws needed to be corrected in the national accounts decision-making process. Fortunately for everyone involved, Franchet and his critics quickly resolved their differences, and used this opportunity to mend their consultation procedures in time for the decisions that were to take place the following year, during the politically charged year of 1997. Third, France Telecom strengthened the technical objectivity of this determination by ratcheting up the political price for any attempt at manipulation by the Commission, or for that matter, by the various member states. The decision-making process for evaluating the national accounts measure of a deficit or debt level was now deeply embedded in the majoritarian based CMFB. If Eurostat reduced its political risk level by following the majoritarian view, CMFB to some extent absorbed that risk, leaving the member states themselves subject to potential press scrutiny for any dubious rulings. Fourth, prior to France Telecom, national accounts decisions were made, as an EMI official noted, "by higher management persons at Eurostat." After France Telecom, decision-making no longer simply resided with a dominant central authority, but both the decision-making and the success of the surveillance process rested with a broader, integrated set of actors.

All this said, it would be truly inaccurate to portray Eurostat as a docile supplicant of the CMFB after France Telecom. CMFB remains an advisory body to Eurostat. It plays the role of a modified veto player in the statistical decision-making process, where its own autonomy is constrained by its own majority voting rules that limit the power of individual member states, by its procedural transparency that enables all participants to observe each member's behaviors and preferences, by the commonality of epistemic and professional values as statisticians, and by the Committee's lack of comitoligical powers that would enable it to appeal Eurostat rulings. Furthermore, Eurostat exercises significant organizational influence over CMFB by building "consensus" among the member states to produce an "optimal" CMFB recommendation, where large majority rulings are provided to both guide and politically shield Eurostat's final rulings. Eurostat, in addition, still provides the principal staff for CMFB, the working parties, and task forces; it determines which member states will be represented on these working parties and task forces, in a way a senior Eurostat official stated, to create "a balanced view." Eurostat frames the technical questions that will be addressed by these working parties and task forces, as well as by the CMFB, and, working with the CMFB chair, it greatly influences the agenda for these various meetings. Eurostat coordinates the agendas and leads the mission visits to the member states. Its technical knowledge of ESA is unmatched in the EU, and according to the Maastricht Treaty, as the principal agent of the Commission, it still retains the ultimate authority for determining how ESA will be interpreted and applied to individual cases. Finally, despite France Telecom, as an organization it remains highly regarded among statisticians in the EU for its technical expertise. Given these many comparative advantages over individual member states that might seek a self-interested ruling, after the France Telecom imbroglio, Eurostat has since successfully encouraged large majority, consensual CMFB decisions on all major rulings.

4.5   Netherlands, Belgium, Italy, Germany, and the Sale of Gold by Central Banks (1996 and 1997)

In these decisions, Eurostat and the CMFB ruled on the direct and indirect sale of gold, and its revaluation, all efforts by EU member states to reduce their deficits.

4.5.1   Belgium (1996)

Between 1995 and 1997, at least four EU member states engaged in the sale of gold by their central banks and the transfer of these revenues to their governments. To varying degrees of public notoriety and contentiousness, these governments attempted to apply these receipts towards their deficit and debt levels. According to ESA 79, there are four categories of gold: financial gold, which may be held by all institutional sectors of the economy; industrial gold for productive purposes; investment gold; and monetary gold held by a central bank used for official reserves. The question at hand was how to classify either a direct or indirect sale of NCB gold under ESA.

In the early 1990s, the NCBs of the Netherlands, Spain, and Belgium sold gold, but the Belgium case became the basis of Eurostat's ruling. The proceeds from these sales, amounting to 236 billion BEF, were placed in an account identified by Belgium's national central bank as an "Undistributable reserve of capital gains on gold." Because Belgium's central bank is half publicly and half privately owned, the government passed legislation asserting that the special account belonged to it. These funds were then used to trim Belgium's foreign currency debt by some 221 billion BEF, or 2.7 percent of GDP. Basing its decision on the notion that this transferring of funds to the state was similar to indirect privatization, Eurostat ruled that this revenue infusion was a financial transaction, the sale of gold was unrelated to the NCB's monetary or exchange rate policies, and thus did not affect the deficit levels of either Belgium or the Netherlands.

4.5.2 Germany (1997)

West Germany's economy was the strongest in Europe during the 1980s, but the burden of reunification in 1990 became a great financial drag. Germany's national debt grew from 41.5 percent in 1991, the eve of Maastricht, to 61.3 percent in 1997, and by 1998 the unemployment rate in the old East Germany reached 21 percent. As Germany's economic situation rapidly deteriorated in 1996, with its deficit reaching as high as 4.2 percent of GDP, Prime Minister Kohl pledged that Germany would qualify for EMU status. This meant reducing the budget deficit from an estimated 3.3 percent of GDP as preparations began for the drafting of the 1997 budget down to at least 3.0 percent.

To accomplish this goal, the 1997 budget reduced spending by 2.5 percent and trimmed the federal workforce by 5 percent over four years. The Transport ministry's budget would be reduced by 9.9 percent, Education and Research by 2.5 percent, and Labor by 2 percent. Kohl cut sick pay by 20 percent, reduced the value of health insurance plans, raised the retirement age from 63 to 65 for men and 60 to 65 for women, raised pension contributions to their highest postwar level, and deferred federal payments to reduce old East German debts. In addition to these efforts, the government required special approval from the Bundestag to override the German constitution. Article 115 of the Basic Law sets out the "golden rule" of German budgeting, that net federal borrowing be less than the amount allocated for investment. Germany's economic woes drove the level of net borrowing past the amount of investment borrowing, thus requiring the special exemption.

Far more publicly controversial and embarrassing to Germany than exceeding the Basic Law, however, was Finance Minister Theo Waigel's attempt to revalue Germany's gold supply, which became a matter of Eurostat and CMFB review. On the very same day that he announced that Germany would experience an 18 billion DM revenue shortfall for 1997, Waigel declared that the government was about to revalue the Bundesbank's 95.2 million troy ounces in gold reserves, from $84.80 an ounce to the current market value of $344.60 an ounce. The difference would add 42 billion DM, or $24.8 billion, to Germany's revenues, and they would be transferred into the newly created "redemption fund for historic burdens" account. In the short term, the government would realize a revenue increase of 11 billion marks for 1997, no less than 0.3 percent of GDP. This was not "creative accounting," Waigel declared, but an "acceptable and legitimate" reclassification.[22]

Nations regularly revalue their gold supplies according to changes in market prices. Italy revalues its gold every three months, and most other EU member states do so once a year. Germany's revaluation, however, would take place as part of the process for transferring national gold reserves to the European Central Bank (ECB) as it assumed monetary responsibility for the EMU. This would require a change in Bundesbank law to permit the revaluation before those conducted by the other EU NCBs and before the rules for revaluation were adopted by the new ECB. Yet Waigel's timing provoked the greatest criticism any government suffered for creative accounting in the critical year of 1997, for Germany's finances ordinarily were beyond reproach and the revaluation was viewed as just an accounting gimmick. After Germany had publicly criticized France over the France Telecom decision, the French were particularly willing to speak out about German gold. "Our German friends," France's Lionel Jospin declared, "who are so rigorous about the criteria, are looking to see if they can't fudge things." Pierre Guidoni, the international secretary of the Socialist party agreed that "Mr. Waigel is ill-placed to give lessons [on meeting the Maastricht criteria] to others, notably France and Italy."[23] The Italian foreign minister, in retaliation for Waigel's criticism of Italy's fiscal policy, announced that Waigel was guilty of "accounting tricks," a charge Waigel retorted was "impertinence."[24] One of the harshest critiques came from Gerrit Zalm, finance minister of the Netherlands. "Germany must meet the criteria in a decent way," Zalm declared. "I cannot conceive that Germany will put its reputation for soundness at risk. I trust that Germany will achieve the goal of a maximum 3 percent deficit for 1997 not through a one-off profit from the Bundesbank, but by restricting spending and raising taxes."[25]

In fact, Kohl and Waigel's plan proved to be exceedingly divisive within Germany. Amid threats that he would resign over the issue, Hans Tietmeyer, president of the Bundesbank, demanded that the deficit goal be fairly met

---

[22] Lionel Barber (1997b). "Boost for Italy's Bid to be in First EMU Wave," *Financial Times*. February 4, p. 4; William Drozdiak (1997a). "Kohl Defies Central Bank by Revaluing Gold," *Washington Post*. May 30, p. A24; Peter Norman (1997a). "German Turmoil Over Gold Plan," *Financial Times*. May 17–18, p. 1; Peter Norman, Andrew Fisher, and Wolfgang Manchau (1997). "Germany's Rift on EMU Deepens," *Financial Times*. May 20, p. 1; Wolfgang Manchau (1997). "Row Creates Dilemma for Financial Markets," *Financial Times*. May 30, p. 2.

[23] David Buchan (1997). "Jospin Raps Germany Over Criteria 'Fudge,'" *Financial Times*. May 29, p. 2.

[24] Tony Paterson and Victor Smart (1997). "Has Germany Kissed the Strong Euro Goodbye?" *The European*, May 22–28, p. 1.

[25] Gordon Cramb (1997). "Dutch Express Alarm at German Gold Scheme," *Financial Times*, May 23, p. 1.

without using the revaluation, in order to prevent the creation of a "soft" euro currency. At stake for Tietmeyer was nothing less than the integrity of the Bundesbank and the credibility of the entire EMU experiment. The uproar in Germany even launched a debate as to whether Germany should delay its entry into the EMU for a year, rather than engage in such budgetary manipulation. Finally, after suffering much abuse, Kohl and Waigel retreated and withdrew their gold revaluation plan in June, compromising with the Bundesbank on a foreign exchange revaluation that would aid Germany's fiscal condition in 1998, after EMU membership was determined, but not before Eurostat too weighed in against the gold revaluation.[26]

Eurostat and the CMFB confronted the statistical question of determining the proper ESA classification for the revaluation of gold or any other form of foreign exchange reserves. This decision affected not only Germany's fiscal standing, but virtually every other EU member state as well. As shown in Table 4.1, of the thirteen states for which data existed, ten EU governments could conceivably revaluate their gold where the difference in revenue gains could prove to be significant, even to the point of ensuring EMU membership. Moreover, if each of the states revalued its gold to the world market price of $344.05, three of the states could be forced to devalue their gold stores, thereby undermining their deficit positions.[27] Given the potentially intense political pressure that might be placed on Eurostat and CMFB by the member states, the Bundesbank's absolute opposition to the gold scheme proved to be invaluable to the statistical community. Moreover, the delight that Kohl and Waigel's foreign colleagues took in Germany's embarrassment meant that these other governments were more occupied adding to Germany's discomfort than they were pressuring Eurostat over this matter for their own benefit. Thus, the politics of the German gold revaluation actually strengthened Eurostat's ability to draw a technical rather than a political decision in this case. That technical ruling declared that such a revaluation simply stood equivalent to the change in the value of shareholdings. Then, taking notice of Germany's "redemption fund for historic burdens," the special account into which the revaluated funds were to be deposited, the Eurostat ruling stated: "The latter includes the counterpart of the revaluation, recorded in the balance sheet on the liabilities side in a reserve account or in a clearing account. Thus, when the central bank pays back to General Government the

[26] Ralph Atkins (1997b). "Waigel Resolves Bundesbank Row," *Financial Times*. June 20, p. 2; William Drozdiak (1997b). "Germany Unveils Plan to Reduce Deficit in Preparation for Common Currency," *Washington Post*. June 20; Matt Marshall (1997). "Germany Scuttles Controversial Plan for Gold Reserves," *Wall Street Journal*. June 4, p. A15.

[27] Wolfgang Manchau (1997). "Row Creates Dilemma for Financial Markets," *Financial Times*. May 30, p. 2.

Table 4.1 EU member state valuation of gold reserves, 1996

	Gold reserves (Troy oz. m.)	National valuation ($bn.)	National valuation ($ per Troy oz.)	Valuation per oz. vs. market price ($344.05 per oz.)
Italy	66.7	25.37	380.40	−36.35
France	81.9	30.37	370.80	−26.75
Ireland	0.4	0.14	350.00	−5.95
Portugal	15.5	4.99	321.90	+22.15
United Kingdom	18.4	5.48	297.80	+46.25
Denmark	2.0	0.59	295.00	+49.05
Spain	15.6	4.22	270.50	+73.55
Finland	1.6	0.40	250.00	+94.05
Netherlands	34.8	8.62	247.70	+96.35
Greece	3.5	0.83	237.10	+106.95
Austria	10.8	1.80	166.70	+177.35
Germany	95.2	8.80	92.40	+251.65
Sweden	4.8	0.24	50.00	+294.05
Belgium	15.4	n.a.	n.a.	n.a.
Luxembourg	0.3	n.a.	n.a.	n.a.

Source: "EU Gold Reserves: Worth A Closer Look," *Financial Times*, May 30, 1997, p. 2.

counterpart of the revaluation of foreign exchange reserves, the value of shareholding is reduced, similar to a capital reduction." Based on a unanimous vote of the CMFB, Eurostat determined the revaluation is a financial transaction, with no affect on the government's deficit or debt.

4.5.3   Italy (1997)

The Italian decision proved to be both more difficult and strenuously contested. The issue in this case consisted of a transaction between the *Banca d'Italia* (BI) and the *Ufficio Italiano dei Cambi* (UIC). Unique among the EU member states, the Italian central bank consists of these two institutions, where the central government has no equity holdings in either entity. The government does, however, receive approximately 60 percent of BI's profits and some 25 percent of UIC's, where this income to the state is classified under ESA as a capital transfer, and thus affects Italy's deficit and debt calculation. In 1996, UIC purchased 540 tons of gold from the BI, to serve as a guarantee for a 2 billion dollar loan from the Bundesbank, and then resold it to BI the following year for 10,500 billion lire. The Italian government then taxed the capital gain on this transaction, equivalent to 7,600 billion lire, which resulted in a tax payment to the state of 3,400 billion lire. This figure amounted to 0.2 percent of GDP, which the Italian government attempted to apply towards its deficit and debt levels. This information came to Eurostat by way of press reports, for, as Alberto De Michelis recalled, "There was somebody inside telling the press something was going on."[28] So, the decision at hand was how to classify the payment to the state in terms of national accounts, as R79 in national accounts terms, as a financial transaction by way of a capital transfer among governmental bodies with no affect on the deficit and debt, or as a tax, R61, which would affect the deficit and debt, and thereby benefit Italy's push towards fiscal convergence.

There were two alternative interpretations of this classification debated among the statisticians. One perspective was that the ruling should be based on the legal status of the two institutions in Italy, such that they are separate organizational units where the Italian government has no equity interests in the organizations or ownership over the gold. ESA states that in order to be classified as independent, an organization must keep a complete set of accounts and exercise autonomous decision-making in its key function. Another aspect of this legal argument for separate institutions rested on the claim that the state held no equity status in the two institutions, and so the gold belonged to and was under the legal control of the BI and UIC. Consequently, according to this interpretation, a sale existed between two independent institutions and the tax payment imposed on this sale at the standard corporate rate of 53 percent should count as revenue to the government, thereby aiding Italy's fiscal status.

The alternative argument rested on an economic rather than legal interpretation of this transaction. While there was widespread agreement that UIC and BI maintained complete accounts, the statisticians were divided as to whether the two entities actually made their decisions separately and autonomously, given that they operated in tandem and shared responsibility for Italy's monetary policy. Further complicating the argument for separate institutions was the fact that the governor of BI also served as the chairman of UIC, and the two organizations produce a consolidated balance sheet. Moreover, the state received, by law, profits from these entities, which indicates that economic

---

[28] Interview with Alberto De Michelis, February 23, 2000.

de facto control remained with the state, which employed the gold for purposes of state economic policy. Thus, UIC and BI, were economically, if not legally, operating as a single entity, where the government, in fact, exercised real control and was indeed the owner of these enterprises and their gold. Thus, the tax was nothing more than the withdrawal of capital from the central bank to the government, which constituted a financial transaction having no affect on the government's fiscal position.

Not surprisingly, the Italian NSI argued vociferously in favor of the first interpretation. The Italians claimed that UIC and BI truly acted as independent entities, where UIC managed foreign reserves and BI set monetary and exchange rate policy. The gold itself was owned by UIC and not by the state, as the state lacked equity shares in UIC, though the only owner of UIC equity was BI. UIC's 25 percent annual payment to the state simply reflected the charges UIC paid for its exclusive rights to control foreign reserves. Thus, the payment from UIC to the state must be counted as a capital gains tax on the gold transaction between UIC and BI, and not as a financial transaction in shares and equities.

Despite this fervently presented argument, Italy lost its case by a vote of twelve to three in a December 1997 meeting of the CMFB, followed by a Eurostat decision declaring the gold transfer a financial transaction. "Eurostat's decision was hotly disputed in Rome," the *Financial Times* reported, "and followed a lively debate among statisticians and strong lobbying by member states eager to clamp down on 'creative accounting' in the race to join monetary union."[29] A senior Italian NSI official, however, viewed this as a "political decision" by the NCB representatives at CMFB "to avoid any affect of movements in gold on deficits, even if a technical, legal interpretation was in favor of Italy." Although Italy strenuously opposed Eurostat's ruling on the UIC and BI gold transaction, by the time the decision was announced to the public on December 17, 1997, Italy was virtually assured of gaining entry into the EMU, and so the adverse ruling had less political consequence than suggested by the intense debate within the CMFB.

4.6   Italy's Eurotax (1997)

Another Eurostat decision concerning Italy was much more warmly greeted by Italian officials; it addressed what many to be Italy's most controversial fiscal policy choice, and it proved to have a much greater effect on Italy's

---

[29] Lionel Barber and James Blitz (1998). "Italy Loses Gold Profits Battle," *Financial Times*. January 28, p. 1.

gaining membership in the EMU. The introduction of the eurotax in 1996 reflected the political and economic turmoil that accompanied Italy's efforts to comply with Maastricht's deficit and debt convergence criteria.

In the month of November, 1996, Italy's EMU prospects appeared bleak. For the first time in recent history, the Italian government was forced to pass its budget in two stages. The initial stage of action on the forthcoming fiscal 1997 that passed in November, required 2,000 separate parliamentary votes cast over eleven days so as to enact 37.5 billion lire ($25 billion) in spending cuts and revenues. The cuts were generated primarily by a 5 percent across-the-board reduction in ministerial accounts, a hiring freeze, closing hospitals, trimming the length of military service by two months, and limiting railroad subsidies. Italy's privatization efforts included the sale of Autostrade, the toll system, and a 41 percent share in the Rome airport. Included in the government's revenue projections were the UIC/BI gold transaction, revisions in income tax, and the introduction of a new consolidating regional tax.[30]

Despite this fiscal package, on November 25, 1996, the European Parliament's Task Force on Economic and Monetary Union released its report on Italy that began, "It is unlikely that Italy will meet the criteria for entry into stage III of Economic and Monetary Union by the 1997 deadline. The genuine improvements in economic indicators, such as inflation and the budget deficit, may be too little too late." The November 26, 1996 weekly barometer, "EMU: Who's going to make it?" published by the *Financial Times*, gave Italy only a 63 percent probability of joining the EMU.[31]

That same week in November, despite the new spending reductions and revenues, the government of Prime Minister Romano Prodi introduced a new one-year tax intended to raise 5,500 billion lire ($3.6 billion), approximately 0.3 percent of GDP, as part of the second stage of his 1997 budget, which altogether aimed at producing 12.5 billion lire in taxes and savings. This creative impost, dubbed the "eurotax," effectively acted as a withholding tax on income generated in 1996 that would be applied in 1997–8, and then refunded in 1999, after Italy's fate regarding EMU membership had been determined. Prodi intended the three-tiered tax to be somewhat progressive in nature, with a rate of 1.5 applied to employee wages of between 23 and 60 million lire, adjusted for families, with a 2.5 percent rate for incomes up to 100 million lire, and 3.5 percent for incomes above 100 million lire. Self-employed workers would find their taxes beginning at 10 million lire, though in a later form, in response to complaints about equity among

[30] Robert Graham (1996a). "Italy Levies 'Euro-tax' in Drive to Meet EMU Targets," *Financial Times*. November 20, p. 2.

[31] "EMU: Who's Going to Make It?" (1996). *Financial Times*. November 26, p. 2.

workers, a single 20 million lire floor would be set for all tax payers.[32] The rebate would take two forms: a direct tax refund, or the option to buy privatization bonds, which allowed the purchase of five times the value of the cost of the bonds. This second option mirrored Prodi's assertion that the bonds should be considered as "dividends" that served as just one benefit stemming from Italy's participation in the EMU.[33] Encouraged by France's successful efforts to apply France Telecom revenues towards its deficit, Romano Prodi declared, "If others carry out window dressing, we can do the same."[34] In any case, perhaps employed to gain an anxious Italian public's acceptance for the impost, the very name "eurotax" reflects its targeted purpose, the first such fiscal measure identified by name with the race to join the EMU.

Italy's eurotax certainly ranks as one of the most cynical fiscal policy schemes undertaken by any EU member state to comply with the Maastricht criteria. The tax fits in nicely with the long list of familiar gimmicks typically employed to evade budgetary deadlines and timetables: Fiscal years are extended or shortened; payments and dispersals are similarly adjusted; revenues are counted in desired time periods; regular operating expenses are transferred off-budget and into capital accounts; and "one-off" spending cuts or revenue measures, such as asset sales, which are enacted to meet the constraints of a current fiscal year with little regard to their long-term effects. Not surprisingly, the eurotax invited widespread criticism throughout the EU. Even Germany's somewhat tarnished Theo Waigel, for example, declared that the tax was simply an "attempt to cook the books."[35] Regardless of the accuracy of these claims, the issue at hand for Eurostat and the CMFB was determining the appropriate national accounts classification for the tax.

Eurostat initially reacted skeptically towards Italy's argument that the revenues gained from the eurotax should be counted towards its deficit and debt. "The main problem in the beginning," recalled Eurostat's De Michelis,

was the presentation made by the Italian authorities and the Ministry of Finance. They said, "Okay, I will raise this tax this year, but I will give you back this tax two years from now." We wrote a letter to the Ministry of Finance, "Look, if there is something in

---

[32] Robert Graham (1996c). "Italy is Pressed to Rethink Euro-tax," *Financial Times*. November 28, p. 3.

[33] Robert Graham (1996a). "Italy Levies 'Euro-tax' in Drive to Meet EMU Targets," *Financial Times*. November 20, p. 2

[34] Lex Column (1996). "Roman Numerals," *Financial Times*. November 20, p. 18.

[35] Tony Paterson and Victor Smart (1997). "Has Germany Kissed the Strong Euro Goodbye?" *The European*. May 22 –28, p. 1.

writing in the law, in the tax law, that you will reimburse this, we will not accept this. This is a financial transaction that will not affect the deficit."[36]

De Michelis' point was that if the reimbursement provisos of the eurotax had actually been codified into law, then the government would have been legally committed to a financial transaction in the form of a financial advance where there would have been no net effect on the government's fiscal position. Financial advances were considered simply as a type of short- or long-term loan, F70 and F80 in terms of ESA, where payments were brought forward ahead of the initial due date of the actual tax, or nonfinancial transaction, that created the payment in the first place. The refund that Prodi promised, however, was never included in the actual legislative text that created the tax. Consequently, as De Michelis informed the press, the refund was "only a political commitment," not a legal one.[37] In fact, De Michelis reported that later in 1999 the Italian government instituted a tax reduction rather than an actual refund, claiming this substitute effectively served as the reimbursement.

The unanimous decision by Eurostat and the CMFB to view the eurotax's refund as an open-ended political promise rather than a legal requirement meant the tax's revenues would indeed count towards Italy's deficit. According to De Michelis,

National accounts reflects a system, the way the government behaves in terms of revenues and expenditures. If there is a new tax [for whatever purpose], this is a new tax with a new revenue. If the year after, or two years after, the government decides to reduce the level of taxes, this will be reflected in the income of government, and national accounts must reflect what the government does. . . . You can say in two years I will reimburse you. This has nothing to do with national accounts.[38]

Therefore, for purposes of ESA, Eurostat and CMFB ruled on a technical basis that the eurotax, regardless of the motivation that initiated it and the gimmickry it produced, served as just another tax with its revenue added to the government's balance sheet. Asserting Eurostat's technical and professional independence in its decision-making, De Michelis professed, "I know some governments are accusing others of cheating, but it does not concern us if there are political considerations."[39]

---

[36] Interview with Alberto De Michelis, February 23, 2000.

[37] Lionel Barber (1997c). "Watchdog Approves Italy's Tax Route to EMU Target," *Financial Times*. February 22–3, p. 24.   [38] Interview with Alberto De Michelis, February 23, 2000.

[39] Lionel Barber (1997b). "Boost for Italy's Bid to be in First EMU Wave," *Financial Times*. February 4, p. 4.

4.6.1   Related Rulings: Wage Fund and *Concessionaire* Taxes

Eurostat and the CMFB ruled on two other Italian taxes based on the eurotax decision.[40] The first tax was in fact a separate provision of the eurotax, and it constituted a tax on wage funds, known as *fondi di quiescenza*, which are accumulated in an enterprise's balances, where employees are required to pay a tax when they withdraw these funds from the enterprise. The 1996 tax law mandated that Italy's enterprises should pay 2 percent of these total wages in taxes to the state in 1997, regardless of whether employees actually attempted to remove these funds. Later, when the workers did in fact leave their place of work, they would pay the balance of the taxes due to the state. This tax in advance, in fact, was larger than the more publicly well-known refund section of the eurotax, as it was projected to produce 6,599 billion lire in revenues, or 0.34 percent of GDP, compared to 4,804 billion lire and 0.25 percent of GDP. As with the more famous section of the eurotax, the national accounts question was determining whether this constituted a financial advance with no influence on the deficit calculation, or as a new tax. As with the refund or wage tax, Eurostat, supported by a unanimous vote of the CMFB, ruled this was a new tax whose revenues were to be included in the deficit calculation.

Another provision of the 1997 tax law addressed the role of nongovernmental tax collectors. Italy relies on financial intermediaries, known as a *concessionaire*, to act as tax collectors. The 1997 tax law expanded the value of the taxes collected by the entities to some 30,000 billion lire. For each collection, the *concessionaire* receives a payment from the state a proportion of the taxes collected. In return for their right to collect taxes and receive a portion of each tax payment, a *concessionarie* must, under the 1997 tax law, pay a fee to the state. Eurostat ruled that these payments should be classified as nonfinancial transactions, thereby effecting the government's deficit calculation. This ruling reduced Italy's deficit by some 0.15 percent of GDP in 1997. Together, therefore, these three decisions on provisions of the eurotax improved Italy's 1997 deficit position by approximately 0.74 percent of GDP.

4.7   Germany's Hospital Debt (1997)

By the summer of 1997, under tremendous domestic political pressure, Prime Minister Helmut Kohl declared that Germany would precisely fulfill the

---

[40] On these rulings, see Eurostat (1998c). "Excessive Deficit Procedure: Statistical Aspects: Mission Report in Italy," February 2.

Maastricht Treaty's 3.0 deficit requirement, not exceeding the convergence requirement by a single tenth of a percent. At the same time, estimates made by such international bodies as the Organization for Economic Cooperation and Development (OECD) projected Germany's deficit to be 3.2 percent. In August of 1997, however, Eurostat made a ruling that subtracted exactly 0.2 percent of Germany's deficit.

The case at hand was determining the national accounts status of Germany's public hospital debt, which served as an example of the difficulty of distinguishing between the government and private sectors under ESA 79. In Germany, private insurance firms purchase services from public sector hospitals, which transforms them into private sector institutions. The question was whether some 5 billion DM ($2.7 billion) of hospital debt would be charged to the national government's finances, or be counted as belonging to the private sector. According to a senior Eurostat official,

Because they have these strange types of organizations in Germany; you can find them in other countries, what they call "grave side" corporations. These are relatively large institutional units, but they have no legal personality, and ESA makes the distinction between corporations and those which are unincorporated. In most countries, institutions have legal personality. But in Germany, you can have very large companies and effectively they have no legal form, and so there is no clear line distinguishing between the owner and the company, in the sense that everything is together. So when the owner pays something to this kind of company, which has no legal personality, it is automatically considered to be a financial transaction.

So, according to this interpretation of ESA, in this case the economic boundary separating the public and private sectors was invisible, with the debt charged to the hospital's private operations. This ruling was discussed at several technical meetings of the working parties, but, noted the Eurostat official, "there was no debate, because it was clearly within ESA. You could not criticize the principle."

What Eurostat did criticize was Germany's timing of its request for the reclassification of its deficit figures. "They promised me," the Eurostat official complained.

Okay, we guarantee we can manage without the reclassification of the hospital debt. Germany will meet its 3.0 target; we don't need to do this exercise. Then suddenly it was a decision by the Ministry of Finance. . . . It was a wrong signal, because then some could say "Also the Germans are attempting to cheat now." This was a very, very bad time, but in terms of statistics we could not say anything to them, because it was correct.

Germany apparently had known for some time that it could classify the hospital's debt as a financial transaction, which meant that it would have no effect on Germany's deficit or debt. Overconfidence, however, caused the delay in making the reclassification, resulting in the press to describe Eurostat's ruling as a "statistical windfall" for Germany, leaving the German MOF to deny any implications that this was simply "creative accounting" on its part.[41]

4.8   The Influence of Eurostat's Rulings on Member State Deficit Calculations for the Stage II Convergence Process

A "compliance information system" describes a segmented monitoring process of gathering, interpreting, and analyzing information to determine the status of compliance or noncompliance with predetermined rules and guidelines. This monitoring and information management function is viewed as a distinct organizational task, one that usually includes some responsibility for assessing the degree and status of compliance. These various monitoring and assessment functions, however, are typically viewed as technical in nature. They are institutionally differentiated and separated from a level of decision-making reserved for significant political actors. The political decisions these actors make, often bounded by a predetermined set of overarching rules, include the final authority to make formal declarations of compliance or noncompliance, and the final authority to determine the extent and timing of sanctions on noncomplying actors. In the case of Maastricht, the Treaty delegated to the EC a monitoring function, while it assigned to the EMI and the Commission the responsibility for providing the Council of Economic and Finance Ministers (ECOFIN) with assessments of the member states' compliance with the Treaty's requirements. The Treaty, however, reserved to the ECOFIN Council the right to make the final political decision in determining EMU membership.

Nonetheless, in practice, Eurostat's statistical case law effectively predetermined the findings in EMI's "Convergence Report" and the EC's "Convergence Report 1998," as well as the outcome of the European Council's decision on EMU membership decision.[42] When taken collectively, these case law rulings

---

[41] Ralph Atkins and Michael Smith (1997). "Germany Set for Unexpected Windfall," *Financial Times*. August 21, p. 2.

[42] European Monetary Institute (1998). "Convergence Report: Report Required by Article 109j of the Treaty Establishing the European Community," Frankfurt, March; European Commission, "Convergence Report 1998: Prepared in Accordance with Article 109j(1) of the Treaty," Brussels, March 25, 1998.

provided the technical basis for admitting or excluding EU member states from the EMU. Yet, in one sense Eurostat's rulings gained their power from neither their technical sophistication nor even the Treaty's reference to ESA as the measure of deficits and debt. Their force and influence ultimately stemmed from the politics of convergence, which in 1998 demanded that member state deficits comply with the 3.0 percent deficit level. The politics of the time essentially prevented the ECOFIN Council from interpreting these deficits any more favorably, regardless of whatever formal leeway the Treaty might grant. Thus, the EMU's fate effectively rested in the hands of EU's statistical technocrats and their March 1998 report, "Statistics on Convergence Criteria, Assessment by Eurostat."[43]

4.8.1   Eurostat's Report: "Statistics on Convergence Criteria"

Eurostat's document compiled the sum of its case law rulings and their effect on the member states. In addition to information on the status of the member states' deficit and debt levels, the report included information on price stability, long-term interest rates, balance of payments, and market integration, all required by the Maastricht Treaty. This analysis also assessed the effects of Eurostat's harmonization efforts on the member states' consumer price indices, budgetary positions, and GDP. On the measure of the Harmonized Indices of Consumer Prices, for example, the report indicated that as of January 1998, only Greece failed to comply with the mandated rate of inflation. The great majority of the report, fifty-nine of eighty-four pages, however, dedicated its analysis to examining the member states' budgetary condition.

Eurostat arrayed its data on deficits and debt in a number of formats for the period 1994 through 1997, with 1994 serving as the baseline, as it was the first year the member states submitted their biannual budgetary information to the Commission. These tables and figures displayed each country's deficit and debt in terms of member state currencies, as a percent of GDP, and as a ratio of the member state's national GDP. All of these budget deficit numbers would have been different, of course, had the member states been permitted to report their deficits on a cash basis of their own choosing, in their individual fiscal years, according to their own understanding of what counted as a revenue or expenditure, without the benefit of a standardized accounting system. Eurostat supplied information in numerical and in graphic form for individual nations and for the EU as a whole. A separate analysis subjected each member

---

[43] Eurostat (1998a). "Statistics on Convergence Criteria: Assessment by Eurostat," Luxembourg, March 25.

state to an examination of the condition, quality, and promptness of its national accounts system. The report noted changes in accounting methodology, procedures for data gathering and record keeping, with particular emphasis paid to the member state's efforts, successful and unsuccessful, in harmonizing its domestic national accounting system with that of the EU's ESA 79. A large section titled "Main Methodological Aspects Affecting the Whole Period 1994–97," assessed how the implementation of Eurostat rulings influenced the member state's deficit and debt levels during these years, followed by another section that identified any exceptional budgetary actions undertaken by the member state for 1997. Eurostat also declared whether the member state's data complied with the methodology and rules of ESA 79, each doing so, and then officially certified the member state's budgetary data. Eurostat next analyzed the condition of the member states' deficit position. In 1994, only four member states fulfilled the Maastricht 3 percent deficit criterion, Denmark, Germany, Ireland, and Luxembourg. By the end of 1997, the booming economic growth in the fourth quarter of the year enabled all countries but Greece to meet the target, with three member states actually running budget surpluses. Even Greece complied with the spirit of Maastricht, as its deficits declined from 10.3 percent of GDP in 1995, to 7.5 percent in 1996, and then 4.0 percent in 1997. The Maastricht Treaty stated that a member state complied if it demonstrated a clear trend in deficit reduction towards the desired 3 percent target. As it evolved, however, the political reality of Maastricht was quite clear: An applicant member state needed precisely to fulfill the targeted deficit at 3 percent or less if it were to be admitted into the EMU.

The member state national debt levels proved to be enforced on a far less rigorous basis. In 1994, four member states, Germany, France, Luxembourg, and the United Kingdom fulfilled the 60 percent of GDP debt criterion. By 1997, still only four nations met the target: Finland, France, Luxembourg, and the United Kingdom. Simply put, if the 60 percent debt barrier had been strictly observed, as had the deficit target, the EMU most likely would never have come into being. In addition to those member states that marginally violated the 60 percent level, Belgium, Greece, and Italy's debt levels far exceeded the 60 percent target, with their debt figures for 1997 standing at 122.2, 108.7, and 121.6 percent of GDP, respectively. Moreover, of the three governments, only Belgium complied with the Maastricht Treaty's admonition that there be a downward trend in national debt levels. Although Greece's debt actually registered at a lower level than Belgium's and Italy's, and its declining trend roughly mirrored Italy's, its deficit level proved to be sufficiently excessive to outweigh its comparatively equivalent performance on the debt criterion, resulting in its exclusion from the EMU. As a Eurostat official observed,

Greece was already out [of consideration for EMU membership because of its high deficit figure]. At that time we had the correct impression, because they were not able to join the first round. We did send a mission to Greece, but they had a lot of problems of getting their numbers right. We had to establish a small [working] group which reviewed all of their statistics. All the figures contradicted.

These general trends in member state budgetary outcomes are now familiar. Yet, the question at hand is assessing the effect of Eurostat's interpretations of ESA on the size of the member states' budgetary outcomes for 1997. Such an assessment necessarily centers on the member states' deficit rather than their debt levels. This is so because by 1998 it was clear to all participants in the convergence process that the dynamics of EU politics demanded that the standard for gaining EMU membership would be the ability of the member states to comply with the 3 percent deficit target, rather than either the size of their debts or trends in debt reduction. The decisions ultimately rendered on the EMU membership of Belgium, Italy, and Greece, certainly indicated this to be the case. Consequently, Eurostat responded to this demand by concentrating its analysis on the member states' deficits. The report Eurostat submitted to the EMI, in fact, offers very few examples of how Eurostat's rulings influenced the member states' debt levels. Only in the case of Denmark does the report cite as many as three relevant rulings where a numerically measurable consequence, stated in terms of debt as a percent of GDP, can be identified, but none at all for such member states as Finland, Germany, Italy, the Netherlands, Portugal, Spain, or Sweden. According to Eurostat's Dieter Glatzel, this difference can be attributed to the clear definitions for debt that existed in the Treaty and in ESA. "For the measurement of debt, there were not so many problems. Debt management was very simple and straight forward. Asset-backed borrowing and securitisation did not exist at that time."[44] By comparison, the report specified thirteen countries, all EU nations except Greece and Luxembourg, where Eurostat's decisions influenced public deficits in some numerically identifiable way.

One significant difficulty arises in assessing the full effect of Eurostat's decisions on the member states' deficits during the period 1993 through 1997. In its convergence report to the EMI, Eurostat frequently reported the effect of its rulings on deficits and debt on an annual rather than a multi-year basis, as throughout the process there simply had been no demand for such data.

---

[44] Interview with Dieter Glatzel, March 19, 2003.

Therefore, there is no systematic way to tell how a ruling applied to the 1995 or 1996 budget might change figures in 1997. For example, Eurostat ruled on Belgium's privatization in 1994, a decision that prevented governments from including revenues derived from indirect as well as direct privatization in the calculation of budgetary deficits. This ruling means there is no change in the deficit the year the revenues are collected, but these same revenues can be employed to reduce the member state's debt, which subsequently reduce its interest payments and hence its deficit in the following year. Yet, the cumulative effect of this critical decision, which may very well be Eurostat's most important national accounts ruling on member states' deficits and debt, is simply unavailable.

This means that the best way to assess the affect of Eurostat's rulings on the convergence process is to examine how rulings actually handed down in late 1996 and 1997 influenced member state budget deficits for 1997. Table 4.2 attempts to do this by identifying the member state involved; Eurostat's applicable ruling; the resulting improvement or deterioration in the budget deficit, in other words, the decrease or increase in the deficit as a percent of GDP; the member state's final 1997 deficit as a percent of GDP; and the difference between this final figure, which is the one that served as the decisive deficit figure employed for determining EMU membership, and what this figure would have been without the various rulings. On a national accounts basis, Austria's deficit for 1997 would have been 2.77 percent of GDP, rather than the official 2.5 percent, without the benefit of rulings that lowered its deficit by 0.27 percent. Finland's official deficit was 0.9 percent, but it would have been 0.68 percent had not Eurostat's rulings increased its deficit by 0.22 percent. Collectively, Eurostat's decisions lowered the deficits of eight countries and increased the deficits of five, with no reported rulings that created numerical differences in the deficits of two of the fifteen EU member states. Eurostat's rulings, moreover, contributed positively if not decisively to Italy, Spain, and France gaining entry into the EMU, while significantly aiding the convergence efforts of Germany.

In the case of Italy, Eurostat's decisions proved to be overwhelmingly beneficial to the government. Indeed, commenting on his country's success, the director of Italy's NSI declared, "I am very happy that all the decisions, with the exception of gold, were in favor of Italy. For gold, there was a large majority [in the CMFB voting] against Italy. So, in CMFB, I have seen a large degree of impartiality."[45] As this statement suggested, the voting within the CMFB on Italy consisted of large majority or unanimous votes, where, except

---

[45] Interview with Enrico Giovannini, May 16, 2000.

Table 4.2 The effect of Eurostat rulings on 1997 EU member state deficits

Member state	Applicable ruling	Improvement (+) or deterioration (−) in budget deficit as percent of GDP	Final 1997 deficit as percent of GDP	1997 deficit without ruling
Austria	Export insurance	−0.02		
	Carry-over losses	+0.15		
	Non-funded pensions	+0.14		
	Net: +0.27		2.5	2.77
Belgium	Capitalized interest	+0.05		
	Linear bonds	−0.04		
	Zero coupons	+0.02		
	Net: +0.03		2.1	2.13
Denmark	Privatization	+0.28		
	Definition of govt. sector	+0.16		
	Deep-discounted bonds	+0.15		
	Pension funds	+0.06		
	Interest	+0.08		
	Time recording of interest	−0.14		
	Linear bonds	−0.02		
	Zero coupon bonds	−0.01		
	Privatization	+0.05		
	War insurance	+0.17		
	Net: +0.78		0.7	1.48
Finland	Swaps	−0.01		
	Short-term interest	−0.04		
	Linear bonds	−0.17		
	Net: −0.22		0.9	0.68
France	France Telecom	+0.5	3.0	3.5
Germany	Hospitals	+0.2		
	Gold	−0.3		
	Subsidy reimbursement	+0.04		
	Net: −0.06		2.7	2.64
Ireland	Swaps	+0.4	0.9	1.3
Italy	Enterprise debt	+0.2		
	Eurotax	+0.25		
	Wage fund tax	+0.34		
	Concessionaire tax	+0.15		
	Capitalized interest	+0.26		

Table 4.2 *Continued*

Member state	Applicable ruling	Improvement (+) or deterioration (−) in budget deficit as percent of GDP	Final 1997 deficit as percent of GDP	1997 deficit without ruling
	Gold	−0.16		
	Export insurance	+0.03		
	Swaps	+0.02		
	Net: +1.09		2.7	3.79
Netherlands	Interest	−0.12	1.4	1.28
Portugal	Capitalized interest	−0.15		
	Linear bonds	−0.05		
	Public enterprise pensions	+0.3		
	Net: −0.10		2.5	2.4
Spain	Debt assumption	+0.3		
	Short-term interest	+0.7		
	Export insurance	+0.1		
	Time recording of taxes	+0.28		
	Timing of 1997 expenditures	−0.25		
	Net: +1.13		2.6	3.73
Sweden	Linear bonds	+0.28		
	Liquidation of assets	−0.3		
	Net: −0.02		0.8	0.78
United Kingdom	Index-linked bonds	+0.2	1.9	2.1

Source: Eurostat, "Statistics on Convergence Criteria: Assessment by Eurostat," Luxembourg, 1998.

in the ruling on gold, the CMFB supported decisions that reduced Italy's deficits. In each instance, Eurostat adopted the CMFB's recommendations on the various decisions shown in Table 5.1, including the eurotax, the reclassification of Italy's railways enterprise debt, and the recording of government payments for export insurance. For 1997, the net effect of these rulings lowered Italy's deficit by 1.09 percent of GDP. Without these favorable interpretations of ESA, Italy's deficit would have been an EMU-excluding 3.77 percent.

Spain and France, too, benefitted from Eurostat's decisions. Eurostat rulings on when social security taxes could be recorded, on the recording of interest on short-term securities, and the treatment of debt assumption, all decreased Spain's 1997 deficit. One decision increased the deficit by 0.25 percent of GDP, as a Eurostat ruling prevented Spain from counting certain expenditures incurred during 1997 in 1998. Altogether, these rulings improved Spain's deficit position by 1.13 percent, without which the government's 1997 deficit would have reached 3.73 percent of GDP. For France, Eurostat's controversial ruling in 1996 on France Telecom enabled that member state to meet the Maastricht deficit target exactly. No other rulings directly affected France's deficit in 1997.

In Germany, an influential lobbying association for the protection of savers criticized the rulings for Italy's eurotax and France Telecom, claiming that without the assistance of special treatment for these revenue raisers, Italy and France would have "significantly overshot" the 3 percent deficit target. Not stopping there, the group also asserted that Germany's entry into the EMU was aided by "special factors," including an increase in social security contributions and extreme controls over investment spending.[46] The group may have wanted to add to their list Eurostat's ruling on the reclassification of the majority of Germany's hospitals from the government to the nonfinancial and quasi-corporations sector. Although Germany's 1997 deficit of 2.7 percent falls to 2.64 percent when the effect of Eurostat's rulings are added in, at the time of the hospital decision Germany's deficit stood at 3.2 percent, and was lowered to 3 percent by Eurostat's decision. The great economic surge occurring throughout most of the industrialized democracies in the third quarter of 1997 is likely the primary cause of the deficit falling to 2.7 percent of GDP.

4.9   Conclusion

From 1994 through the early months of 1998, Eurostat engaged in fiscal rule-making in the form of administrative statistical case law. Lacking the capacity to scrutinize every budgeting and economic transaction taking place in the EU, Eurostat directed its surveillance efforts towards a core group of "big issues" that, in effect, sampled a significant amount of fiscal activity occurring in the member states. Some of these cases focused on ongoing practices, such as privatization, which deserved attention because of the significant number and size of these transactions. Determining the classification of privatization relatively early in the surveillance process also helped affirm Eurostat's authority in

---

[46] Ralph Atkins (1998). "Euro Doubts Raised in Bonn," *Financial Times*. March 12, p. 3.

interpreting ESA for a revenue gathering activity that clearly played a central role in the member states' fiscal practices. Other cases, constituting the "gray areas" of national accounts, addressed new forms of economic transactions, including the use of the eurotax and the emergence of swaps, which deserved attention because ESA 79 proved to be an unreliable guide as to whether they should be classified as a financial or nonfinancial transaction.

Perhaps the most important of Eurostat's rulings was that of France Telecom. Eurostat learned from that case to avoid taking the lead on highly controversial rulings, which only raised the specter of bias and favoritism and the charge of autocratic decision-making. All of Eurostat's rulings following France Telecom conformed to the majority opinions voted by the member states represented in the CMFB. Widespread and transparent consultation characterized the decision-making processes leading to these rulings. There would be no replay of the France Telecom fiasco throughout the remainder of the convergence process. "The procedure established after the 'FT affair,' " the Italian NSI director concluded, "demonstrated its value, reinforcing the cooperation between the NCBs, NSIs, Eurostat and the European Monetary Institute (now the European Central Bank) and improving the quality of European economic and financial statistics."[47] More than symbolic is the fact that the president of CMFB during 1997 was the director of the United Kingdom's NSI, John Kidgell, who drafted the CMFB's reform procedures in the wake of France Telecom. Kidgell's presence both helped ensure that CMFB exercised its independence when developing its national accounts recommendations to Eurostat, and, given his nationality and the United Kingdom's position on EMU membership, that these decisions were reasonably impartial towards the various member states. At the July 1999 meeting of the CMFB, Kidgell relinquished his presidency after holding that position for two years. Reflecting on this period, he observed that although it seemed to be a "near miracle," Eurostat and the CMFB's rulings went unchallenged from within the EU or by the press. Moreover, as the meeting's minutes noted, "Kidgell stressed that CMFB was a highly respected statistical body, in terms of credibility, transparency, and independence."[48] Thus, after France Telecom, Eurostat's caution in building consensus among the EU's statisticians and CMFB's new-found assertiveness created a type of check and balance system that enhanced the credibility, and ironically the autonomy, of Eurostat's final decisions.

[47] Enrico Giovannini (2003). "The 'France Telecom Affair': A Night at the Bundesbank," in Alberto De Michelis and Alain Chantraine (eds.), *Memoirs of Eurostat: Fifty Years Serving Europe*. Luxembourg: Office for Official Publications of the European Communities, p. 144.

[48] "Minutes, Meeting of the Committee on Monetary, Financial and Balance of Payments Statistics (CMFB)," Luxembourg, July 1–2, 1999, p. 3.

An additional consideration that furthered Eurostat's independent rule-making was its relationship with the press. Again, following its bitter experience in the France Telecom debacle, Eurostat recognized that its public reputation for integrity and the credibility of its data had been seriously undermined and its standing with the press greatly damaged. To remedy the situation, Eurostat initiated a campaign to repair its relations with the press, beginning with an effort to explain the logic of its rulings and the institutional framework of its decision-making process in a series of news releases.

Eurostat's efforts with the press appear to have been somewhat successful, gaining it hard won credibility.[49] Though some of the press still questioned Eurostat's complete independence from the Commission, the agency escaped the kind of skeptical, if not cynical, media coverage it received in the aftermath of France Telecom for the remainder of the convergence process. As Eurostat gained a degree of credibility and attention from the press, it also gained independence. For as Franchet and the members of the CMFB recognized, this coverage insulated them somewhat from external interference, as offending third-parties would fear being exposed and embarrassed by the press. Of course, the press continued to portray any number of fiscal and budgetary decisions of the EU member states as "cooking the books" and "creative accounting." The overtly manipulative efforts of the member states to reduce their deficits and debt by way of reclassifying their gold supplies and dubious tax increases only furthered the press's legitimate accusations of questionable, if not duplicitous, budgetary behavior. Nonetheless, the press rarely challenged the integrity of either Eurostat's rulings or its decision-making process following France Telecom. There were no exposés or stories of disgruntled, alienated statisticians with behind-the-scenes tales of fraudulent national

---

[49] Interview with Lionel Barber, September 6, 2002. Barber served as a lead reporter for the *Financial Times* throughout the convergence process, covering many of Eurostat's major rulings, including France Telecom, German and Italian gold, and the Italian eurotax. Displaying a reporter's very appropriate skepticism, Barber had this to say about Eurostat:

For those of us who followed EMU through the seven years from 92 to 99, we looked at this largely as a political and macroeconomic process. . . . [Eurostat] was headed by a Frenchman, the French had a huge stake in making EMU work. It was also a Commission body, and the Commission obviously had a huge stake in making EMU happen. So no matter how much Yves Franchet and his people would come out and describe themselves as independent statisticians, I think there were always doubts in our minds about how strict they were actually going to be when it came to assessing whether countries genuinely met the convergence criteria, or whether they were cutting corners. . . . I thought they did a good job [at the press conferences, presenting technical information] but I was left with some doubts. . . . They didn't completely rollover [on decisions such as the German and Italian gold cases] and let their tummies be tickled by everybody. That was important, yes. To be fair to Franchet and the others, they did actually try and stand up a bit here. . . . [Eurostat's technical decisions] carried a degree of credibility.

accounts classifications, or of logrolling and side-payments disbursed among CMFB members to produce favorable interpretations for desperate member states. Instead, the veracity of Eurostat's decisions went largely unchallenged and its statements accepted as the last word on these matters by the press. What mattered in the long run, however, was not how the press viewed Eurostat, but how Eurostat's rulings affected the ability of the member states to comply with Maastricht's convergence criteria.

There is an obvious question that underlies all of Eurostat's statistical rulings, especially those taking place during Stage II convergence when EMU membership was at stake: Did Eurostat rig, perhaps at the urging or demand of some higher authority, the outcome of these decisions to ensure that certain member states qualified for entrance into the Economic and Monetary Union? "No," replies Yves Franchet. "It would have been known everywhere, and it would have destroyed the process completely, and my commissioner [economic Commissioner Yves-Thibault de Silguy] understood that very well. The problem of reliability in statistics is that it takes years to build and minutes to lose, and once you've lost it, you've lost it for twenty years."[50] "One should not forget one thing," adds Dieter Glatzel. "In 1997 when we made the convergence report, we were still operating under ESA 79. At that time, of all these rulings, the only case which was a little bit shocking was the case of France Telecom, where we made some kind of problematic decision. All the rest, we used a very open policy [of decision-making]."[51]

There is much to be said in support of Franchet and Glatzel's interpretation of events. Following the mismanagement of the France Telecom ruling, Eurostat did indeed reform its decision-making process, formalize its procedures, work with the member states to revitalize the CMFB, expand consultation, and enhance transparency by improving access and clarifying rulings for the press. The ability of Eurostat to make an overtly biased ruling, as in the case of France Telecom, after 1996 appears highly unlikely. Simply put, too many members of the expanded EU epistemic statistical community would learn of this behavior, report it to the various member states, and leak this information to the press. Even if some member states actively supported or participated in the ruling, other governments could challenge it in CMFB and, again, leak Eurostat's action to the press. As Franchet stated, everyone would know and the surveillance process would be publicly compromised.

That some member states might react with hostility to such a move by Eurostat may be seen from the reaction of many governments to suggestions

---

[50] Interview with Yves Franchet, March 19, 2003.
[51] Interview with Dieter Glatzel, March 19, 2003.

that the Stability and Growth Pact be scrapped or greatly modified. As the eurozone economy weakened beginning in 2000, Germany, France, and Italy, in particular, and even EC President Romano Prodi, recommended that the Pact's deficit requirements be made more "flexible," with Prodi at one point calling the law "stupid." A number of the smaller governments, especially Austria, Finland, the Netherlands, Spain, and even Greece, fiercely resisted this idea.[52] A similar reaction is also likely to occur at CMFB, where in addition to these member states the ECB also strongly opposes modifying the Pact. "Even if there is an interest for one member state to have a ruling in its favor," Dieter Glatzel suggests, "all the others which are more strict, who have reduced their deficits, they say 'We don't see why there should be exceptions made for someone else. We want to keep a strict ruling on this.'"[53] As indicated, however, by the large majorities voting in favor of the vast majority of rulings at CMFB since France Telecom, these smaller states clearly supported the decisions issued by Eurostat.

Finally, not all observers will agree with each of Eurostat's rulings. The decision on Italy's eurotax, for example, certainly appears to permit, if not encourage, governments to engage in what is commonly viewed as fiscal gimmickry. The ability of governments to make laws that purposively skirt around target dates, such as fiscal years, to lower their deficits on a temporary basis, certainly promotes budgetary mismanagement, if not gimmickry. Nevertheless, despite how one might question the logic of these rulings, what matters is that the EU statistical community supported these decisions by large majorities, they constitute part of the ESA statistical case law that governs the calculation of member state deficits and debt for the excessive deficit procedure, and they continue to play a role in the domestic political life of the member states that pledge to keep their deficits contained.

---

[52] Tony Barber and James Blitz (1999). "Prodi's Rhetoric Highlights Public Disunity on Euro," *Financial Times*. June 23, p. 2; Nicholas George and George Parker (2002). "Finns Insist EU Pact Must Be Protected," *Financial Times*. September 4, p. 2; George Parker, Ian Bickerton, and Tony Major (2002). "Brussels Plan Upsets Smaller Countries," *Financial Times*. September 26, p. 4; Thomas Fuller (2002). "Rift Widens On EU Deficits," *International Herald Tribune*, September 26, p. 11; James Blitz (2002). "UK Wants Tougher Rules on European Government Borrowing," *Financial Times*. October 21, p. 2; George Parker (2003b). "Greece Warns On Easing of Stability Pact," *Financial Times*. July 30, p. 3; Tony Major (2002). "ECB Mounts Defence of 'Indispensible' Stability Pact," *Financial Times*. October 25, p. 6.   [53] Interview with Dieter Glatzel, March 19, 2003.

5

European Statistical Case Law For Stage III Monetary Union, 1998–2004

Following the entry of the first eleven member states into the Economic and Monetary Union (EMU), three significant events occurred in the surveillance process. First, the incentives for an EMU member state to incur excessive deficits and debt actually increased after March 1998. The sanctions associated with violating the excessive deficit procedure centered on the reputational and financial penalties established by the Stability and Growth Pact, rather than exclusion from EMU membership stemming from the failure to comply with the Stage II convergence process. Clearly, the sanctions associated with the Pact could be much more easily endured by a government than outright rejection from participating in the EMU. Second, by the third quarter of 2000, it became increasingly apparent that the economies of the euro-zone peaked after three years of growth, creating yet another incentive for some of the member states to engage in stimulative fiscal policies and for others to violate the Pact because their deteriorating economic situations severely undermined revenues.[1] In 2001, based upon the Commission's recommendation, the Council of Economic and Finance Ministers (ECOFIN) directed its first formal public reprimand issued under the Pact to Ireland. Despite Ireland's healthy budget surpluses of 4.3 percent of GDP in 2000 and 1.1 percent in 2001, the ministers feared the inflationary effects of its expansionary fiscal policy.[2] The ECOFIN Council's future reprimands, however, and its initiation of the excessive deficit procedure against Germany, France, and Portugal,

---

[1] Tony Barber (2000a). "Euro-Zone's Output Growth Shows Signs of Peaking," *Financial Times.* July 4, p. 2; Tony Barber (2000b). "Economic Indicators Cast a Pall Over the Euro-Zone's Prospects," *Financial Times.* September 27, p. 2.

[2] *International Herald Tribune.* "EU Faults Irish Inflation Policy," February 13, p. 11; Peter Norman (2001a). "EU Reprimands Ireland Over 'Inflationary' Budget," *Financial Times.* February 13, p. 1.

stemmed from their rapidly rising deficits incurred largely as a result of economic contraction rather than expansion.

Third, during Stage III, Director General II for Economic and Financial Affairs (DG ECFIN) came to play an increasingly important role in European Union (EU) macroeconomic policy coordination. As noted in Chapter 2, Eurostat gained the upper hand in the Stage II surveillance process over DG ECFIN by way of its right to interpret European System of Integrated Accounts (ESA). "To get back into the game," as one Eurostat official observed, during the drafting of the Stability Pact DG ECFIN reasserted its place in the surveillance process by emphasizing the role of cyclical economics and cyclical forecasts for surveillance purposes. DG ECFIN's economic forecasts and analyses of member states' stability programs periodically alert the ECOFIN Council to potential deviations from the Pact during Stage III, and act as the basis for the Commission's frequent and highly publicized early warnings, opinions, and recommendations about wayward member state fiscal behavior. In this regard, the broad economic policy guidelines are also more important in Stage III than in Stage II. In Stage II, these guidelines were often vacuous in their directions for member state fiscal convergence policies, and they had no enforcement power. There were no penalties, in terms of member states obtaining EMU membership, for ignoring the guidelines. The only enforcement stemmed from Eurostat's rulings on national accounts, which could and did determine if a member state complied with budgetary Treaty requirements. For Stage III, where denial of EMU membership as a sanction is not available, the Commission's recommendations on guidelines and warnings serves as potential reputational sanctions against member states incurring excessive deficits or violating the Pact's call for balanced budgets. Nonetheless, as the Commission's Legal Service pointed out, "These forecasts are not legally binding documents and in elaborating them the Commission may use information in its possession, provided for by the Member State in question."[3] Thus, although DG ECFIN has become the more prominent player publicly and within the Commission for purposes of the surveillance process, Eurostat's certification of member states' deficit positions continues to play a critical role in activating the excessive deficit procedure and in determining whether a member state may be financially sanctioned under the Stability and Growth Pact. According to the Treaty, member states must continue to submit their reports in a manner consistent with ESA, subject to Eurostat's monitoring and review.

---

[3] Letter from Hans Peter Hartvig and Miguel Diaz-Llanos La Roche to Mr Klaus Regling, Director General, DG Economic and Financial Affairs (2002). "Subject: Portugal—Derogation on the Application of Regulation (EC) 2516/2000," Brussels. European Commission Legal Service, May 6, p. 3.

Eurostat's technical rulings, therefore, matter greatly. Indeed, as examined in the following sections, the agency issued several major rulings in 2000 and 2002 on the allocation of mobile phone licenses, swaps, and securitization that significantly influence the member states' fiscal positions. The swaps case is particularly interesting, for, as did the France Telecom decision, it reveals the sometimes contentious nature and constraints of the oversight and influence exercised by principals and the efforts of agents to build autonomy. Two more major rulings in 2003 and 2004 on unfunded pension obligation payments and public–private partnerships may dramatically improve the deficit position of member states in violation of the Stability and Growth Pact. Finally, Eurostat's exercise of its power to refuse to certify the budgetary statistical data supplied by a member state in its biannual report led directly to the initiation of the excessive deficit procedure against Portugal and France.

5.1   The Allocation of Mobile Phone Licenses (2000)

In the months immediately following the admission of the euro-eleven member states into the EMU, many of these governments urgently looked for new revenues to fund new initiatives and expand existing programs, often ignoring the pleas of the European Central Bank (ECB) and the Commission to follow a path of fiscal austerity. In France, for example, after the privations suffered during the convergence years, the five leftist parties that constituted the governing coalition called upon Prime Minister Jospin to increase pensions, unemployment benefits, and public sector jobs.[4] The Italians searched for new revenues not only to fund government programs, but also to meet EU demands that it lower its public debt and fulfill their pledge to reduce the budget deficit to 0.8 percent of GDP. As Vincenzo Visco, Italy's finance minister, warned against right-wing efforts to lower taxes, "The choice is simple. Either the EU will be forced to bring Italy back into line using the rules of the stability pact, or the right changes its policies."[5] The Germans, meanwhile, looked for ways to fund new infrastructure spending for railways and roads, education programs in its eastern territories, and research on new energy sources, all of which might cost 2 billion marks.[6] In the year 2000, these and the other EU states thought they had found their treasure trove of new revenues in the sale of mobile phone licenses.

---

[4] Robert Graham (2000). "Jospin Under Pressure to Boost Social Spending," *Financial Times*. November 8, p. 6.

[5] James Blitz (2000*a*). "Italy Set for Mobile Phone Bonanza," *Financial Times*. June 19, p. 2.

[6] Haig Simonian (2000*b*). "Germany to Fund Extra Spending with Mobiles Cash," *Financial Times*. October 12, p. 2.

In the spring of 2000, virtually the entire telecoms industry of the EU sought new profits and opportunities for expansion in the rapidly emerging third generation mobile phone market. With the European Commission (EC) urging the member states to open up their phone networks and continue their privatization efforts, the EU's revenue hungry governments were only too happy to oblige. By summer, following Britain's very successful auctioning of five phone licenses to nine bidding companies for 22.5 billion pounds, the Dutch projected the sale of their licenses to produce revenues approximately a third of that amount. Germany's Ministry of Finance (MOF) expected that the sale of as many as six licenses to generate as much as 120 billion marks, with 20 billion marks assumed as revenues for the drafting of the 2001 budget. The actual amount, reached after 173 rounds of bidding conducted over fourteen days, totaled 89.8 billion marks.[7] The Italians, meanwhile, estimated they would raise at least 20,000 billion lira with the auctioning of their licenses, and the French, relying upon fixed-cost sale prices rather than auctions, initially estimated their sales would exceed 50 billion francs.[8] Of the EU states engaged in allocating licenses, only Finland, Norway, and Sweden decided to offer the licenses for free, where they were allocated on the basis of a comparison of offers, on the grounds that this was the best way to encourage the industry's growth. By the end of the year the frenzy in purchasing licenses had abated, leaving a number of these governments, Italy and the Netherlands in particular, realizing less revenues than projected. Nevertheless, their sales generated significant income for the member states, leaving the issue facing Eurostat of how they should be classified in terms of national accounts.[9]

Before making its ruling, Eurostat first consulted its National Accounts Working Group and the Committee on Monetary, Financial, and Balance of Payment Statistics (CMFB).[10] Two issues that need to be addressed were whether to classify the asset being sold as a financial or nonfinancial asset, and to determine if these transactions were sales or rents. According to national accounts, the direct sale of an intangible asset, such as equities in the case of privatization, constitutes a financial transaction with no resulting effect on the calculation of the deficit. If a mobile phone license were ruled

---

[7] Bertrand Benoit and Haig Simonian (2000). "German Mobile Phone Auction Raises $46bn," *Financial Times*. August 18, p. 1.

[8] James Blitz (2000a). "Italy Set for Mobile Phone Bonanza," *Financial Times*. June 19, p. 2; Peter Ehrlich (2000). "Germany Expects DM2obn from Auction," *Financial Times*. June 19, p. 2; Joseph Fitchett (2000). "France is Torn over Potential Windfall," *International Herald Tribune*. May 31, p. 1.

[9] James Blitz (2000b). "Italian Deficit Reduction on Track Despite 3G Debacle," *Financial Times*. November 2, p. 4; Tom Buerkle (2000). "Mobile Auction Frenzy Wanes Across Europe," *International Herald Tribune*. July 12, p. 1.

[10] See Eurostat press release (2000b). "Eurostat Decision on the Allocation of Mobile Phone Licences (UMTS)", N. 81/2000, July 14.

the equivalent of an equity, then these revenues could not be applied to the member states' deficits. The CMFB and the working group determined, however, that the physical properties of the electromagnetic spectrum or wave itself were being sold, not the license. Thus, the governments were engaged in nonfinancial transactions, and the revenues generated from these sales were included in the deficit calculation, which improved the member states' fiscal positions.

The second issue rested on whether the transaction constituted an outright lump-sum sale of the asset, or a distributive transaction, where the government retained the ownership of the asset and effectively rented it to the purchaser. An example of a distributive transaction is when a government rents a license to a telecom provider for a set number of years, where the issue at hand is determining how a government should count the flow of revenues over time. Eurostat, following the recommendation of the CMFB and working party, ruled that in the case of an outright sale, revenues would be counted and applied to the government's deficit in the year of the sale, and in the case of a distributive transaction revenues should be counted in accrual terms over the lifetime of the rental. This decision by Eurostat on the mobile phone licenses significantly improved the deficit and debt positions of a number of EU member states. A different ruling, one that stated these sales constituted a financial transaction, would, by contrast, have had dire political and fiscal consequences for the member states. Yet, by removing the fiscal incentive to charge large auction fees for the licenses, such a ruling might have encouraged the method of allocation of licenses adopted by the Scandinavian countries, thereby aiding the diffusion and privatization of this aspect of the EU telecoms industry.

5.2   Revising ESA: The Case of Swaps and the Lessons of Building Autonomy (2000)

Throughout much of the Maastricht Stage II convergence process and into Stage III, the European statistical community worked busily to update the ESA 79 manual to reflect new forms of transactions and economic activity within the EU. The financial and national accounts working parties, various task forces, National Statistical Institutes (NSIs) and Eurostat officials, and the CMFB toiled in this effort, employing what they learned from the deficit and debt rulings offered during the surveillance process. Their labors eventually came to fruition with the creation of ESA 95, codified in Council Regulation 02223/96 issued in 1996, and later in the *ESA 95 Manual on Government Deficit and Debt*, which appeared in 2000. This manual serves as a supplement to ESA

95, and incorporates Eurostat's various rulings since the mid-1990s, clarifying its critical decisions on such matters as the treatment of gold sales, capital injections, and privatization. The drafting of the ESA 95 manual also offered the member states an opportunity to reconsider the case of swaps, an experience that taught Eurostat a critical lesson in building institutional autonomy.

What makes swaps significant is that they provide governments with a very useful financial tool in debt management. A swap occurs when two parties contractually agree to exchange the streams of payments on equivalent amounts of debt. There are two forms of swaps, interest rate and currency swaps, which may be used, for example, by governments to extend the time period for payments on interest and principal. In the first category, the parties exchange the flows of different types of interest payments on debt, such as various combinations of floating and fixed exchange rates to reflect the risk of the swap. In the second category, debt denominated in different types of currencies are exchanged, where, again, the agreement between the parties provides for flows of interest and repayment. The smaller EU countries in particular, including Ireland, Finland, and Sweden, often employed currency swaps prior to monetary union due to the limited size of their national currencies. So too do larger states, as in the case of Italy, where some ten percent of that government's debt is denominated in foreign currency.[11] Swaps among EU member states and other national governments in international financial markets employing euro currency are, of course, also possible.

Eurostat initially addressed the issue of swaps in 1997 because, given its dated framework, ESA 79 said little about how to interpret this type of transaction. To classify swaps, Eurostat and CMFB turned to ESA 95, which defined swaps as a type of financial derivative where streams of net interest payments resulting from swap agreements would be recorded as property income. The standard question facing Eurostat at the time was whether these swap arrangements should indeed be included in a government's debt and deficit calculations. Council Regulation 3605/93 simplified the matter to some extent, as it

---

[11] A case that attracted Eurostat's attention occurred in 1995, when Italy engaged in a 200 billion yen bond swap, when the yen–lira exchange rate stood at L19.3. After the yen depreciated during the next year, dropping the rate to L13.4, the Treasury locked in the rate by converting its yen obligations to lira. Critics of the swap later announced this constituted nothing less than Enron accounting, with one critic declaring, "It is clear that the existence of the yen bond was merely a convenient pretext for Italy to borrow money that it could then misclassify as a hedge, just as Enron's commodities trades were a pretext for its own disguised borrowing." Eurostat, however, knew about the transaction as it transpired and accounted for it in its general ruling on swaps. James Blitz (2001b). "Italy Rebuts Swap Contract Claims," *Financial Times*. November 6, p. 6; Benn Steil (2002). "Enron and Italy," *Financial Times*. February 21, p. 13; Peter Norman (2001b)."Rome 'Did Not Cheat Over Deficit,' " *Financial Times*. November 6, p. 6. See Eurostat news release (1997a) "Eurostat Rules On Accounting Issues," N. 10/97, February 3.

made no mention of including financial derivatives in a member state's debt calculation. Therefore, any interest rate gains derived from the swap could not be employed to reduce a member state's debt figure, though the liability that existed before the transaction occurred would naturally be factored in to that amount. Regarding the deficit calculation, based on ESA 95, Eurostat ruled, as indicated in the Appendix, that the revenue gains or losses realized from swaps would be limited to the net difference between the interest flows agreed to in the exchange. Changes in capital gains or losses, however, would be excluded from the calculation. As shown in Table 4.2, this ruling influenced in a minor way the deficit and debt calculations of Ireland, Italy, and Finland for purposes of the convergence requirement. More generally, Eurostat's ruling limited the ability of member state governments to employ swaps as a device to improve their budgetary positions.

5.2.1 Swaps and the Lessons of Building Autonomy

Although Eurostat ruled on swaps in 1997, in its ongoing efforts to improve ESA 95 the matter remained under discussion. One motivation to revisit swaps was the EU statistical community's desire to harmonize ESA with the world's premier national accounting standard, the United Nations' System of National Accounts and Supporting Tables (SNA). In September 1999, to consider this and other statistical matters, Eurostat held a meeting of its various working parties, with representatives from the International Monetary Fund (IMF), the Organization for Economic Cooperation and Development (OECD), the World Bank, and the UN statistics office in attendance. The discussion on swaps focused on whether the net difference in interest rates would continue to be counted as property income, a type of nonfinancial transaction, or as a financial derivative, a form of financial transaction included in financial accounts. If this net difference were considered a financial derivative, according to Regulation 3605/93, it would no longer be included in the deficit and debt calculations. This treatment, however, would be consistent with SNA. The epistemic community of statisticians agreed that Eurostat should propose draft legislation to the European Council to amend ESA 95 to bring its understanding of swaps into harmony with SNA.[12]

---

[12] On the statistical community's opposition to the debt managers' position on swaps, see, for example: Letter from A. De Michelis to Mr. Cabral—DG ECFIN and MR. Chatzidoukakis—ESTAT R-4, "Subject: Amendments to ESA 95 (Swaps)," Eurostat, February 4, 2000; Eurostat (2000a). "Some Options Concerning Swaps for General Government in ESA 95," March 9, 2000; "Minutes of the CMFB Plenary Meeting Held in Luxembourg on 1–2 July 1999, prepared for the 19th Meeting of the Committee on Monetary, Financial and Balanced Payments Statistics," January 27–8, 2000, pp 10–13; "Revised Minutes of the Financial Accounts Working Party Meeting, Luxembourg, 21–22 October 1999, prepared for the Financial Accounts Working Party," March 16–17, 2000, pp. 7–8.

This potential loss of swap flexibility deeply upset the member state debt managers. These managers were organized as the Brouhns Group on EU Government Bonds and Bills, which reported to the ECOFIN Council. They preferred a specific reference in the regulations that counted swaps as interest, a form of distributive transaction, rather than as a financial derivative. As one senior Eurostat official commented, "There are units in finance ministries that do nothing else than arrange swaps. If swaps are harmonized, then they say, 'All our work is below the line and is worthless.'" The consequence of following the debt managers' preference, however, would be that swaps arranged by governments would be classified differently than swaps agreements arranged from other types of economic institutions, and the EU would stand out separately from nations that adhered to SNA. Eurostat contended that the debt managers were "freezing ESA in time," making it obsolete, undermining "the coherence of the system as a whole."

Nonetheless, the Brouhns Group successfully used Eurostat's own efforts to update the Maastricht surveillance legislation to achieve its ends. As part of this effort, Eurostat proposed that Council Regulation 3605/93, which defined the calculation of deficit and debt and outlined the member states' biannual reporting requirements, be revised to accommodate the change from ESA 79 to ESA 95. During this legislative process, which requires a proposal by the Commission and the approval of the European Council and Parliament, the debt managers exerted their influence with the ECOFIN Council. The Brouhns Group persuasively claimed the member states benefitted significantly from the existing status of swaps for purposes of debt management. Thus, despite Eurostat's opposition, when Council Regulation 3605/93 was amended by Council Regulation 475/2000, the new definition of government deficit declared "the interest comprised in the government deficit is the interest (D.41), as defined in ESA 95." In ESA 95, the provision "Interest D.41" includes swaps.[13] "Statisticians have the desire to bring ESA 95 in line with SNA," a chagrined Eurostat official proclaimed, "but the finance ministries and politicians don't care." "We were trapped," another Eurostat official said. "The only way out was to say okay, we amended the ESA but we keep a separate ruling for the recording of the deficit."

Eurostat and CMFB learned a painful lesson in autonomy building from this experience with swaps, which they later applied to securitization and other future rulings. In their drive to codify this transformation in national accounts and ESA, the statisticians realized they were politically vulnerable during the legislative process for two reasons. First, the EU legislative process

[13] Council Regulation (EC) No. 475/2000, February 28, 2000; Eurostat (1996). *European System of Accounts, ESA 1995.* Luxembourg: Office for Official Publications of the European Communities, p. 72.

is remarkably long, with legislation taking as long as two years before it is finally approved by the European Parliament. During this period, those in opposition to legislation would have ample time to form coalitions and mobilize to defeat Eurostat's proposals. Second, as a Eurostat officer observed, "You're not entirely sure if independent statisticians could be successful before the Council, as, say, compared to the ministries of finance." This is particularly true when desperate member states search for ways to comply with the Maastricht Treaty and the Stability and Growth Pact, and the possibility of compliance lies with making favorable changes in statistical case law. To avoid the dangers of the legislative path exemplified by the swaps "trap," the EU's statisticians learned to rely upon the delegated wall of legal autonomy already erected for them by the Maastricht Treaty and supporting legislation. "We don't amend ESA 95, we just interpret it," announced a Eurostat officer. "And we can do this within the community of statisticians. We don't go to the Council. If we would go to the Council, it would certainly be a difficult story. But for the time being, we keep this in ESA, and we need some kind of interpretation. And that's how we solve the case." As long as Eurostat's statisticians and their member state colleagues interpret ESA, as called for by the Treaty, they may render relatively independent judgments on the member states' deficits and debts. Thus, in the case of Italian securitization, although it represented a new form of transaction, Eurostat simply chose to interpret its proper classification, rather than seek to incorporate a change in the national accounts framework and amend ESA 95 by way of a Council regulation.

5.3   Italian Securitization Operations (2002)

The year 2002 was not a particularly happy one for Italian national accounts. Critics twice charged the Italians engaged in "Enron accounting," once in a prominent editorial critical of Italy's 1996 swaps transactions, the second time most remarkably by Eurostat's own Director General, Yves Franchet.[14] In 2002, Eurostat delivered a severe fiscal setback to Italy. An agency ruling forced Italy to adjust its reported 2001 deficit upwards from 1.6 percent of gross domestic product (GDP) to 2.2 percent, at the same time as Italy's Prime Minister Silvio Berlusconi's government's proclaimed its intention to drive its 2002 deficit down to 0.9 percent of GDP. This ruling also contributed to Italy's

---

[14] Benn Steil (2002). "Enron and Italy," *Financial Times*. July 21, p. 13. Leading up to this editorial, see James Blitz (2001). "Italy Rebuts Swap Contract Claims," *Financial Times*. November 6, p. 6, and Peter Norman (2001). "Rome 'Did Not Cheat Over Deficit,'" *Financial Times*. November 6, p. 6.

2.3 percent deficit.[15] What prompted Franchet's remark and Eurostat's decision was Italy's selling of securitized debt and recording it as off-balance sheet borrowing. More simply, in 2001, Italy issued bonds backed by assets in the form of real estate sales and lottery tickets, which constituted government borrowing against anticipated revenues rather than backed by assets in-hand.[16] As the euro-zone economies began to sink in 2000, both private and public entities extensively turned to asset-backed financing to meet their borrowing needs, with more than 92 billion euros worth of securitized debt sold in Europe in 2002.[17] Five EU member states, Austria, Finland, Greece, Ireland, and Italy, employed securitized debt as part of their public finances, but none as extensively as Italy. Vito Tanzi, a senior Italian Treasury official, indicated that real estate securitizations would serve as the government's "main tool" in the crafting of its fiscal policy aimed at balancing the budget in 2003, while another official described securitisations as a "highly innovative operation."[18] Altogether, these lottery and real estate securitizations trimmed Italy's 2001 deficit by approximately 7 billion euros, with the government planning on some 7.7 billion euros derived from securitization for its 2002 budget.

In deciding on this matter, Eurostat had to rule on several questions unaided by the new ESA 95, which was already dated, as the world's financial markets rapidly developed new and elaborate forms of economic transactions. As occurred several times during the convergence process in 1997 when ESA failed to provide adequate guidance, Eurostat developed its rulings by first creating a technical working party and by surveying the CMFB. The survey asked such questions as, should these securitized activities be classified as government borrowing, such that it influenced the calculation of a member state's deficit and debt? Should the "unit" that purchases the right to the future proceeds from the securitized sales, such as a bank or a pool of investors, which is termed the "special purpose vehicle" (SPV) in national accounts language, be categorized as governmental in nature, and be included

[15] See Eurostat press release (2002). "Securitisation Operations Undertaken By General Government," N. 80/2002, July 3. Also, CMFB conducted a survey of its membership on securitization and issued to the group several statements on the topic: "Consultation of the CMFB on the Treatment of Securitisation Operations Undertaken by General Government," 12 June 2002; "CMFB Opinion on the Treatment of Securitisation Operations Undertaken by General Government," 2 July 2002; and "Consultation of the CMFB on the Part V of the ESA 95 Manual on Government Deficit and Debt on Securitisation Operations Undertaken by Government Units," 3 February 2003.

[16] James Blitz (2001a). "Italy Looks to Real Estate Sales to Meet Budget Targets," *Financial Times*. September 11, p. 2.

[17] Rebecca Bream (2002). "Asset-Backed Proves Port In Storm," *Financial Times*. October 9, p. 24.

[18] Daniel Domby and Gavin Jones (2002). "Eurostat Warns Portugal Deficit May Be Higher," *Financial Times*. March 22, p. 2; James Blitz (2001). "Italy Looks to Real Estate Sales to Meet Budget Targets," *Financial Times*. September 11, p. 2.

in the governmental sector's balance sheet, or as a non-governmental unit? Should the revenues from these securitized sales be counted in one lump-sum payment, as Italy was attempting to do, or over time as they are collected?

After consulting with the CMFB, Eurostat answered the first question, as to whether this type of transaction should be classified as government borrowing, by declaring that anticipated securitized sales from such activities as lotteries and real estate sales, which are not tied to pre-existing assets, or, in effect, collateral, are the equivalent of borrowing against future revenues, thereby affecting the deficit and debt calculation.[19] Eurostat then answered the second question about whether an SPV should be classified within the governmental sector. This was an important question because if the SPV were classified outside the government, so too would its liabilities and debt. The central issue here was the element of economic risk. "The question we ask," noted Eurostat's Dieter Glatzel, "is the risk still with the government or is it transferred? What is the price at which the asset was transferred? If the risk is still with the government, it is [included] in the government deficit."[20] If a government were to sell an asset where there is a complete transfer of ownership to an SPV, this means there is a full transfer of "risk and rewards."

Consequently, the buyer is truly separate from the seller, and they should in this case be classified in different economic sectors within the national accounts framework. If, however, the government provides guarantees in the performance of that asset, say the sale of lottery tickets, then there is no full transfer of risks and rewards, and the SPV should be classified within the governmental sector. Thus, the SPV's transactions should be regarded as government borrowing. The last question addressed the recording of revenues. Eurostat declared that initial revenues paid by the SPV to the government must be recorded at that time, but future additional payments must be recorded as they occurred, not in a single upfront, lump-sum total.

The effects of these decisions were, first, to require that the government's securitized bonds be included in Italy's deficit and debt calculations, and, second, that the value of the revenues derived from the lottery and real estate sales be allocated over the time period in which they were derived. Italy's deficit, therefore, grew to 2.2 percent, as 5.3 billion euros worth of securitized debt that had been counted as off-balance sheet borrowing had to be included in the government's balance sheet and in its borrowing totals. In addition, the lottery and real estate revenues would be counted over the three-year period

---

[19] Eurostat news release (2002). "Securitisation Operations Undertaken by General Government," No. 80/2002, July 3.   [20] Interview with Dieter Glatzel, March 19, 2003.

in which they would be collected, rather than simply aggregated in a lump-sum figure and included in the 2001 budget.[21]

Meanwhile, EC authorities attempted to prevent a public relations fiasco by calming the furious Italians who bitterly resented Yves Franchet's analogy between their accounting and Enron's. Even *The Economist*, in a story warning of a member state's "clear incentive to cheat" over its budgetary statistics, described Franchet's remarks as "a wicked libel," "rashly" made.[22] Since the France Telecom decision, Franchet's management of the surveillance process proved to be politically sophisticated and sure-footed, but his remarks about Italy created a mini firestorm of very unwanted controversy. In response, a representative for EC President Romano Prodi declared the president "regretted" the connection, by announcing that "On the one hand we are talking about fraudulent and possible criminal activity. On the other, we are talking securitization and its treatment in statistics. They could not be any more different."[23] In an effort at damage control, Franchet also distanced himself from his remarks comparing the Italians' budgetary accounts to those of Enron. In a letter to the *Financial Times*, Franchet outlined Eurostat's role in the surveillance procedure and its responsibilities for national accounts harmonization:

The EU has set up over the years procedures for the collection of public account data that are reliable and transparent. Of course, the world moves on and the rules cannot cover everything. Last year a number of countries carried out securitisations in the financial markets. Such transactions were not covered by the existing ESA 95 rules and, as a result, countries initially treated them differently for national account purposes. Some reduced the deficit, some their public debt, while others kept them outside the government sector. In order to ensure equal treatment and avoid uncertainty, Eurostat set up this year a special working group together with the European Central Bank and member states' statistical offices to examine the particularities of such transactions. A similar approach was taken with the accounts treatment of UMTS auctions receipts two years ago. The result is clear and transparent rules that do not forbid securitisation

---

[21] James Blitz (2001a). "Italy Looks to Real Estate Sales to Meet Budget Targets," *Financial Times*. September 11, p. 2; (2002). "EU Ruling Raises Italy's Deficit Level," *International Herald Tribune*. July 5, p. 12.

[22] *The Economist*. "Roll Over, Enron," August 3, 2002, p. 42. Though sympathetic to the Commission's monitoring problem, *The Economist* exhibited limited knowledge about how Eurostat's surveillance worked and of Eurostat's authority in the process: "Countries collect their own numbers and report them to the European Union. Given the penalties for transgression, there is clear a incentive to cheat. . . . There's little Eurostat can do. It has a plan to harmonise the statistics, but it can't go in and audit for itself." As has been shown, Eurostat, in fact, exercises significant authority in analyzing and certifying the member states' budgetary data.

[23] Fred Kapner and George Parker (2002). "Angry Italy Agrees to EU Guidelines on Accounts," *Financial Times*. July 5, p. 2.

transactions as such but ensure that, when carried out, they are treated equally across the EU for public accounts purposes.[24]

Franchet promised that by the end of 2002 that ESA 95 would be revised to account fully for the use of securitization in the EU.

5.4   Crossing Over the 3.0 Percent Tripwire: Eurostat Rulings Initiate the Stability and Growth Pact's Excessive Deficit Procedure Against Portugal and France (2002 and 2003)

5.4.1   The Stability and Growth Pact's Surveillance Procedures and the Notification Process of the Excessive Deficit Procedure

Before examining Eurostat's rulings that resulted in the initiation of the excessive deficit procedure against Portugal and France, there is some value to reviewing the relevant provisions of the Maastricht Treaty and the Stability and Growth Pact. The Treaty requires that the member states avoid excessive deficit and debt levels of 3 and 60 percent of GDP, while the Pact calls upon the states to achieve and maintain their budgets "close to balance or in surplus." The Pact, furthermore, requires that member states provide annual stability programs that outline how their fiscal policies will enable them to realize these budgetary goals. The budgetary data and economic categories in these programs, it should be noted, are organized on the basis of ESA classifications and codes. These data, in turn, are those employed in DG ECFIN's econometeric modeling. Council Regulation 1466/97 directs the ECOFIN Council to assess these programs, taking "into account the relevant cyclical and structural characteristics of the economy of each Member State." Council Regulation 1467/97 states that during this assessment the Council may decide that an excessive deficit "shall be considered exceptional and temporary" if it results from circumstances outside a member state's control, and if "budgetary forecasts as provided by the Commission indicate that the deficit will fall below the reference value following the end of the unusual event or the severe economic downturn."[25]

These notions of cyclical economic characteristics and budgetary forecasts were introduced by DG ECFIN staff during the drafting of the Pact, which enables it to play a much greater role in the Stage III surveillance process than

---

[24] Yves Franchet (2002b). "Eurostat's New Rules on Securitisation Transactions," *Financial Times.* July 6, p. 6.

[25] The cyclical reference is found in Section 14 the preamble of Council Regulation (EC) 1466/97; the role of forecasting is in Council Regulation (EC) 1467/97, Section 1, Article 2.

during Stage II. For the practical purpose of determining fiscal convergence, the Stage II surveillance process relied almost exclusively on Eurostat's management of ESA interpretations of member state fiscal positions. In addition to relying upon Eurostat's function, the Stage III process calls upon DG ECFIN's abilities in econometric forecasting and evaluating cyclical economic conditions in assessing the member states' stability programs. Perhaps the most important of DG ECFIN's econometric calculations is that of the cyclically adjusted budget balance. This calculation attempts to identify the cyclical element in a member state's actual deficit, thus separating the component of the deficit that is due to structural or policy considerations, from that component due to cyclical changes in the economy. The cyclical element improves with the economy, while the structural element remains and must be countered with corrective fiscal policy. The econometrics underlying this measure is complex. As the ECOFIN Council's advisory Economic Policy Committee warned, "Annual changes in the structural fiscal balance should be interpreted with caution, since they do not fully reflect discretionary fiscal policy measures nor the precise impact of fiscal policy on aggregate demand."[26] In 2001, DG ECFIN replaced its econometric model with another, as well as the format and content of the member states' stability programs, in an attempt better to assess the member states' cyclical budget balances. So, if the model works, the added value of DG ECFIN's enhanced participation in the surveillance process is that presumably its forecasting can alert EU officials to prospective excessive deficits and debt before they occur, long before the member states produce data on their actual and planned deficits in their biannual reports to Eurostat.

Nonetheless, either the presence of an actual excessive deficit or the forecast of one is sufficient to initiate the excessive deficit procedure. The Treaty's Articles 99 and 104 describe the procedure's notification process. Article 99 declares that the Commission may recommend to the ECOFIN Council that a member state may be deviating from the budgetary targets set in its stability program, and that the Council may then send an early warning to a member state. This warning may be followed by an ECOFIN Council recommendation to the state to take appropriate corrective measures. This early warning, therefore, may be sent even if the member state's deficit is far below the 3 percent of GDP reference value, as the member state is also held responsible for meeting the Pact's close to budgetary balance or surplus mandate. Where Article 99 is replete with the conditional "may," Article 104, which contains the specific

---

[26] Economic Policy Committee (2001). "Report on Potential Output and the Output Gap," ECFIN/EPC/670/01/en, October 25, p. 9. On cyclically adjusted budgets, see Director General for Economic and Financial Affairs (2002). *European Economy: Public Finances in EMU 2002, No. 3/2002.* Brussels: European Communities, pp. 54–61.

provisions of the excessive deficit procedure, is more definitive, requiring that the Commission and the ECOFIN Council "shall" take various actions to notify and recommend corrective action to the member states. Article 104(3) states that the Commission shall prepare a report, presumably drafted by DG ECFIN, if a member state's deficit or debt is excessive or if there is a risk of such an occurrence. This report is merely factual, and the ECOFIN Council is required to form an opinion as to whether it agrees with the report. The next steps, described in Articles 104(5) and (6), requires the Commission to determine if an excessive deficit exists, and to provide the Council with an opinion and a recommendation to that effect.

The ECOFIN Council then renders a decision as to whether it concurs with that assessment. If it does, according to Article 104(7), the ECOFIN Council must provide the member state with a recommendation on how it should rectify its budgetary condition within a given period of time. Council Regulation 1467/97 indicates the nature of this time frame outlined in the recommendation. The member state must take action, such as making policy and programmatic changes, within four months, and achieve its corrective goals within the following year. Article 104(8) provides for the ECOFIN Council, again presumably with Commission assistance, to establish whether a member state complies with these recommendations. Article 104(9) then states that the Council may give the member state notice that it should take this corrective action within a specified timetable. The remaining sections of the article address the application of financial and other penalties for noncompliance, and the termination of such penalties with the correction of the actual excessive deficit.

The notification provisions of the excessive deficit procedure, therefore, provide roles for both DG ECFIN and Eurostat. Either a DG ECFIN forecast of an excessive deficit or Eurostat's reporting of an actual or planned excessive deficit may inaugurate Article 104's procedures, with DG ECFIN producing the various opinions, reports, and recommendations for the ECOFIN Council's use. The data and findings from both Commission agencies may determine whether a member state is compliant or noncompliant throughout the excessive deficit procedure. Before the penalty phase begins, however, Council Regulation 1467/97 Article 10 specifies that there must be the determination that an actual excessive deficit exits, which depends upon Eurostat's certification, as does the cessation of whatever penalties may have been imposed.

5.4.2 Portugal (2002)

In February 2002, Yves Franchet wrote to Commissioner Solbes, warning him that Portugal's biannual statistical report was in arrears. If the data were not submitted immediately, Eurostat would be unable to certify Portugal's figures for the March report. More important, for three years the Portuguese NSI repeatedly failed to provide Eurostat with requested information on government subsidies granted to seven major public enterprises, including *Metro Lisboa*, to an amount of some 7.3 billion euros. "The overwhelming majority of these transfers," Franchet noted, "have been treated by the Portuguese authorities as equity acquisitions, therefore, without having any impact on the deficit. However . . . there is legitimate ground for suspicion that at least some of these capital injections should have been treated as capital transfers as they were granted to enterprises on a regular basis to cover accumulated losses."[27] When a government purchases shares to increase their equity holdings, such that there is a true increase in assets, this purchase is considered a financial transaction with no effect on the government's net borrowing/net lending calculation. When, however, a government simply injects capital into an enterprise as a form of financial assistance, so that the government does not increase its equity holdings and its payment is essentially unrequited, this capital injection is considered a nonfinancial transaction that does effect the deficit calculation. In these particular cases, Eurostat required that Portugal reclassify its presumed equity purchases as capital injections.[28]

Eurostat's refusal to certify these data came at a very sensitive time, as the Portuguese planned to hold a general election in March, with the condition of Portugal's economy and budget playing a central role in the campaign between the incumbent Socialist government and the Social Democrats. Like many other EU countries, Portugal's economic health declined dramatically beginning in 2001, in terms of GDP, gross fixed investment, private consumption, and domestic demand.[29] As a result, Portugal's deficit climbed, with the nation's political parties pledging its reduction. The Socialist plan focusing on spending reductions and the Social Democrats proposing significant corporate tax cuts that would stimulate the economy, thereby producing greater tax

[27] Yves Franchet (2002a). "Note for the Attention of Mr. Pedro Solbes, Subject: Portugal—Debt and Deficit Issues," 21 February.

[28] On this point, see Eurostat (2000b). *ESA 95 Manual On Government Deficit and Debt*, chapter II.3 Capital Injections. Luxembourg: Eurostat, pp. 47–54.

[29] For an assessment of Portugal's economy, see ECFIN's "Report From the Commission: Excessive Deficit in Portugal—Report Prepared in Accordance With Art. 104.3 of the Treaty," September 9, 2002, ECFIN/436/02-en. On page 12, the report also observed,

The monitoring of the execution of multi-annual budgetary plans is made difficult due to lack of timely data for the social security sector, local authorities and most autonomous funds and services. The recent approval of a "budgetary stability law" has strengthened information requirements for local authorities and autonomous funds and services, which could facilitate fiscal management by shortening the recognition lag for the identification of budgetary slippages and the implementation lag to adopt corrective measures.

revenues.[30] In what may be either, or perhaps both, an apparent effort to mask the extent of its fiscal problems or simply sloppy record keeping, the incumbent Socialist government misclassified budgetary data and failed to share it with Eurostat on a timely basis.

The budget figures initially submitted to Eurostat in 2001 by the government showed that year's deficit to be 2.2 percent of GDP with the planned 2002 deficit set at 2.6 percent. Eurostat directly challenged these numbers for the reasons Franchet cited, including Portugal's underestimation of local government deficits, overestimation of tax receipts, the imprecise recording of EU Third Community Support Programme funds, the improper inclusion of receipts derived from the liquidation of an industrial development fund counted as government revenue, and the above mentioned misclassification of government capital injections as the acquisition of shares.[31] For 2002, the applicable error centered on the liquidation of development funds, which amounted to some 139.5 million euros, or 0.11 percent of GDP for 2002. This recalculation raised the deficit for that year to 2.7 percent.[32]

Much more troubling for Portugal, the revisions forced by Eurostat boosted the 2001 deficit from a reported level of 2.2 percent to an astonishing 4.1 percent, a clear violation of the Stability and Growth Pact. Eurostat later raised this figure to 4.2 percent of GDP, as shown in Table 5.1.[33] The difference between the 2.2 and 4.2 percent was accounted for the following fashion: 0.4 percent due to improperly classified capital injections; 0.1 percent due to local deficits; 0.3 percent caused by under reported expenditures caused by a switch to accrual accounting; 0.6 percent due to a revision of overestimated tax collections in conformity with Council Regulation 2516/2000, which extended ESA 95 to certain taxes and social contributions; 0.2 percent due to the revision of state accounts; and 0.4 percent due to the revision of autonomous funds and

---

[30] Peter Wise (2002a). "Portugal Gets No Reprieve at Home Over Budget Deficit," *Financial Times.* February 13, p. 2; Peter Wise (2002b). "Candidates in Portugese Polls Turn Guns on Budget Dilemma," *Financial Times.* March 4, p. 4.

[31] For details on these dubious classifications, see: Yves Franchet (2002c). "Note A L' Attention de Monsieur P. Solbes, Membre De La Commission, Objet: Procedure de deficit excessif—cas du Portugal," Eurostat, February 5; Bart Meganck (2002b). "Note for the Attention of Mr. Cabral, Director, Directorate B, ECFIN, Subject: Portugal—Excessive Deficit Procedure," Eurostat, April 10; Bart Meganck (2002c). Letter to Professor Doctor Paulo Gomes, Presidente Instituto Nacional de Estatistica, "Subject: Statistical Aspects for the Excessive Deficit Procedure," Eurostat, May 3, 2002; Hans Peter Hartvig and Miguel Diaz-Llanos La Roche (2002). "Note for the Attention of Mr. Klaus Regling, Director General, DG Economic and Financial Affairs, "Subject: Portugal—Derogation on the Application of Regulation (EC) 2516/2000," European Commission Legal Service, May 6.

[32] See Eurostat news release (2003a). "Euro-Zone Government Deficit at 2.2% of GDP and Public Debt at 69.1% of GDP," N. 30/2003, March 17; Daniel Dombey and Gavin Jones (2002). "Eurostat Warns Portugal Deficit May Be Higher," *Financial Times.* March 22, p. 2.

[33] Eurostat news release, ibid.

Table 5.1 Budget deficits in the euro-zone, 1997–2003, as a percent of GDP

	1997	1998	1999	2000	2001	2002	2003
Austria	−1.9	−2.4	−2.3	−1.5	+0.2	−.02	−1.1
Belgium	−2.0	−0.7	−0.5	+0.2	+0.5	+0.1	+0.2
Finland	−1.5	+1.3	+2.0	+7.1	+5.2	+4.3	+2.3
France	−3.0	−2.7	−1.8	−1.4	−1.5	−3.2	−4.1
Germany	−2.7	−2.2	−1.5	+1.3	−2.8	−3.5	−3.9
Greece[a]	−4.0	−2.5	−1.8	−2.0	−1.4	−1.4	−3.2
Ireland	+1.2	+1.2	+2.3	+4.4	+1.1	−0.2	+0.2
Italy	−2.7	−2.8	−1.7	−0.6	−2.6	−2.3	−2.4
Luxembourg	+3.4	+3.1	+3.5	+6.3	+6.3	+2.7	−0.1
Netherlands	−1.1	−0.8	+0.7	+2.2	0.0	−1.9	−3.0
Portugal	−2.7	−2.6	−2.8	−2.8	−4.1	−2.7	−2.8
Spain	−3.2	−2.6	−1.1	+2.4	+2.8	+2.8	+2.9

[a] Greece joined the euro-zone in 2001.

Source: Eurostat News Releases, "Euro-zone Government Deficit at − 1.2% and Debt at 72.2% of GDP in 1999," N. 34/2000, March 13, 2000; "Euro-zone Government Deficit at 2.7% of GDP and Public Debt at 70.4% of GDP," N. 38/2004, March 16, 2004; and "Greek Government Deficit at 3.2% of GDP and Public Debt at 103.0% of GDP," N. 62/2004, May 7, 2004.

services accounts. Under pressure from the Commission, Portugal's newly created Commission for the Analysis of Public Accounts resubmitted a new biannual report for the preceding years, which Eurostat then certified. Given the shocking state of Portugal's statistics, however, Commissioner Solbes declared that Portugal suffered from "serious omissions in the production of government deficit and debt data."

Under our Community system of European and Monetary Union (EMU) statistics, Member States are fully responsible for the collection and compilation of national statistics, which are then controlled with regard to their classification by Eurostat. Budgetary surveillance cannot function properly unless member states and their statistical offices pay the utmost attention to this task. It is not possible to substitute at European level for national shortcomings. I therefore call on the Portuguese government to make sure that the necessary resources and effort are put into place to ensure that general government deficit and debt are properly collected in the future.[34]

[34] Pedro Solbes (2002). "Statement by Commissioner Solbes on the Portuguese Deficit Data," EU Press Releases, IP/02/1168, July 7, 2002; Mark Landler (2002). "EU Faces Major Test on Deficit in Portugal," *International Herald Tribune*. July 27–8, p. 1.

Portugal's election resulted in a victory for the Social Democrats and their new prime minister, Jose Manuel Durao Barroso. Barroso, who argued during the election that the Socialists under reported the government's deficit, agreed that the government's data were unreliable, and he pledged the government's accounts would be audited and properly organized.

Meanwhile, between September and October 2002, DG ECFIN responded to Portugal's budgetary position by submitting to the ECOFIN Council reports that activated the excessive deficit procedure, declared the existence of an excessive deficit, and recommended corrective action to the Council. Though earlier in the year, in February, the Council rejected a Commission recommendation that Portugal be issued an early warning, it now agreed with the Commission's opinion, formally reprimanded Portugal, and gave its government a year to bring its finances in order. Prime Minister Barroso promised to bring the government's deficit under control, declaring "The pact sets out rules for the sound management of the economy that I would be following even if we were not part of the euro."[35] Portugal did indeed take action, and reduced its deficit to 2.7 percent of GDP for 2002.

5.4.3 France (2003)

At the same time Eurostat issued its public revision of the Portuguese deficit in March 2003, it did so for France. Though at that time France's fiscal position proved to be not nearly so precarious as Portugal's, it too suffered from growing budgetary deficits and debt. Like a number of other EU member states, France's economy began to stutter, reducing both GDP growth and government revenues. As a result, the steady decline in France's deficit from 5.8 percent of GDP in 1994 to 1.4 percent in 2000 came to an end in 2001. In response to France's weakening circumstances, Prime Minister Lionel Jospin announced in October 2001 that the government would engage in a program of fiscal stimulus to boost the economy. This plan called for an overall expansion in the budget of some 2 percent, including spending 30.5 million euros to create 50,000 public jobs. Coupled with the effects of the weakening economy on revenues, the added spending raised the 2001 deficit slightly to 1.5 percent of GDP. Despite this reversal, at the March 2002 Barcelona conference the French nevertheless pledged with the other EU member states to bring their countries' budgets into balance

---

[35] *The Economist.* "Too Much Red Ink For the Euro-Zone," July 6, 2002, p. 47; *International Herald Tribune.* "EU Reprimands Portugal Over Budget Deficit," November 6, 2002, p. 11; Peter Wise (2003). "Portugal Learns to Love Stability Pact," *Financial Times.* January 29, p. 4.

by 2004.[36] Furthermore, Jospin's effort at fiscal stimulus failed to protect him politically, as in the spring elections of 2002 President Jacques Chirac's Gaullist Rally for the Republic (RPR) party gained control of the government.

Though Chirac bitterly opposed the Socialists' fiscal policies, during the election he nevertheless promised to provide stimulative tax cuts amounting to 30 percentage points by 2007 that would induce higher deficit spending. By September 2002, his government announced that France would break the balanced budget pledge made at Barcelona, and that deficit spending was "likely to remain beyond 2006."[37] From that point on, through 2002 and into 2004, Chirac's government repeatedly clashed with EU officials and many of the smaller member states over France's rapidly expanding deficit. In November 2002, a day after the Commission recommended to the ECOFIN Council that it issue an early warning to France, Finance Minister Alain Lambert admitted the deficit would grow to 2.8 percent, up from a previous estimate of 2.6 percent. Still, Lambert declared that the government would not exceed the 3.0 percent level, as the French government bluntly informed the Commission that it would ignore demands that it bring the deficit under control. The ECOFIN Council responded in January 2003 by issuing to France the first early warning message ever delivered to a member state under the excessive deficit procedure. The March 2003 biannual report submitted to Eurostat, in fact, indicated the 2002 deficit to be exactly 3.0 percent.[38]

This deficit figure soon crossed over into the range of an excessive deficit, however, as Eurostat found itself at odds with the French NSI over one transaction that soon required the upward revision of France's deficit figures. For some six years the French government classified its financial assistance to the state railway, *Reseau ferre de France* (RFF), as a financial transaction.

---

[36] *International Herald Tribune*. "President Assails Jospin's Economic Policies," July 16, 2001, p. 7; Robert Graham (2001a). "Jospin Opts to Increase Budget," *Financial Times*. July 18, p. 2; Robert Graham (2001b). "France to Create 50,000 Temporary Jobs," *Financial Times*. October 3, p. 7; Robert Graham (2001c). "Fabius to Introduce Fiscal Stimulus," *Financial Times*. October 16, p. 4; Victor Mallet (2002a). "France Set to Break Pledge on Balanced Budget Target," *Financial Times*. May 12, p. 1.

[37] Liz Alderman (2002). "Fiscal Fisticuffs for Europe?" *International Herald Tribune*. May 14, p. 13; Barry James (2002). "France to Cut Taxes Despite Jump In Deficit," *International Herald Tribune*. June 21, p. 11; Paul Betts (2002). "France Backs Tax Cuts At the Expense of Balanced Budget," *Financial Times*. September 25, p. 6; Victor Mallet (2002b). "French Deficit 'Likely to Remain Beyond 2006,'" *Financial Times*. September 26, p. 4.

[38] Francesco Guerrera (2003). "France May Ignore Order To Cut Deficit," *Financial Times*. January 22, p. 4; *International Herald Tribune*, "Public Deficit Is Flirting with EU Limit, France Says," February 5, 2003, p. 10; Francesco Guerrera and Jo Johnson (2002). "France Refuses To Take Steps To Curb Budget Deficit," *Financial Times*. February 26, p. 8; Eric Pfanner (2003a). "France, Foe of Unilateralism, Stands Alone on EU Debt," *International Herald Tribune*. February 27, p. 5; *International Herald Tribune*. "France Lifts Outlook for Deficit to 2.8% of GDP," November 21, 2002, p. 11; Victor Mallet and George Parker (2003). "France 'To Breach Deficit Limit This Year,'" *Financial Times*. February 5, p. 4.

When Eurostat examined the RFF's accounts, it found the railway sustained enormous losses that essentially equaled the amount of the state's payments. Given the revision in ESA 95 that addressed capital injections, this transaction clearly needed to be reclassified as a nonfinancial transaction, as had similar state support to public railways in Portugal and Greece. Consequently, Eurostat added the 2002 capital injection of 1.362 billion euros to the deficit calculation, raising it for that year to 3.1 percent of GDP.[39] Forced to recalculate its deficit, the French warned that its 2003 deficit might reach 3.4 percent. Based upon this information, in May 2003 Commissioner Solbes announced that France would continue to exceed the Stability and Growth Pact with projected deficits of 3.7 percent of GDP in 2003 and 3.6 percent in 2004. The Commission determined that France's deficit was excessive and recommended that the ECOFIN Council makes its own recommendation as to what corrective action should be taken.[40] The ECOFIN Council responded by declaring in June that an excessive deficit existed in France, and recommended that the government should take all necessary action to avoid exceeding the 3.0 percent deficit level in 2003, and that these measures should reduce the cyclically adjusted deficit by 0.5 percent. The government was ordered to make its policy and program changes by October 3, and end its excessive deficit condition by the end of 2004.

Throughout the summer and early fall, the Commission and the French government repeatedly clashed over France's fiscal position. DG ECFIN charged that despite France's budgetary problems becoming evident in 2002, the government failed to take appropriate corrective measures. "Moreover," the agency claimed, "they have failed to engage in an constructive dialogue at EU level on the pace of budgetary consolidation towards the 'close to balance or surplus' requirement" in the Stability and Growth Pact.[41] Though acknowledging that its deficit would remain excessive through 2005, in September 2003 the French government approved a tax cut of 3.3 billion euros. Finance Minister Francis Mer defended his government's stimulative policies, declaring,

[39] Eurostat news release (2003a). "Euro-Zone Government Deficit at 2.2% of GDP and Public Debt at 69.1% of GDP," N. 30/2003, March 17. Also, letters from Yves Franchet to Jean-Michel Charpin, Director General of the French NSI, "Dotation en capital dans RFF," March 4, 2003; and "Notification PDE de la France—1 mars 2003 Communique de presse Eurostat," March 13, 2003. Eurostat further clarified its position on capital injections, as in the case of FFR, in its news release, (2003c). "Capital Injections by Government Units Into Public Corporations," No. 98/2003, August 21.

[40] Eric Pfanner (2003b). "EU Warns France on Breaching Deficit Limit," *International Herald Tribune.* March 8–9, p. 15; George Parker and Robert Graham (2003). "France 'Could Be in Deficit For Three Years,'" *Financial Times.* April 3, p. 4; Paul Meller (2003). "EU Orders France to Cut Its Deficit," *International Herald Tribune.* May 8, p. 1.

[41] European Commission: Directorate-General for Economic and Financial Affairs (2003). *Public Finances in EMU.* Brussels, p. 48.

"Stability is imperative, but you must not forget growth."[42] Increasingly irritated, Commissioner Solbes responded to France with the announcement that "I am not in favor . . . of applying sanctions against France. However, if the day comes and we have to apply sanctions, then we have to apply them. . . . I am convinced that we have to have this framework. It makes sense. I will carry on defending the Pact. I don't think we have an alternative."[43]

The Commission publicly registered its displeasure in its evaluation of France's compliance with the ECOFIN Council's order that corrective budgetary action be completed by early October. The Commission first reported France made minor programmatic adjustments, such as tobacco tax increases, the cancellation of state sector credits, and the termination of certain drug reimbursements, but, in total, the government took "no effective action" to reduce its deficit.[44] As a result, the French would be unable to eliminate their excessive deficit by 2004, as previously called for by the Council. To counter the growing fiscal imbalance, the Commission recommended to the Council that France reduce its cyclically adjusted deficit by 1 percent of GDP in 2004, which meant undertaking deeper budget reductions amounting to 0.4 percent of GDP more than provided for in the government's June budget. The recommendation also required the French to submit a compliance report by December 15, with four implementation reports during the coming two years. Yet, the great significance of the Commission's recommendation was that these additional changes would bring the deficit below 3 percent in 2005, not in 2004, which meant that France would incur an excessive deficit for the third consecutive year. Furthermore, while citing France's deteriorating economy and cyclical conditions, the Commission's recommendation effectively postponed the next stages of the excessive deficit procedure, which included imposing financial penalties on France.

5.5   The ECOFIN Council's Conclusions on France and Germany

In November, in a startling decision that elicited cries that the EU had witnessed the death of the Stability Pact, the ECOFIN Council rejected both the Commission's assessment of France's budgetary behavior and its recommendations for corrective action. With Belgium, Germany, Greece, Ireland, Italy, Luxembourg, and Portugal voting in favor, the Council adopted a set of

---

[42] Ed Crooks (2003). "Eurozone Enforcer Prepares to Strike First Blow," *Financial Times*. September 3, p. 6.   [43] Euobserver (2003a). "Sobles Hits Back At France," September 30.

[44] European Commission (2003d). "Commission Asks France to Take New Measures to Reduce the Budget Deficit in 2004," IP/03/1420, Brussels. October 21.

conclusions that suspended the excessive deficit procedure against France. The majority of member states ruled that France's deepening economic problems and falling real GDP were "abrupt and unexpected," and that the government's September deficit reduction measures amounted to a cyclically adjusted 0.7 percent, a figure larger than the Commission's June recommendation of 0.5 percent.[45] Given these circumstances, the Council asked France to increase the 2004 reduction to 0.8 percent, and the 2005 reduction at least to 0.6 percent, which would bring the deficit below 3 percent, with continued annual cyclical reductions of 0.5 percent until the budget fulfilled the Stability and Growth Pact's target of being close to or in balance.

5.5.1 Germany

In the cases of Portugal and France, Eurostat played a direct role in activation of the excessive deficit procedure by challenging the member states' biannual report deficit figures. Eurostat's refusal to certify their budgetary data forced these member states to revise their numbers, placing them in the position of incurring excessive deficits. Germany's data, however, required no revisions. Eurostat found Germany's biannual report in compliance with ESA 95's guidelines, and certified that its budgetary position violated the excessive deficit procedure and Stability and Growth Pact.

Like several of its fellow EU member states, Germany experienced the heady fiscal euphoria of the late 1990s, only to fall into fiscal crisis. In 1999, Finance Minister Hans Eichel predicted that Germany's deficit would fall to 1.5 percent of GDP in 2000. In fact, the government far surpassed that target, as the budget produced an astonishing 1.1 percent surplus, leaving an ebullient Eichel to predict significant debt reduction, tax cuts, and even spending increases.[46] Within a year these happy plans were scrapped, as Germany slipped into a recession in the third quarter of 2001, with the deficit predicted to grow to 2.5 percent in 2001. In August, Eichel stunned the EU by raising the topic of revising the Stability and Growth Pact, focusing its effort on controlling spending targets rather than deficits, only to recant soon after and pledge, "We are firmly sticking to our goals of balancing the budget by 2006."[47] Nevertheless, with DG ECFIN predicting the 2001 deficit would grow

[45] Council of Economic and Financial Affairs (2003). "2546th Council Meeting," C/03/320, Brussels. November 25, p. xv.

[46] Uta Harnischfeger (1999). "German Deficit Falling 'Faster,'" *Financial Times*. July 5, p. 3; Haig Simonian (2000). "Eichel Predicts Future Budget Surpluses Could Cut Debt," *Financial Times*. November 10, p. 6.

[47] Haig Simonian (2001). "Germany Slips Into Recession in Third Quarter," *Financial Times*. November 23, 6; Haig Simonian and Gerrit Weismann (2001). "Germany Revises Down Its Deficit

to 2.7 percent, the Commission urged the ECOFIN Council to issue Germany, as well as Portugal, an early warning reprimand for failing to rein in its deficit. Rather than impose this highly embarrassing sanction on Germany, the founder of the Pact, in February 2002 the ECOFIN Council ministers instead reached an "agreement" in which Germany "confirms its endeavor" to reduce its deficit and honor the goal of balancing its budget in 2004. Rather than single out Portugal for an early warning, the ECOFIN Council also permitted the Portuguese to commit themselves to the agreement. The ministers apparently spared Germany this rebuke in order to protect Chancellor Gerhard Schroeder from popular retribution in the September elections.[48]

Despite the agreement, Germany's deficit continued to grow, with the German government promising more tax cuts to encourage the economy. In November, the Commission initiated the first stage of the excessive deficit procedure against Germany, and in January declared its deficit to be excessive. The ECOFIN Council concurred and accepted the Commission's recommendation that Germany take corrective action by May to lower its excessive deficit to 2.75 percent for 2003. To accomplish this, Germany would have to make changes in fiscal policies amounting to 1 percent of GDP. For their part, the Germans admitted in their biannual report they submitted to Eurostat that the 2002 deficit reached 3.6 percent of GDP, with expectations that the 3.0 deficit level would again be breached in 2003. From Eurostat's perspective, unlike the Portuguese and the French, the Germans submitted appropriately classified budgetary figures in their biannual report, thereby willingly exposing themselves to these reprimands and sanctions. Chancellor Schroeder, moreover, acknowledged that his government would fail to balance its budget as promised at Barcelona, leaving Commissioner Solbes to warn, "If the deficit is above 3 percent in 2004 as well, a [financial] penalty could be imposed in January

Forecasts," *Financial Times*. November 27, p. 6; Claus Hulverscheidt and Daniel Dombey (2001). "German Finance Chief Hints At Changes to Key European Pact," *Financial Times*. August 17, p. 12.

[48] Peter Norman (2002a). "Germany May Take Its Own Medicine," *Financial Times*. January 20, p. 2; John Schmid (2002a). "EU to Scold Berlin, But Gently," *International Herald Tribune*. January 31, p. 2; John Schmid (2002b). "EU Rebukes Germany As Deficit Nears Limit," *International Herald Tribune*. January 31, p. 9; John Schmid (2002c). "Berlin Will Partly Dodge EU Deficit Warning," *International Herald Tribune*. February 12, p. 1; Peter Norman (2002b). "EU Avoids Vote in Compromise Over Finances," *Financial Times*. February 13, p. 2; Peter Norman (2002c). "Protagonists Each Claim Satisfaction From Accord," *Financial Times*. February 13, p. 2; Hugh Williamson (2002). "Berlin Attacked Over Stance On Deficit,'" *Financial Times*. February 13, p. 2; Council of Economic and Finance Ministers (2002). "Statement by the Council (ECOFIN) on the Budgetary Situation of Germany," Brussels. February 12; John Vinocur (2002). "Pure Politics Drove EU to Be Lenient on Berlin," *International Herald Tribune*. February 13, p. 1.

2005."[49] In November, the Commission notified the ECOFIN Council that Germany's deficit would remain excessive in 2003 despite its policy changes. For Germany to remedy its excessive deficit position, an additional deficit reduction of 0.8 percent of GDP would be required in 2004 and 0.5 percent in 2005. Rather than eliminate its excessive deficit in 2003 or 2004 as called for earlier by the Council, the Commission recommended that Germany, like France, be permitted an additional year to accomplish this task.

5.5.2   The Council's Conclusions and the Commission's Reaction

The Council's reaction stunned the Commission. Again, as with France, a majority of the Council rejected the Commission's findings and recommendations, as Belgium, Greece, France, Ireland, Italy, Luxembourg, and Portugal voted to suspend the excessive deficit procedure against Germany. The Council determined that the German government complied with its January recommendations that budget changes amounting to 1 percent of GDP be enacted within the allowable time frame. Thus, where the Commission recommended a 0.8 percent cyclical deficit reduction in 2004, the Council indicated 0.6 percent would be appropriate. Germany's excessive deficit, the Council concluded, stemmed not from a lack of political will but from a failing economy and a 2 percent drop in GDP. Since even the Commission acknowledged that an attempt to terminate the excessive deficit would undermine long-term economic recovery, the Council ruled that Germany be granted the extra time required to bring this condition to an end by 2005. Finally, the Council unanimously agreed to this statement:

The Council recalls the central role played by the Stability and Growth Pact in ensuring an improvement in the overall budgetary situation in the EU, and encouraging the development by the Member States of sound and sustainable budgetary policies; [the Council] reaffirms its commitment to the Stability and Growth Pact as the framework for the coordination of budgetary policies in the European Union with the particular objectives of achieving budgetary positions of close to balance or in surplus over the business cycle and public finances that are sustainable in the long term.[50]

---

[49] George Parker, Haig Simonian, and Tony Major (2003). "Brussels to Warn Schroder Over Deficit Rule Breach," *Financial Times*. January 8, p. 4; Mark Landler and Paul Meller (2003). "EU Warns Berlin, Paris, and Rome," *International Herald Tribune*. January 9, p. 1; George Parker, Haig Simonian, Victor Mallet, and Tony Barber (2003). "EU Orders Berlin to Curb Budget Deficit," *Financial Times*. January 9, p. 4; Betrand Benoit and Daniel Dombey (2003). "Schroder Drops Budget Pledge," *Financial Times*. May 12, p. 3.

[50] Council of Economic and Financial Affairs (2003). "2546th Council Meeting," C/03/320, Brussels. November 25, p. xx.

Outraged, the Commission refused to accept the ECOFIN Council's conclusions peacefully. The Commission first countered with its own addendum to the Council's statement: "The Commission deeply regrets that the Council has not followed the spirit and the rules of the Treaty and the Stability and Growth Pact that were agreed unanimously by all Member States. Only a rule-based system can guarantee that commitments are enforced and that all Member States are treated equally." The Commission argued that the Council failed to provide an "adequate explanation" for rejecting its recommendations, and threatened that it would examine the Council's conclusions "and decide on possible subsequent actions."[51]

The Commission made clear what was meant by its "subsequent action," when in January President Prodi announced that the Commission would challenge the ECOFIN Council's conclusions in the European Court of Justice. In particular, the Commission objected to the Council's decision to suspend, or hold in "abeyance," the excessive deficit procedure against France and Germany while keeping these rules intact when considering the remaining member states, its failure to state "unambiguously" on economic grounds why the Commission's recommendations were rejected, and its stepping outside the set of procedures called for in the Treaty and Pact. The Council's decision undermined the efficacy of the surveillance process, Commissioner Sobles declared, making the appeal necessary:

We all know that the Council could have adopted the substance of the ECOFIN conclusions in the form of Council recommendations, which is what the Treaty provides for in this area. But Member States deliberately chose to take an intergovernmental position. This changes the nature of the budgetary surveillance and it is therefore useful to have the Court's ruling in order to clarify surveillance for the future.[52]

Prodi and Sobles promised that the Commission would continue its surveillance of the member states' budgetary positions in accordance with the Treaty and the Pact, especially France and Germany's compliance with the Council's conclusions. They also pledged to develop a new framework for economic governance that would strengthen and balance the terms of the Stability and Growth Pact and the use of broad economic policy guidelines. Given DG ECFIN's likely role in helping to draft these reforms, the new framework is likely to stress the role of economic forecasting and cyclical budgetary

---

[51] Council of Economic and Financial Affairs (2003). "2546th Council Meeting," C/03/320, Brussels. November 25, p. xxi.

[52] European Commission (2004). "Commission Sets Out Strategy for Economic Policy Coordination and Surveillance," IP/04/35, Brussels. January 13.

adjustments in any revision of the surveillance procedure. Meanwhile, the initiative would place more emphasis on national debt levels and sustainability, stricter surveillance of member state budgetary policies during periods of economic well-being, and do more to recognize member state differences while providing for more rigorous enforcement procedures. Finally, despite expectations that the Stability and Growth Pact would be immediately scrapped, both Ireland, the incoming member state president of the EU, and the ECOFIN Council declared that revisions in the Pact would not occur until 2005.[53]

5.6   Additional Significant Eurostat Rulings: Pension Funds and Public–Private Partnerships (2003 and 2004)

As the Commission and DG ECFIN pressed the surveillance procedure against France and Germany, Eurostat adopted two significant rulings that carry with them the potential to reduce dramatically, perhaps ending, the member states' excessive deficit condition. The first ruling permits certain public enterprise one-time, lump-sum payments to member states be counted as new revenues; the second allows governments under certain circumstances to exclude debt from the net lending/net borrowing calculation.

5.6.1   Unfunded Pension Obligations: France Telecom Revisited (2003)

In October, Eurostat ruled on whether in the transfer of unfunded public enterprise pension obligations to a government, the payments it receives in the transaction may be counted as revenue for the calculation of its deficit.[54] These payments commonly exist when a government decides to absorb the pension liabilities of its enterprises, thereby relieving them of this burden, and in return receives a negotiated lump-sum payment. The governments gain these revenue transfers, but they also incur new pension liabilities and must make the appropriate long-term payments to the pension's beneficiaries. An unfunded program is one where the operator of the plan is not required to

---

[53] Euobserver (2003b). "Ireland Set to Leave Euro Rules Alone." Euobserver.com. December 19; George Parker and Haig Simonian (2004). "EU Nations Call for Delay to Fiscal Reforms," *Financial Times*. February 2, p. 2; George Parker (2004). "EU Ministers Will Not Rewrite Pact Until 2005," *Financial Times*. April 3–4, p. 2.

[54] Eurostat news release (2003d). "Payments to Governments by Public Corporations in the Context of the Transfer to Government of Their Unfunded Pensions Obligations," N. 120/2003, October 21.

build pension reserves and the pension participants hold no legal claims for their benefits. In 2003, a number of governments engaged in such transfers. Most notably, the French government initiated such a transfer of pension obligations for revenue transfers for two of its major enterprises prior to their proposed privatization, *Electricité de France* (EdF) and *Gaz de France* (GdF). The payments from these public enterprises to the government may top those of France Telecom, possibly in the range of 7.2 billion euros, with the government absorbing these enterprises' massive unfunded pension obligations. Such an amount could reduce France's budgetary imbalance by some 0.5 percent of GDP, nearly eliminating its excessive deficit. As *The Times* noted, "The French government is forecasting a budget deficit of 3.6 percent of GDP for next year, and a lump sum from EdF would bring this down towards the 3 percent ceiling." This payment could range between 8 and 10 billion euros, an amount sufficient to help reduce France's deficit to 2.9 percent of GDP from the estimated 3.6 percent.[55] In July 2003, Portugal's government received 1.2 billion euros during the transfer of the CTT telecoms-postal pension fund obligations to its CGA state pension fund. The initial pension plan was unfunded, relying upon a company financial reserve to pay beneficiaries. The effect of such a transfer would cut Portugal's deficit by nearly one percent of GDP, saving it from violating the excessive deficit procedure. Belgium's government undertook a similar transfer from Belgacom, where the government absorbed the telecom's pension obligations during its privatization. The Germans may benefit from such transfers from the reform of Deutsche Post and its railway system.[56]

Technically, Eurostat's ruling essentially reaffirmed the controversial France Telecom decision of 1996, which also addressed the effect of a government's absorption of public enterprise pension schemes. As in France Telecom, the CMFB proved to be significantly divided. Fourteen NSIs and national central banks (NCBs) voted in favor of counting these transactions as nonfinancial transactions, with eleven votes supporting an interpretation where these cash transfer payments between a government and its public enterprises would be classified as financial transactions, and thus excluded from the deficit calculation. Eurostat ruled with the majority, declaring these payments to be nonfinancial capital transfers, having a one-time positive effect on the deficit. Eurostat, however, warned in its ruling that these payments may fail to reflect properly the huge future pension burdens assumed by the member states.

[55] Lea Pearson (2003). "Eurostat Ruling May Resolve French Row," *The Times*, October 23, p. 23.

[56] "Portugal Says Eurostat Backs Deficit-Cutting Move," *Reuters Limited*. October 21, 2003; "Eurostat Rules on Booking Pension Fund Transfers," *Reuters Limited*. October 21, 2003; "Eurostat Pension Fund Rule Confirms Belgium's View," *Reuters Limited*. October 22, 2003.

5.6.2 Public–Private Partnerships (2004)

In February, Eurostat provided an important ruling on the proper classification of infrastructure financing. In traditional financing, the state assumes the full cost of capital in its balance sheet, thus adding to its public debt. In December 2003, the European Council adopted the European Growth Initiative, which promotes the use of public–private partnerships to increase and improve the amount of public infrastructure in the EU. In such partnerships many of these infrastructure costs, such as those due to construction delays, are assumed by the private partner. Encouraged by the initiative, a number of EU governments, particularly Ireland, Portugal, and Spain, planned major infrastructure improvements using the partnership framework. The question facing Eurostat was how to classify these costs and subsequent debt; whether to continue assigning them to the government or to the private enterprise.

Eurostat, supported by a 26 to 1 vote of the CMFB, decided that according to national accounts the central issue in making that classification is determining which party bears the risk for the cost of developing the assets in the partnership. Three categories of risk exist: construction risk, which includes construction delays, late delivery, and technical deficiencies; availability risk, where a partner fails to meet standards or performs inadequately; and demand risk, which applies to the variability of demand due to market trends, competition, or technological developments. Risk analysis of contracts will determine which party absorbs the risk in these circumstances. If, for instance, a government continues to make payments to a private partner even if the partner fails to meet construction deadlines, then the risk is assigned to the public partner. Eurostat ruled that in the final classification, the debt would be assigned to the private partner if it bears the construction risk and at least one of the other two forms of risk. So, if two of the three forms of risk are underwritten by the private partner, then the debt incurred by the government is not counted in its net lending/net borrowing calculation. Eurostat's ruling, therefore, is likely to stimulate private funding for public construction projects throughout the EU, while providing significantly greater opportunities for governments to remain in compliance with the excessive deficit requirement and the Stability and Growth Pact.[57]

---

[57] Eurostat news release (2003e). "Treatment of Public–Private Partnerships," N. 18/2004, February 11. Peter Chapman (2003). "Infrastructure Finance Guidelines Promised," *European Voice*. October 23–9, p. 38; John Murray Brown, Nicholas Timmins, and Peter Wise (2004). "Brussels Acts to Exclude Private Finance for Public Works from Stability Pact Rules," *Financial Times*. February 7, p. 2.

5.7   Conclusion

The surveillance process is marked by rising tension between the Commission—especially DG ECFIN—the ECOFIN Council, and the member states. The Commission's disappointment began with the ECOFIN Council's refusal to accept its recommendation to issue early warnings to Germany and Portugal. If the Commission failed to make these recommendations, DG ECFIN concluded: "The whole process of multilateral surveillance and economy policy coordination would have been called into question. Unless the Commission took action in such clear-cut cases . . . it is difficult to see when an early warning could ever be issued."[58]

The credibility in the rules-based framework was not aided by the Council's failure to issue an early warning in February 2002, not the subsequent ratcheting up of projections for the deficit level throughout 2002. This called into question the reliability of budgetary statistics and forecasts underlying the EU surveillance process, and indicated a lack of capacity and willingness on the part of the Member States to deal with growing budgetary imbalances.[59]

For DG ECFIN, the Council's failure to issue the early warnings signaled its reluctance to pressure the member states firmly enough to ensure budgetary compliance. The almost predictable result came with the Council's decision in November 2003 to hold the excessive deficit procedure in abeyance in the cases of France and Germany.

Next, DG ECFIN questioned the veracity of the member states, declaring that many failed to run appropriate budgetary policies during both good and bad economic times, thus avoiding the implications of cyclical effects on their budget deficits. Real discrepancies existed between the governments' publicly declared fiscal commitments and their actual policies. These governments, moreover, overestimated revenues and GDP growth, while underestimating expenditures in their budget plans. In particular, they pushed estimated program costs into the future, thereby understating their true fiscal effects and economic burden. DG ECFIN laid part of the blame for the member states' unsustainable policies on the technical difference between the nominal 3.0 percent of GDP deficit reference value enshrined in the excessive deficit procedure and the balanced budget called for in the Pact, as compared to the

---

[58] European Commission: Director-General for Economic and Financial Affairs (2002). *European Economy: Public Finances in EMU 2002, No. 3/2002.* Brussels: European Communities, p. 50.

[59] European Commission: Directorate-General for Economic and Financial Affairs (2003). *Public Finances in EMU, 2003.* Brussels, p. 47.

Pact's implication that the member states' stability programs should be evaluated in terms of their cyclically adjusted budget balances. The cyclical adjustment better reflected the effects of the economy on fiscal policy and planning. The broader use of cyclically adjusted budget balances would elevate the Commission's ability to evaluate the direction of the member states' fiscal policies and plans, while enhancing DG ECFIN's role in the surveillance process.

Then DG ECFIN also publicly rebuked its fellow Commission agency, Eurostat. The member states, specifically Portugal, were blamed for submitting deficient biannual reports to the Commission. These reports subsequently required revisions, which delayed the Commission's evaluation of the member states' budgetary positions. Nevertheless, according to DG ECFIN, all this was made possible by Eurostat's failure to monitor the member states' national accounts more effectively and promptly. "The decision making processes of Eurostat on the classification of certain budgetary operations could be speeded up."[60] These assessments of Eurostat's performance perhaps reflect the fact that its surveillance unit continues to be understaffed and lacks Slavic speaking personnel to accommodate fully the EU's current and expected expansion.

Yet, questions were also raised by the press and by Germany about DG ECFIN's own lack of political impartiality and technical objectivity. The *Financial Times* observed that DG ECFIN's Director General, Klaus Regling, served as a leading member of Germany's conservative opposition to Chancellor Schroeder and his tax cuts. Regling acted as a "driving force" behind the push to increase the level of Germany's deficit 0.3 percent requirement beyond what the Commission previously recommended, which would force Schroeder to delay or cancel the tax cuts, his "only remotely popular policy."[61] In addition, German authorities rejected DG ECFIN's calculation of what constituted the structural element of its cyclical deficit calculation. An imprecise calculation could unnecessarily increase the level of deficit reduction mandated by the Commission. "The whole notion of structural deficit is very shaky," a German economist noted, "A lot of questionable assumptions go into these calculations."[62] Indeed, even DG ECFIN acknowledged in 2002 that employing its econometrics techniques in the early years of Stage III "proved difficult in the absence of an agreed method to calculate cyclically-adjusted budget balances." Moreover, DG ECFIN's cyclically adjusted budget

---

[60] Ibid., p. 52.

[61] Wolfgang Munchau (2003). "A Treaty to Undermine the Eurozone," *Financial Times*. December 1, p. 15.

[62] Bertrand Benoit (2003). "Surprise at Eichel's 'Emotional Response,' " *Financial Times*. November 26, p. 4.

deficit levels differed significantly, though less negatively, from those of the OECD and IMF, thus suggesting the difficulty of employing such models when measuring tenths of a percent of GDP.[63]

Regarding DG ECFIN's claim that Eurostat neglected to classify Portugal's national accounts data in a timely fashion, it is worth recalling that DG ECFIN staff participate in all mission visits to Portugal, attend CMFB meetings, and are aware of the variation in the quality of the member states' budgetary statistics. Moreover, DG ECFIN, not Eurostat, evaluates the member states' broad economic policy guidelines for the Commission and the ECOFIN Council. It operates member state "desks," whose staffs' sole function is to monitor the economic conditions within individual members states, and who maintain their own set of professional and personal relationships with member state officials. DG ECFIN also designs and runs the Commission's macroeconomic and cyclical econometrics models. Despite its technical expertise and access to data, DG ECFIN estimated Portugal's 2001 deficit at 2.2 percent of GDP while the actual total reached 4.1 percent.[64] DG ECFIN's models, therefore, misforecast Portugal's deficit by nearly 100 percent. Eurostat's refusal to certify its biannual report forced Portugal to revise its data, not DG ECFIN's forecasting and more active role in the surveillance process.

For its part, Eurostat remains a central player in the Stage III surveillance process. Eurostat's rulings triggered the excessive deficit procedure against Portugal and France, and it issued a number of national accounts decisions that may significantly improve the budgetary positions of a number of member states. Its decisions on the sale of mobile phone licenses and the infusion of unfunded pension program payments add substantially to member state revenues, while its ruling on public–private partnerships potentially reduces member state debt. If the France Telecom decision is any guide, the effect of Eurostat's pension ruling may enable a member state to reduce its deficit by as much or more than half a percent of GDP.

[63] European Commission: Directorate-General for Economic and Financial Affairs (2003). *Public Finances in EMU*, 2003. Brussels, p. 51. On the variation in models, see European Commission: Director-General for Economic and Financial Affairs (2002). *European Economy: Public Finances in EMU 2002, No. 3/2002*. Brussels: European Communities, p. 57.

[64] European Commission: Directorate-General for Economic and Financial Affairs (2003). *Public Finances in EMU*, 2003. Brussels, p. 65.

6

Credibility, Institutionalization, and Europeanization

Through its management of the Maastricht Treaty's surveillance procedure, Eurostat played a critical, though largely unnoticed, role in the creation of the Economic and Monetary Union (EMU), while its monitoring duties continue to promote the institutionalization and integration of Europe. Eurostat's statistical case law serves as the authoritative measure for calculating and harmonizing the budgetary consequences of the member states' fiscal policies. Because the Treaty requires each state to produce these statistical data, this harmonizing effect applies to all European Union (EU) member states and candidate countries, regardless of their EMU status. When one of these states publicly announces its deficit and debt, and submits these data to Eurostat, it does so according to the standards of the European System of Integrated Economic Accounts (ESA). During the convergence process, Eurostat and its technical decisions served as the EU's gatekeeper against member states with excessive deficits from gaining EMU membership. Under the Stability and Growth Pact, the member states must submit stability programs to Directorate General II for Economic and Financial Affairs (DG ECFIN) that conform to ESA categories and classifications. Furthermore, Eurostat must certify that a member state's deficit exceeds the 3.0 percent of gross domestic product (GDP) level before the Council of Economic and Finance Ministers (ECOFIN) may impose full sanctions. The consequences of Eurostat's rulings, therefore, extend beyond its surveillance function; they serve as a sanction in their own right, regularly affecting of the politics of the EMU and the budgetary practices and policies of the member states.[1] Yet, before further examining the surveillance procedure's

---

[1] Consider the cases of how Eurostat's budgetary statistics influence Austria, Spain, and Greece. In June 1999, Austria adopted its own version of the Stability and Growth Pact, complete with sanctions that would apply to each level of government. The law requires internal bargaining among the federal, state, and local government levels over their shares of the fiscal financial burden, deficit quotas,

influence on European integration, the integrity of Eurostat's role in the process deserves additional attention. For despite its accomplishments, scandal at Eurostat tarnishes its reputation and raises questions about its credibility, and, thus, the credibility of the surveillance procedure.

6.1   Scandal at Eurostat: Institutional Autonomy and the Credibility of Eurostat's Statistics for the Excessive Deficit Procedure

On May 16, 2003, Eurostat's employees gathered together in a glorious celebration of their agency's fiftieth anniversary. Following a full day of speeches, receptions, and festivities, Grand Duke Henri of Luxembourg served as the guest of honor at a splendid dinner attended by Commissioner for Economic and Monetary Affairs Pedro Solbes, and Jean-Claude Juncker, the prime minister of Luxembourg. To add to the stature of the event, the agency released a handsome, 200-plus page history, *Memoirs of Eurostat: Fifty Years Serving Europe*, dating its founding to the legendary Jean Monnet.[2] Yves Franchet, who simultaneously celebrated his sixteenth year as Eurostat's director general, acted as the grand master of ceremonies. Just five days later, however, Franchet resigned his position, following allegations that under his direction, Eurostat awarded fraudulent contracts to statistical consulting companies beginning approximately in 2000, after the Stage II convergence process.[3]

and burden of sanctions. The activation of these sanctions depends upon Eurostat's certification of Austria's general government deficit. Regarding Spain, on March 13, 2000, Eurostat released new calculations of the member states' deficit based on the shift from ESA 79 to ESA 95. In these figures, Spain's deficit for 1997 climbs to 3.2 percent of GDP, an amount that would have excluded it from EMU membership. The political sensitivity of this information was such that Yves Franchet decided to delay its public release until after Spain's spring elections. See Eurostat news release (2000*a*). "Euro-Zone Government Deficit at −1.2% and Debt at 72.2% of GDP in 1999," N. 34/2000, March 13. Regarding Greece, in August 2003, Eurostat's mission visit and subsequent rulings turned that country's much heralded budget surpluses of 2001 and 2002 into deficits, forcing the 2003 deficit to run larger than expected, which greatly embarrassed the government, exposing it to charges that it deceived the public about the country's finances. Also see footnote 11 for more on Greece's deficit.

[2] Tobias Buck (2003*a*). "Comment and Analysis: 'To Safeguard the Interests of the Institution'—but was Action Taken Quickly Enough?" *Financial Times*. June 17, FT.com web site; Alberto De Michelis and Alain Chantraine (2003). *Memoirs of Eurostat: Fifty Years Serving Europe*. Luxembourg: Office for Official Publications of the European Communities.

[3] Rumors of financial irregularities at Eurostat circulated throughout the EU for at more than a year preceding the celebration. Dorte Schmidt-Brown, a Danish economist employed at Eurostat, reported to Commission officials that the agency improperly awarded a 250,000-euro contract to Eurogramme, a Luxembourg-based statistical consulting firm. After complaining to her superiors, the whistleblower declared that Commission Vice-President Neil Kinnock failed to protect her, leaving her subject to "moral harassment," causing her to leave the organization on an invalidity pension. By mid-March of 2003, Luxembourg police began investigating these allegations, followed by similar proceedings initiated by French officials. In June, the EC acknowledged that allegations of

The Eurostat scandal ranks as one of the worst in Commission history, to be compared with the financial mismanagement and corruption that forced the mass resignation of President Jacques Santer's Commission in 1999. The matter at hand, however, is assessing whether this incident fatally undermines the credibility of the agency's regular activities, including its conduct during the

fraudulent behavior at Eurostat proved to be "far more significant than we had known," and that there existed "a vast enterprise of looting of EU funds." A month later, based on preliminary analysis from the Commission's Anti-Fraud Office (OLAF), Kinnock announced that Eurostat engaged in the "relatively extensive practice" of employing secret bank accounts that held millions of euros that vanished into the hands of statistical contractors. In September, Commission President Romano Prodi presented to the Conference of Presidents of the European Parliament the results of three reports investigating Eurostat. Prodi informed the Conference that due to the Commission's growing administrative burdens, many of the directorates general increasingly turned to the outsourcing of their administrative functions to private firms in order to supplement their staff. Weak or inadequate management controls, however, often accompanied these contractual relationships. In Eurostat's case, this contracting outside the organization eventually led to the scandal. Ironically, Yves Franchet's efforts to strengthen Eurostat's internal management practices and auditing identified the mismanagement that resulted in his suspension. ["Report of the Eurostat Task Forces (TRES), Summary and Conclusions," European Commission, Brussels. September 24, 2003. This report states:

The period from 1999 to 2003 is marked by progressive improvements in the management environment in Eurostat. These improvements are closely linked to implementation of Commission reform, but also predate it. Particular note should be taken of the creation by the Director General of Eurostat of an audit function in which was gradually reinforced in terms of human resources over time in line with the reform. . . . It is this audit function which has facilitated the identification of problems in financial management and programme implementation in Eurostat.

See points 1.3 and 1.4.] OLAF, nevertheless, found significant conflicts of interest occurring between Franchet and the awarding of Eurostat's contracts. Franchet, for example, helped to establish Eurocost, one of the statistical consulting firms receiving a Eurostat contract. Because of this intimate connection, OLAF concluded that "the Director-General of Eurostat could not have been unaware of the many irregularities detected that harmed the European Commission in its relations with Eurocost." ["Summary of the Eurostat Cases Now Closed," European Anti-Fraud Office (OLAF), European Commission, Brussels. September 24, 2003, p. 2.] The Internal Audit Service added, "Even if, as claimed by the Eurostat's former senior management, the irregular funding obtained through the above practices was solely intended to be used to make up for the chronic lack of resources, the lack of control with which those funds were managed creates an unacceptably high exposure to the risk of fraud and irregularities." ["Eurostat Briefing Note: Based on Second Interim Progress Report by the Internal Audit Service," European Commission, Brussels. September 24, 2003, p. 6.] Although the Audit Service conceded that "we cannot give an opinion on the possibility of fraud involving personal enrichment," President Prodi blamed Yves Franchet for Eurostat's problems: "The first person [responsible] was clearly none other than Eurostat's Director-General himself." [Ibid., p. 6; Romano Prodi (2003). "'The Eurostat Case,' Statement of the President of the European Commission," Conference of Presidents of the European Parliament, Strasbourg, September 25.] Martin Banks (2003). "Whistleblower Claims Trigger Eurostat Fraud Investigation," *European Voice*. June 20–6, p. 1; Stephen Grey (2003). "Kinnock Under Fire for Rebuffing Second Fraud Whistleblower," *Sunday Times*. March 16, FT.com web site; Tobias Buck (2003*b*). "Eurostat Faces Paris Corruption Probe," *Financial Times*. May 16, p. 1; Tobias Buck and George Parker (2003*a*). "Eurostat Scandal Draws in Prodi and Kinnock," *Financial Times*. June 17, p. 1; Tobias Buck and George Parker (2003*b*). "Brussels Attacked Over Alleged Fraud," *Financial Times*. June 18, p. 1; George Parker (2003*a*). "Passing the Buck on Eurostat," *Financial Times*. June 18, FT.com web site; Stephen Castle (2003). "New Fraud Inquiry Into Missing EU Money," *Independent*. June 18, FT.com web site; George Parker, Tobias Buck, and John Prideaux

surveillance process. One note of skepticism, for example, comes from the European Parliament, which considered, but rejected in May 2004, an act to censure the Commission over this matter: "Whatever the outcome, economists and policymakers will want to know which contracts were carried out by the companies under investigation," declared Parliament member Chris Heaton-Harris. "Politicians will demand assurances that all Eurostat statistics are reliable."[4] By implication, Heaton-Harris challenges the integrity of the surveillance procedure itself and virtually every decision made by the Commission in its treaty guardian role since the mid 1990s. This is so, as, clearly, Eurostat's national accounts decision-making and the data it certifies serve as the cornerstone of the entire surveillance process. Thus, Heaton-Harris' demand that the EU be assured these data are reliable, deserves attention. Is Eurostat's national accounts rulings, and thus its data, for the surveillance procedure credible?

To help answer that question, it is useful to reassess Eurostat's relationship with other EU institutions in terms of principal-agency theory. For Eurostat to conduct its rulings on a professional, technical, and impartial basis, it must be insulated from the intervention and demands of its EU principals. Yet, due to the specter of Eurostat's financial mismanagement, this concern for autonomy must certainly be countered by the principals' right to exercise appropriate control and oversight over their agent to guarantee its integrity. In the words of European Parliament member Heaton-Harris, the principals must be assured of Eurostat's statistical reliability. Thus, to ensure the trustworthiness of the surveillance procedure, a balance must exist between the principals' necessary right of oversight and the agent's independence of action while conducting its task as a treaty guardian.

6.1.1   Eurostat's Sources of Autonomy

A review of the major sources of Eurostat autonomy helps to address whether the agency has the capacity to engage in credible decision-making. Eurostat's

---

(2003). "Prodi Orders Disciplinary Action for Directors," *Financial Times*. July 10, p. 3; Tobias Buck, George Parker, and John Prideaux (2003). "Brussels Finally Moves to Quell Critics Over Financial Scandals at Eurostat," *Financial Times*. July 10, p. 3; Tobias Buck and George Parker (2003c). "Brussels Widens Fraud Probe," *Financial Times*. July 17, p. 1; Tobias Buck (2003c). "Four Companies Suspected in Eurostat Affair Lose Contracts," *Financial Times*, July 24, p. 4; George Parker and Raphael Minder (2003). "Brussels Seeks to Limit Fallout Amid Eurostat Affair," *Financial Times*. September 24, p. 5; Giles Merritt (2003). "Scandal May Topple Prodi's Team," *International Herald Tribune*. August 7, p. 6; Chris Heaton-Harris (2003). "Brussels Must Stop Burying Bad News," *Financial Times*. September 22, FT.com web site.

[4] "Commission Faces Vote of Censure from MEPs," Euobserver.com, April 20, 2004; On May 4, 2004, the European Parliament voted 88 in favor, 515 opposed, with 63 abstaining on a motion of censuring the Commission. The motion is contained in, The European Parliament (2004). *Motion of Censure*, B5-0189/2004, Brussels. April 16.

agency's autonomy stems from a variety of sources consistent with principal-agency theory, including rule-based delegation, the arrangement of organizational structures, and independence won through bureaucratic politics.

Eurostat's independence begins with the Maastricht Treaty and its supporting legislation, which delegates to the European Commission (EC) the responsibility for managing the surveillance procedure, for gathering member state economic and fiscal data, and for analyzing it according to the standards of the ESA. Additional secondary legislation, such as Commission Decision 97/28EC and Council Regulation 322/97, complement Treaty Article 285 and provide further legal basis for Eurostat's independence, declaring these statistical data should be reliable, objective, and impartial.

Eurostat's independence also stems from its successful foray into bureaucratic politics. Yves Franchet's aggressive, entrepreneurial leadership, in direct competition with DG ECFIN, enabled Eurostat to become the lead agency in the surveillance procedure for the Stage II convergence process. Franchet forcefully argued that his agency deserved this responsibility by invoking Eurostat's technical mastery of the ESA. This argument eventually won the support of Commissioner for Economic and Monetary Affairs Yves-Thibault de Silguy. Silguy's endorsement of Eurostat constituted the Commission's formal delegation of authority to the agency in its role as the final interpreter for the ESA over DG ECFIN, and offered Franchet another critical source of organizational autonomy.

The technical and procedural aspects of the surveillance process also promoted Eurostat's decision-making independence. Initially, the ESA itself proved to be confusing, generating as it did so many "gray areas" between ESA 79 and the later version ESA 95. The rapid evolution of forms of economic and financial transactions now require more current interpretations of ESA 95. Thus, Eurostat's technical capacity produces its own form of autonomy, as certainly no other institution within the EU possesses the capacity to challenge its expertise in national accounts. Similarly, Eurostat's expertise extends to its management of the surveillance process and the monitoring techniques it employs, including the interpretation of the member states' biannual reports, Eurostat's right to reject or certify these data as being acceptable and properly submitted, and Eurostat's management of the mission visits to the various member states.

Eurostat benefits greatly from its formal and informal sources of control over the European Statistical System (ESS). Formally, Eurostat either directly manages or staffs every decision-making and policy-setting committee in the ESS. None of these committees, including the Committee for Monetary, Financial, and Balance of Payments Statistics (CMFB), possess comitological status, and thus they lack the formal authority to appeal a Eurostat ruling to a higher power.[5] Even after France Telecom, Eurostat exercises significant influence with the CMFB by way of setting agendas, framing questions, and managing the consultative process among the membership. Furthermore, in a formal sense, CMFB acts in an advisory capacity, and its opinions serve only as recommendations to Eurostat, not directives. The collective decision-making process that produces CMFB opinions also buttress Eurostat's independence. Almost always passed by large majority votes, these recommendations represent the agreement of the member states, who are represented on the committee by their technical experts of the various national statistical institutes (NSIs) and national central banks (NCBs). The transparent nature of these decisions, based on extensive consultation with the member states through surveys and the use of working parties and task forces, adds substantially to their credibility and legitimacy, thereby making them very difficult to challenge.

In addition to these formal sources of independence, Eurostat enjoys the informal rewards of being the center of gravity of the epistemic community of EU statisticians. These statisticians are united by profession, training, technical values, and a sense of personal and professional collegiality. Therefore, rather than creating a surveillance regime built on entirely new relationships and institutions, Eurostat began its task with established associations, organization goals, lines of communication, common frames of reference, and a shared language of statistics and national accounts. These connections, simply put, make Eurostat's monitoring responsibilities significantly easier. Statisticians, furthermore, derive their status, in part, by how they are perceived by their international colleagues. Although the NSI and NCB members of the CMFB certainly represent and advance their home countries' interests in these meetings, they must do so in a manner that is consistent with the logic of the ESA. Arguments that are far-fetched and defy believability act to undermine a member state's position and the long-term status of that member state's representatives. Thus, Eurostat benefits by the connectedness of this epistemic community both in the administration of the surveillance process and in the sense that individual member states, or even a few member states agreeing on a particular interpretation of ESA, must gain the approval of this collective community to gain a favorable ruling.

Finally, Eurostat's autonomy is linked to international press coverage of its national accounts rulings. The press provides Eurostat with an important and reasonably rapid form of information about the member states' economic and

---

[5] Consider how important comitology is for standard interpretations of how the EU as principal controls the Commission. See, for example, Mark A. Pollack (2003). *The Engines of European Integration*, ch. 2. New York: Oxford University Press.

financial transactions. Press coverage of Eurostat, however, also offers it a form of independence, as rumors of external pressure on Eurostat to produce favorable rulings would certainly receive public notice that could prove quite harmful to Eurostat's principals.

6.1.2   The EU's Sources of Control and Oversight

To counter Eurostat's autonomy, EU officials and the member states rely upon a number of familiar institutional devices, including designing rules that govern the nature of their delegation of tasks, participating in the national accounts decision-making process, monitoring Eurostat's behavior both directly and indirectly through various "fire alarm" warnings, and imposing negative sanctions and distributing rewards to the agency.

The first source of the EU principals' controls over Eurostat is the power to design and enact laws and rules that define the nature of the surveillance procedure and the agency's role in that procedure. Beginning with the Maastricht Treaty, these rules define what constitutes member states' deficits and debt, require the calculation of these figures according to ESA 79, indicate the use of biannual self-reports, specify the requirement that calendar rather than fiscal years be employed, and delegate to the Commission the responsibility for managing the surveillance procedure. Through secondary legislation, these rules could be extended to constrain Eurostat's rule-making authority, and even to eliminate it altogether from the procedure.

Next, the member states' active participation in national accounts decisions through their representatives on the CMFB significantly enhances their ability to oversee Eurostat's activities. The CMFB members select the committee's president, the membership is formally consulted as part of the rule-making process, they serve on working parties and task forces that help in the first stages of developing these rules, and they vote on CMFB's recommendations to Eurostat. Though Eurostat makes the final ruling on national accounts and interpreting ESA, certainly following France Telecom, these rulings are completely consistent with the majority votes of the member states.

Principal EU institutions such as the ECOFIN Council and the member states possess multiple ways of monitoring Eurostat's behavior. In addition to the member states, various EU institutions are also represented at CMFB, including DG ECFIN and the European Central Bank (ECB), as well as statistical representatives from the EU candidate countries and from such international organizations as the International Monetary Fund (IMF), Organization for Economic Cooperation and Development (OECD), and United Nations. A number of these institutions are also represented at the various working group and task force meetings. These additional representatives generally possess the technical skills required to assess the validity of Eurostat's national accounts rulings. If the logic of such rulings violated ESA standards, or if the decision-making at these meetings ran counter to appropriate procedure, then these representatives, serving as part of a of information feedback loop, certainly could alert their principal organizations. Information concerning dubious rulings or questionable member state data may also be revealed though monitoring by the press, and by way of leaked sources, such as whistleblowers, within any of the many institutions involved in the surveillance procedure. Finally, it is important to recall that Eurostat is the most heavily seconded agency within the Commission. Member state statisticians constantly rotate in and out of Eurostat. This is also true for unit B-4, which is responsible for the surveillance procedure and included seconded personnel throughout the Stage II convergence process and continues to do so into Stage III. These personnel provide the member states with a powerful safeguard against dubious national accounts rulings.

Another form of organizational control, EU officials may impose negative sanctions and offer rewards to Eurostat to encourage desired behavior. Positive and negative sanctions take many forms. On the one hand, Commission President Romano Prodi, for instance, promises that "Eurostat must be thoroughly overhauled and refocused on its tasks," in response to the hidden bank account scandal.[6] The nature of this "overhaul" is not yet clear, but reorganization and changing responsibilities among administrative staff are likely. On the other hand, more specifically regarding Eurostat's surveillance task, EU principals regularly praise their agent's performance. In just one example, the ECOFIN Council issued the following statement in February 2000:

The Council welcomes the extensive work done during recent years by Eurostat in co-operation with national authorities—according to a procedure involving the Committee on Monetary, Financial and Balance of Payments Statistics (CMFB) and other advisory groups—to resolve methodological issues for the comparability of public finance data used in the context of the excessive deficit procedure. The Council urges Eurostat to pursue such work, together with national authorities, to deal with any technical difficulties which may be raised by the amendment of regulation 3605/93 and the switchover to ESA 95.[7]

This declaration certainly constitutes a reward for service, and indicates the Council's satisfaction with Eurostat's performance in its monitoring duties and with the credibility of its decision-making process.

---

[6] Romano Prodi (2003). "'The Eurostat Case,' Statement of the President of the European Commission," Conference of Presidents of the European Parliament, Strasbourg, September 25.
[7] Council of the European Union (2000). "Statement for the Council Minutes," Interinstitutional File: 99/0196 (CNS), Brussels, February 17.

In summary, what emerges from these various rules, procedures, and practices is a principal-agency relationship that simultaneously promotes institutional autonomy and control, while protecting the interests of both the principal and agent. The EU's interest is that Eurostat create a reliable compliance information system, where the member states' fiscal behavior is monitored, budgetary data are collected and harmonized according to objective measures, and a transparent, technically based decision-making process resolves disputes over statistical issues. Eurostat's interest is that it be allowed to carry out these tasks according to the shared standards and practices of its epistemic community, such that its rulings are viewed as authoritative and credible. Given the immense political stakes and pressures involved, particularly during Maastricht's Stage II convergence phase, as it has evolved over time, this relationship of control and autonomy is working well for both principal and agent. Moreover, this combination promotes European integration through institutionalization and Europeanization.

6.2   Promoting Institutionalization and Europeanization

The Maastricht Treaty promotes institutionalization and Europeanization on a grand scale through the creation of economic and monetary union, but it also furthers these processes, albeit in a far more subtle fashion, through the Treaty's surveillance procedure. The standardizing effects of ESA and the national accounts decision-making process managed by Eurostat encourages institutionalization through the expansion of supranational authority within the EU, and Europeanization by way of the harmonizing influence of EU rules and practices on the member states. Formal rules serve as the cornerstone of these two process through their embedding, enmeshing, integrating effects on the member states.

6.2.1   Institutionalization

Eurostat contributes significantly to the EU's institutionalization through the surveillance procedure. It does so through its supranational rule-making authority, which in this context the rest of the Commission, and specifically DG ECFIN, does not possess. Under the Stability and Growth Pact, the Commission may make recommendations to the ECOFIN Council regarding the status of member state deficits and suggest corrective action, but it is Eurostat that creates independently generated supranational rules that interpret ESA. According to Stone Sweet and Sandholtz, as part of the process of institutionalization, supranational rules resolve "differing technical standards" and "divergent" regulations, while providing dispute resolution mechanisms.[8] Eurostat's national accounts case law rulings and the procedures by which they are created fulfill each of these characteristics. Eurostat's supranational rules resolve the differing technical standards that exist in the field of national accounts, first, between ESA 79 and ESA 95, and, second, between ESA and the accounting practices employed by the member states. Eurostat's case law decisions constitute administrative regulations that both clarify the budgetary status of the member states and effectively sanction them for budgetary action that falls outside the Maastricht Treaty's grand bargain. Eurostat, furthermore, manages a dispute resolution mechanism though the CMFB and its supporting working parties and task forces that serves and satisfies the interests of the EU and the member states. The credibility of this process is such that the member states accept it as the authoritative body for evaluating their budgetary status, both for purposes of the Stage II convergence process and the Stability and Growth Pact, without appealing its decisions either to the ECOFIN Council or to higher authorities within the Commission.

The ECOFIN Council's February 2000 statement praising Eurostat actually reflects a broader commitment by the EU for Eurostat in the future coordination and institutionalization of member state fiscal policies. In preparation for Maastricht's Stage III with its emphasis on stability rather than convergence, the ECOFIN Council approved a number of action plans for EMU's statistical requirements, including the production of "short-term" statistics.[9] Where the Treaty ordered the member states to present only broad budgetary data on a biannual basis, these EU harmonized, short-term public finance statistics are produced quarterly, and in far greater detail. Based on ESA 95, the requested information includes data on taxes, social contributions, and social benefits. The ECOFIN Council and the Commission may employ these data to gauge the member states' fiscal behavior, in part to fulfill the goals of the Lisbon Summit of 2000. At this summit, the European Council adopted guidelines

[8] Alec Stone Sweet and Wayne Sandholtz (1998). "Integration, Supranational Governance, and the Institutionalization of the European Polity," in Wayne Sandholtz and Alec Stone Sweet (eds.), *European Integration and Supranational Governance*. New York: Oxford University Press, p. 11.

[9] On relevant legislation, see Commission Regulation (EC) N. 264/2000 of February 3, 2000 on the implementation of Council Regulation (EC) N. 2223/96, with regard to short-term public finance statistics. Creating these data imposes tremendous workload pressures on the member state NSIs, regional, and local governments where, for example, the Maastricht Treaty specifies that a member state's debt calculation is based on the nominal or face value of government financial instruments, the short-term calculation is determined on more difficult to assess market values. Such a calculation, which must be determined for all forms of government securities, may prove to be politically sensitive for the member states. It may raise the size of a member state's public debt, even though these short-term figures are not considered for purposes of the Stability and Growth Pact.

for questioning not only whether a member state's deficits and debt reflect a "sound financial position," but also if the "quality" of a government's fiscal policy is being met, in terms, for example, of whether there is sufficient spending on such growth oriented programs as human and physical capital and research and development.[10] Though the ambitions of the Lisbon summit appear to be diverted as a number of member states struggle with their deficits and weak economies, they do point to the possibility of greater fiscal and programmatic integration within the EU, which Eurostat helps to make possible through its harmonization of member state budgetary data.

6.2.2 Europeanization

The surveillance procedure and Eurostat's rule-making also promote Europeanization. The process of Europeanization is reflected in part by member state compliance with EU rules, member state incorporation of EU rules, and the adaptation of member state organizational practices and procedures to fulfill EU tasks. First, with a few notable exceptions, the member states routinely comply with the technical aspects of the surveillance procedure itself, such as the requirement that member states submit timely and accurate biannual budgetary data consistent with ESA. Adapatational pressures vary among the member states, of course, as intense domestic pressures for some governments may lead NSIs to argue for favorable interpretations of ESA in the calculation of their deficit and debt figures. In more severe cases of adaptational pressure, the "misfit" between EU standards and member state preferences may take the form of questionable and even deceptive accounting procedures. This is true in the cases of Portugal and Italy in 2002, where charges of Enron accounting were directed at Italy, and Eurostat refused to certify Portugal's biannual figures. Most recently, Eurostat's May 2004 mission visit to Greece revealed extensive misclassifications in that member state's postal savings bank, military, and social security budgets. Consequently, under pressure from Eurostat, Greece revised its 2003 deficit figure from −1.7 percent of GDP to −3.2 percent.[11] As in the case of Portugal, an electoral change in governments

---

[10] On the Lisbon Summit's goals, see "Report: The Contribution of Public Finances to Growth and Employment: Improving Quality and Sustainability," Commission and Council of the European Union to the European Council, Brussels, 6997/01, March 12, 2001; Tim Jones (2000). "Lisbon Summit to Sanction Tighter EU Budget Surveillance," *European Voice*. March 9–15, p. 1.

[11] Eurostat news release (2004b). "Greek Government Deficit at 3.2% of GDP and Public Debt at 103.0% of GDP," N. 62/2004, May 7. Greece prefinanced its military expenditures with financial advances that were never recorded in its accounts as expenditures, while its social security surpluses were achieved through the misclassification of certain public sector pension funds. Although the deficit's growth is also partly explained by unexpected costs associated with the Olympics, Eurostat

appears to be promoting greater cooperation between the Commission and the member state in these accounting issues. In these three cases, the top-down pressures exerted by the EU eventually resulted in member state compliance in their accounting practices.

Second, another measure of Europeanization is the incorporation of Eurostat's national accounts decisions and interpretations of ESA into the member states' own accounting rules and procedures. Europeanization in this regard actually serves the member states' own interests. By incorporating Eurostat's rules, the member states gain a true understanding of the national accounts implications of their own budgetary policies. The member states' ministries of finance (MOFs) and NSIs, moreover, frequently turn to Eurostat to inquire about how possible budgetary actions might be classified according to ESA. As Dieter Glatzel observed, the members states contact Eurostat, asking, "Will this have an impact on the deficit?" "There is an enormous awareness among the member states that there are some common rules, and these common rules are important for the standing of the euro. Sometimes you have the feeling they are happy the ruling comes from outside. 'Okay, we couldn't do anything else. They have imposed it on us.' It's an easy way out."[12] Particularly in the areas of privatization and outsourcing of government contracts, member states have been known to delay, terminate, or reconfigure their activities. Thus, regardless of the institutional design of the member states' budgetary processes, compliance with the Treaty's institutional framework and ESA may at some point require adjustments in domestic fiscal decisions.[13]

Third, Europeanization includes adapting domestic institutions to meet EU demands, which in this case means collecting, formatting, and analyzing budgetary data, and submitting them to Eurostat. These states have reacted to these tasks in the training of their statistical personnel in national accounts techniques, which means seconding them with the Eurostat so that they can learn EU principles, procedures, and practices. This secondment exposes and perhaps even socializes the member states' personnel to Eurostat's standards of what constitutes "impartial, reliable, objective, and independent statistics," as called for in Article 285 of the Treaty Establishing the European Economic Community (EEC). Furthermore, the member state NSIs often adapt their administrative structures to meet the EU's statistical workload demands.

forced Greece to resubmit its data on earlier years, causing its budget surpluses for 2001 and 2002 to be recalculated as deficits. "Olympic's Cost Pushes Greece Over EU Deficit Limits," (2004). *International Herald Tribune.* May 8–9, p. 11.

[12] Interview with Dieter Glatzel, March 19, 2003.

[13] For an institutional analysis of how the member states altered their budgetary processes during these years, see Mark Hallerberg, *Domestic Budgets in a United Europe: Fiscal Governance from the End of Bretton Woods to EMU.* Ithaca: Cornell University Press, 2004.

Member state NSIs have redeployed staff, created new units, and reallocated funds to meet these bureaucratic requirements. In these ways, therefore, the surveillance procedure and Eurostat have encouraged Europeanization within segments of the member states' institutional apparatus.

These three forms of Europeanization suggest that the member states passively adopt the EU's top-down pronouncements and rulings. More than top-down pressure, however, is at work in promoting Europeanization. The member states exert their own influence through bottom-up pressures on the Commission, where their bottom-up strategies include the uploading of member state preferences into the surveillance procedure's evolving decision-making process. Ironically, as a result of Eurostat's top-down ruling on France Telecom, the member states uploaded a more rigorous deliberative process that enhanced member state participation in the CMFB, thereby reinforcing a stricter interpretation of ESA. The CMFB serves as both a policy advisory body and a dispute resolution forum. Although Eurostat determines the final ruling on national accounts issues, since France Telecom every one of these rulings has conformed with the member states' majority vote in the CMFB. Individual member states, of course, may seek self-interested rulings. Yet, overwhelming majority votes by the member states serve to constrain these efforts, and by their very active participation in CMFB the member states contribute significantly to the legitimacy of Eurostat's rulings. Thus, the national accounts decision-making process reflects a dynamic combination of top-down and bottom-up influences and pressures that contribute to Europeanization.

Finally, it is important to note that the integrating effects of institutionalization and Europeanization due to the surveillance process apply not only to EU member states, but also to EU candidate countries. Every EU member and candidate state, regardless of its EMU membership, must comply with the Maastricht Treaty's demand for these ESA harmonized budgetary data, as certified by Eurostat. Certainly, these data are necessary for any EU member state that seeks EMU status through the convergence process.

6.3 Conclusion

There are several conclusions that may be derived from the EU's experience with the surveillance procedure. First, the member states were not free to pursue whatever policies they desired to fulfill the Treaty's Stage II convergence requirements. The Maastricht Treaty's framers understood the nature of the compliance problem they created when they added provisions for a surveillance procedure and powerful exclusionary sanctions for EMU membership.

The compliance information system organized by Eurostat to make the procedure work proved to be much more than simple monitoring. Serving in its role as a delegated treaty guardian, Eurostat created a body of statistical regulatory case law that harmonized the member states' budgetary data. These rules, at the same time, influenced the content of the member states' fiscal practices, and effectively determined which of these states qualified for EMU status.

Second, Eurostat's rule-making continues to influence the future of the EU and EMU. Eurostat's rules still set the standard for harmonizing member state budgetary data, and its certification of member state biannual reports is required before the full financial sanctions of the Stability and Growth Pact may be imposed on noncompliant governments. Furthermore, all EU candidate countries must submit biannual reports to Eurostat, and those new member states eventually seeking EMU status must fulfill the Maastricht Treaty's convergence requirements. So, just as in 1998, Eurostat will file a report that will significantly determine whether these countries should be admitted into the EMU on the basis of their fiscal behavior. In addition, the creation of short-term public finance statistics may be used by the ECOFIN Council to evaluate the content of member state budgetary policies, as well as the size of their deficits and debt. The member and candidate states, meanwhile, continue to integrate Eurostat's rulings into their own accounting rules. Through their active participation in Eurostat's decision-making process, these governments legitimize, lend credibility to, and lock-in Eurostat's supranational authority over budgetary statistics, thereby reinforcing the tendency towards European integration.

Third, although some academic literature suggests the EC acts as a fully independent "trustee" in its treaty guardian role, this description does not fully describe the Commission's role in the Treaty's surveillance procedure. Rather, there are key decision points where the Commission enjoys autonomy that resembles trustee-like independence, but the overall process is one that combines moments of trusteeship and a principal–agent relationship. Those moments of autonomy include Eurostat's authority to make final national accounts rulings, deny certification to member state budgetary data, and submit convergence reports. The Commission's authority includes its right to evaluate member state stability programs, and recommend warnings, calls for corrective fiscal action, and the imposition of financial penalties to the ECOFIN Council. At the same time, however, the member states play a critical role throughout the surveillance procedure. Their NSIs collect and submit the biannual budgetary data that serve as the basis for the procedure's information compliance system. Their representatives serve on the CMFB and develop what have become nearly binding national accounts recommendations to Eurostat. They engage in the interactive process of submitting stability programs to DG ECFIN and responding to the Commission's set of budgetary policy recommendations. The member states' finance ministers, of course, sitting as the ECOFIN Council ultimately determine positive and negative sanctions under the Treaty and Pact.

Fourth, despite the attempt by both member states and the Commission to create prescient rules and decision-making processes for the surveillance procedure, the procedure itself is heavily influenced by contingent and dynamic events.[14] The Treaty's rules provided for a surveillance procedure, specified ESA 79 as the standard for measuring deficits and debt, and delegated to the Commission the task of collecting and analyzing these budgetary data. The procedure is also marked by contingent events producing unexpected outcomes. These events include Director General Franchet's successful assertion that Eurostat deserved a place in the surveillance procedure; Eurostat's unforeseen preeminence within the Commission during the Stage II convergence process; the unexpected influence of Eurostat's rulings in determining what constitutes acceptable member state fiscal actions for reducing deficits and debt; the effect of Eurostat's national accounts decisions and convergence report on the member states' EMU membership status; and DG ECFIN's effort to regain influence in Stage III though its inclusion of cyclical requirements for the Pact's surveillance procedure. The EU responded to Eurostat's expanding functions through adaptation and inclusion by accepting its role, strengthening its position compared to that of DG ECFIN, and acknowledging the force of its rulings over the member states. None of these events could be predicted from the Maastricht Treaty's simple requirements that the Commission collect member state budgetary data that conformed to ESA 79. As a result, what has occurred is less a fully anticipatory set of institutionally controlling rules than an adaptive response by the member states to Eurostat's activities, particularly through the CMFB.

Fifth and finally, regardless of the reforms that may be incorporated into the Treaty and the Stability and Growth Pact, they must include a credible and reliable surveillance procedure to be effective as a trustworthy enforcement instrument. As a result of the ECOFIN Council's rejection of the Commission's recommendations in November 2003, there will likely be significant revisions in the Pact. Such revisions could include, for example, an expansion of Council Regulation 1467/97's provisions on what constitutes an exceptional and acceptably temporary budget deficit in the face of economic difficulties. This alteration could simply mirror the Maastricht Treaty's original intent of

---

[14] On the rational design of institutions, see Barbara Koremenos, Charles Lipson, and Duncan Snidal (2001). "The Rational Design of International Institutions," *International Organization*, 55(4), 761–99.

setting the 3.0 percent deficit level as a reference value, rather than an absolute target. The politics of the time reified the 3.0 percent target as absolute, not the Treaty. These reforms, moreover, should recognize the significant difference in the sanctioning force of the convergence process that may exclude a member state from the EMU, as compared to the Pact's relatively weaker reputational and financial penalties. The Pact, of course, called for balanced budgets as a target, which could be maintained as a policy goal, but as recent member state deficit levels suggest, the current set of sanctions lack the power to force the member states to realize this target. These revisions might also reflect DG ECFIN's desire to emphasize cyclically adjusted budget calculations in evaluating member state stability programs and in determining excessive deficits. In 2003, however, German authorities charged that DG ECFIN's econometric modeling and the calculation of the cyclically adjusted budget deficit is suspect.[15] Clearly, if this methodology is to play a significant role in the Pact's surveillance procedure, these concerns about DG ECFIN's reliability and the transparency of its decision-making process must be addressed. Whatever the nature of the alterations finally introduced into the Treaty and Pact, they will still demand a surveillance procedure that produces credible and reliable statistical budgetary data. Eurostat contributes to this process by providing such data through a decision-making process, one tested and reformed as a result of the France Telecom ruling. Fortunately, these reforms came into being before the making of the convergence process's most delicate national accounts decisions in 1997. Since then, Eurostat has avoided charges that its rulings are biased or unsubstantiated according to the logic of the ESA. In this way, Eurostat adds to the credibility and effectiveness of the surveillance procedure, and its statistical rules contribute to the ongoing, integrative processes of institutionalization and Europeanization.

---

[15] Wolfgang Munchau (2003). "A Treaty to Undermine the Eurozone," *Financial Times*. December 1, p. 15; Bertrand Benoit (2003). "Surprise at Eichel's 'Emotional Response,'" *Financial Times*. November 26, p. 4.

7

Postscript

Is the Maastricht Treaty's surveillance process sustainable despite member state noncompliant behavior? The EU's answer to this question is one of reaffirmation and accommodation. During the summer of 2004, two events occurred that significantly affect the Treaty's budgetary surveillance. First, on June 17 and 18, the EU Intergovernmental Council, consisting of the heads of government of the member states and acceding states, unanimously adopted the draft text of the new European Constitution, Europe's latest grand bargain. The Constitution's chapter on Economic and Monetary Policy incorporates the excessive deficit procedure, including its provisions requiring that the European Commission monitor the budgetary conditions of the member states.[1] Thus, the new Constitution calls for the continuation of the surveillance process analyzed in this book.

Second, a similar reaffirmation occurred on July 13, 2004, when the European Court of Justice issued its judgement upholding the EC's claim that the Council of Economic and Finance Ministers exceeded its authority in declaring the Maastricht Treaty's excessive deficit procedure in "abeyance."[2] The EC sought this ruling following the ECOFIN Council's decision in November, 2003 rejecting the EC's recommendations that Germany and France be directed to take additional fiscal action to reduce their budget deficits. At the same time, ECOFIN announced that the excessive deficit procedure would be held in abeyance in the cases of these two member states. The Court annulled this action, pronouncing that the "Council cannot depart from the rules laid down by the Treaty or those which it set for itself in [the

---

[1] The European Convention (2003). "Draft Treaty Establishing a Constitution for Europe," Brussels, July 18, Part III, Title III, Chapter II, Section 1, Articles III-70–76.

[2] The European Court of Justice issued its judgement as this manuscript was going into final galley form. The author greatfully thanks Oxford for permitting the addition of this postscript very late in the publication process. European Court of Justice (2004). "Judgement of the Court of Justice in Case C-27/04," Luxembourg, July 13, Press Release No. 57/04.

Stability and Growth Pact]." The Court, therefore, preserved the Pact's sanctions and reaffirmed the EC's responsibilities in the surveillance process, namely its "right of initiative" to submit recommendations to the Council.

The Court also declared, however, that "Responsibility for making the Member States observe budgetary discipline lies essentially with the Council." So, said the Court, it is the Council's prerogative to reject the EC's recommendations: "The Council has a discretion in this field, as it can modify the measure recommended by the Commission on the basis of a different assessment of the economic data, of the measures to be taken and of the timetable to be met by the Member State concerned." The Court's ruling offers consolation to both the EC and ECOFIN. The EC continues to exercise its responsibility to conduct budgetary surveillance and make its recommendations to the ECOFIN Council, and the ECOFIN Council, as long as its decisions comply with the Treaty and Pact, exercises its own right to accept or reject these recommendations.

The EC, meanwhile, is considering ways to reform the Pact by accommodating the interests of powerful Germany and France. Joaquin Almunia, the Commissioner for Economic and Monetary Policy, proposes four ways in which the Pact might be reformed.[3] First, incentives should be offered to the member states to consolidate their fiscal policies during periods of economic growth by running budget surpluses, thus enhancing fiscal sustainability during a weak economy. Second, more attention should be paid to country-specific circumstances when determining budgetary goals. Third, while maintaining the Treaty's 3 percent deficit and 60 percent debt reference values, EC recommendations should take economic conditions more strongly into account, thus offering greater flexibility to the member states. Fourth, national debt rather than budgetary deficits should become the focus of the excessive deficit procedure, which also sets a reference value for the debt level. Supporting the last recommendation, one observer notes, "The only way to get to grips with unsustainable public finances is an approach based on qualitative assessments of the development of public-sector debt as opposed to hard and fast rules. Who would be in charge in charge of making such assessments?"[4]

---

[3] Jaoquin Almunia (2004). "Press Conference on Public Finance Report Communication," Brussels, June 24, Speech/04/330. Other suggested reforms include those offered by Austria's finance minister Karl-Heinz Grasser, who recommends strengthening positive incentives for budgetary compliance by providing member states with enhanced EU budgetary resources for research or other activities, and by changing the nature of negative incentives by punishing noncompliant members states with reduced voting rights.

[4] Wolfgang Munchau (2004). "Europe Needs A Strategy, Not Looser Fiscal Rules," *The Financial Times*, May 24, p. 13.

Almunia's last recommendation and this observation return us to the surveillance procedure and the importance of Eurostat's technical national accounts decisions. Even if the numerical reference values in the excessive deficit procedure, the "hard and fast rules," were set aside, EU decision makers would still require the budgetary data generated by Eurostat's compliance information system. Eurostat's rule making process, therefore, would continue to influence budgetary decisions and assessments of member state treaty compliance. The 1994 ruling on privatization, for instance, states that in most cases the revenues generated from privatization may not be used to reduce the size of budget deficits, but they may be applied to the calculation of government debt. Consequently, where privatization offered little benefit to the member states for complying with the Treaty's convergence process that concentrated on the size of budgetary deficits, privatization under a revised Stability and Growth Pact would be greatly encouraged.

Making the revisions in the Treaty and Pact as Almunia suggests may be difficult. A unanimous vote of all 25 EU member states would be required for such a decision. Although several euro-zone member states openly violate the Pact, five other member states within the zone and three other EU member states run budget surpluses, and these states may not take kindly to scrapping or neutering the rules.[5] Member states that could benefit by some revisions may object to other changes. A revision in the Pact that emphasizes the size of a member state's national debt, for instance, would likely be opposed by high debtor states such as Italy and Greece. The Pact may be revised, but how and when remains to be seen. Thus, despite pronouncements that the Stability and Growth Pact is dead, the new European Constitution and the Court of Justice's ruling reaffirm, and, at least for the immediate future, lock in the EU's fiscal rules, including their provisions for ongoing budgetary surveillance.

[5] The euro-zone member states recording surpluses are Spain, Belgium, Ireland, Finland, and Luxembourg; outside the zone, so too are Sweden, Denmark, and Estonia.

Appendix: Other Eurostat Stage II Decisions, 1995–7

A.1   Three Categories of Lesser Rulings

In addition to their major national accounts rulings, Eurostat and the Committee for Monetary, Financial, and Balance of Payment Statistics (CMFB) considered a number of lesser cases that also influenced the deficit and debt calculation of the European Union (EU) member states that directly influenced the Stage II convergence process. Many of these lesser rulings stemmed from questions raised by the National Statistical Institutes (NSIs) themselves during the Eurostat mission visits of 1996 and 1997, and both the more prominent and the less well-known decisions may be divided into three categories. First, there are decisions related to the classification of transactions of government, where they are regarded as financial transactions with no effect on the deficit or debt calculation or nonfinancial transactions that do influence the calculation. The Belgium privatization, France Telecom, the various gold cases, and central bank payments to the state, as well as those indicated in the table, fall under this category. Perhaps most significant of these lesser decisions concerned state guarantees on public enterprise debt, which lowered Italy's deficit by 0.2 of gross domestic product (GDP) for the critical 1997 fiscal year. Another Italian case that attracted significant public attention concerned currency and interest rate swaps, and is described here in some detail. Second, there are decisions related to the time of recording transactions, as in the cases of Ireland and retroactive accounting, the treatment of interest, and the timing of payment dates for taxes, including the eurotax. Last, there are decisions related to the classification of units inside or outside of general government, as, for instance the German hospitals case, where a distinction must be made between those activities falling within the governmental sphere, which therefore affect the deficit calculation.

Sources: Eurostat news releases and CMFB minutes.

A.1.1   Decisions Related to the Classification of Transactions

1. *Interest Rate and Currency Swaps:* In the case of interest rate swaps, only the net payments of interest between the two parties to the swap should be recorded. The influence on a government deficit would be limited to the difference between the interest flows agreed to in the exchange. In the case of currency swaps, any outside foreign currency debt will be valued according to the market exchange rate and not the exchange rate in the swap contract. The existence of a swap agreement has no effect on the valuation of outstanding debt in a foreign currency. This interpretation raised Ireland's 1997 deficit by .4 percent and lowered its 1997 debt by 1 percent of GDP; it increased Finland's 1997 deficit by 0.1 percent, and lowered Italy's deficit by 0.02 percent in 1997.

2. *The Italian Interest Rate and Currency Swaps Case:* In November 2001, the *Financial Times* reported on allegations made by the International Securities Market Association that Italy improperly counted the gains from an exchange and interest rate swaps deal as revenues for calculating its 1997 deficit and debt figures.[1] In such a swap, a government may issue a security in a foreign currency as a way to manage the public debt and the government's foreign exchange reserves, and later elect to swap that security for its own national currency in order to realize the gains from trade. In 1995, the Italian government issued a three-year bond for 200 billion yen, with the yen valued at 19.3 lira. Although the bond matured in September 1998, these liabilities would be counted at the end of 1997 and applied towards that year's deficit and debt because, as Article 1 of Council Regulation 3605/93 requires, "liabilities denominated in foreign currencies shall be converted into the national currency at the representative market exchange rate prevailing on the last working day of each year." Consequently, any unexpected appreciation in the yen would contribute to an expansion in Italy's deficit and debt above its 1996 level, as the yen were converted into lira. Rather than risk this possibility, the Italians incorporated into the terms of these securities anticipated rates of exchange and interest over the lifetime of the bond.

Critics of this financial structuring claimed it to be "creative accounting," no better than that perpetrated in the Enron scandal in the United States.

The contract required Italy to make negative interest payments to the bank of Lira Libor minus an astounding 1,677 basis points in 1997 (meaning that Italy received funds) and then in effect to reverse the payments in September 1998. This reduced Italy's official deficit in 1997 only by raising it in 1998. . . . The damning part of this explanation is

---

[1] James Blitz (2001). "Italy Rebuts Swap Contract Claims," *Financial Times*, November 6, p. 6.

the admission that Italy was taking a cash advance against an expected foreign exchange profit in 1998. . . . It is clear that the existence of the yen bond was merely a convenient pretext for Italy to borrow money that it could then misclassify as a hedge, just as Enron's commodities trades were a pretext for its own disguised borrowing.

Although Eurostat was not mentioned by name, the author inferentially referred to the agency by asking, "who shall guard the guardians?"[2]

The problem for Eurostat in evaluating this aspect of Italy's financial activities was that ESA 79, the outdated national accounting standard set by the Maastricht Treaty, made no mention of swaps transactions, thus making the transaction fully allowable. Moreover, the replacement set of rules, ESA 95, did consider swaps, but had yet to be formally adopted. Eurostat subsequently consulted with the CMFB, whose advice led Eurostat to conclude that nothing had been specified in either set of national accounting rules that prohibited the Italian Treasury from structuring the bond as it did. In a manner explicitly consistent with Regulation 3065/93, the valuation of the liability had to converted into the domestic currency, with its effect on the deficit calculation limited to the difference between the interest flows specified in the bond. In any event, the effect of the transaction improved Italy's deficit by 0.02 percent, not an amount that would influence Italy's entry into the EMU.[3]

3. *Financial Leasing:* All leasing transactions shall be treated as operating leasing. So, if a government sells fixed assets and then leases these assets with the intent of reacquiring them, this constitutes an operating lease. The sale of these fixed assets constitutes the direct sale of nonfinancial assets, and receipts from this sale may be applied to the government's deficit calculation. The obligation to repurchase these assets at the end of the lease is a contingent liability and is not included in the government's debt calculation.

4. *Financing and Exploiting of Public Infrastructures by the Enterprise Sector:* Three cases fell under this category. In the first case associated with the United Kingdom, an enterprise constructs the infrastructure and then operates it while receiving annual payments from the state for services produced with the infrastructure. After the agreed upon period expires, the infrastructure is turned over to the state. Supported unanimously by the CMFB, Eurostat ruled that only the annual payments shall be counted towards the deficit calculation. The actual acquisition of the infrastructure has no effect on the government's debt calculation. The second case applies particularly to the construction and prefinancing of at least twelve roads in Germany, which in 1997 total some 4–5 billion DM. In these instances, the enterprise is required to build and prefinance a fixed asset

[2] Benn Steil (2002). "Enron and Italy," *Financial Times.* July 21, p. 13.
[3] Peter Norman (2001). "Rome 'Did Not Cheat Over Deficit,'" *Financial Times.* November 6, p. 6.

for the state, where the state becomes the owner of the asset as it is constructed. This investment in gross fixed capital formation should be recorded in the general government sector S60, and included in the public deficit calculation, but excluded from the debt calculation. The third case addresses similar situations occurring in the United Kingdom, Denmark, and Sweden, where an enterprise is required to build a fixed asset, operate it, and retain ownership of the asset. In the case of Denmark and Sweden, for example, a bridge was constructed in 1996 by a public corporation where the finances were backed by state guarantees. In each case, gross fixed capital formation is recorded in the enterprise sector with no effect on the public deficit.

5. *State Guarantees on Public Enterprise Debt:* Supported by a large majority vote of the CMFB, Eurostat ruled that public enterprise debt guaranteed by the state shall be included in the calculation of the government's debt when, first, the law authorizing the issuance of this debt indicates the government's repayment obligation, and, second, when the government's budget specifies the annual amount of repayment. This rule applies to the case of the Italian railroad, the *Ferrovie dello Stato*, whose debt issues since 1981 have been authorized by law by the Ministry of Finance. Consequently, the government's debt was reclassified to reflect an increase for each year the railroad's debt increased, while the government's deficit was reduced to reflect the amortization of old debt. For the period 1993–7, this reclassification increased Italy's collective debt by 13.51 billion lire, and reduced its collective deficits by 2.4 billion lire. For the 1997 fiscal year specifically, there was no effect on the debt and an improvement in the deficit of 3.687 billion lire, or 0.2 percent of GDP.

6. *Export Insurance Guaranteed by the State:* In each EU member state there are export insurance enterprises that benefit from state guarantees, which in ESA are classified in either the insurance sector S50 or general government sector S60. All flows from these firms, premiums and indemnities, will be recorded as nonfinancial transactions. Consequently, losses incurred by the state on guaranteed payments will also be recorded as nonfinancial transactions, and must be included in the calculation of the public deficit. This ruling reduced Spain's 1997 deficit by 0.1 percent, and increased Austria's deficit by 0.02 percent of GDP.

A.1.2   Decisions Related to the Time Recording of Transactions

1. *Capitalized Interest on Deposits and Other Financial Instruments Covered by ESA79:* In the case of deposits or similar financial instruments that act as government liabilities, the capitalized interest will recorded as government expenditure, which contributes to the budget deficit, when interest is paid to holders of these instruments. Interest will be recorded separately from the

principal, and will be recorded when the capitalized amount falls due for payment, rather than distribute it to different periods. This ruling increased Portugal's 1997 deficit by 0.15 percent and decreased Italy's 1997 deficit by 0.26 percent of GDP.

2. *Treatment of Fungible Bonds Issued in Several Tranches:* In the case of fungible bonds, that is, bonds that are issued in tranches at different points in time without change in the coupon payment date, the accrued coupon will be recorded as a short-term liability under the heading "accounts receivable and payable," which therefore does not enter into the calculation of government debt. This reduced the French 1996 deficit by 0.18 percent of GDP.

3. *Treatment of Interest for Short-, Medium-, and Long-Term Bonds:* To harmonize bills and short-term bonds across the EU member states, they are defined as those with a maturity up to and including twelve months. For these short-term bonds, the difference between the issue price and the nominal value will be regarded as interest recorded at the issuance of the bonds. This difference will influence the calculation of a government's deficit. For medium- and long-term bonds, the difference between the issue price and nominal price will not be regarded as interest, but as holding gains and losses. This difference will not affect the calculation of a government's deficits. This ruling increased Finland's 1997 deficit by 0.04 percent of GDP.

4. *Treatment of Interest for Linear Bonds:* Like many other unconventional bonds, linear bonds are not addressed in ESA 79. Consequently, Eurostat ruled on how to classify the difference between the nominal value and price at issue for linear bonds, those fungible bonds issued in several tranches from the same lineage with the same nominal interest rate as well as identical dates for coupon payments. All the difference between the nominal value and issue price must be considered as interest recorded at the time of the coupon payments, such that this difference must be included in the calculation of the public deficit. Linear bonds are used particularly in Belgium, Denmark, Finland, Portugal, and Sweden. As a result of this interpretation, Belgium's deficit for 1997 was increased by 0.04 percent, Denmark's by 0.02 percent, Finland's by 0.17 percent, Portugal's by 0.05 percent, while Sweden's deficit was reduced by 0.28 percent.

5. *Treatment of Interest In the Case of Zero Coupon Bonds:* The difference between the issue price and redemption price of a zero coupon bond is to be treated as interest, to be recorded as interest paid at the bond's maturity. Interest is defined as a payment at predetermined dates of a fixed percentage of the nominal value of the asset, so the price difference is interest. This interpretation raised Denmark's 1997 deficit by 0.01 percent of GDP.

6. *Changes in the Due for Payment Dates for Taxes, Salaries, Social Contributions, and Benefits:* Transactions can be recorded at three different points in time: When amounts are cashed, as in a cash payment; when amounts are due, as in due for payment date; and when activities giving rise to transactions occur, on an accrual basis. In 1996, Sweden reduced by one month the time-lag for its value-added tax (VAT) payments granted to large enterprises. This measure led in the Swedish public accounts to cashed amounts corresponding to thirteen months of VAT receipts in 1996. During the same year under the same set of circumstances, Portugal reduced the time-lag for VAT payments by ten days. Both cases raised the matter of whether the government's deficit position is improved by this additional period of VAT payments. In the same context, Eurostat considered the national accounts effect of the time of certain government expenses, particularly public employee salaries and social benefits, and the imposition of certain taxes and social contributions. In making its ruling, supported by the near unanimous opinion of the CMFB, Eurostat distinguished between taxes tied to production and imports, and those taxes on income, wealth, salaries, social contributions, and benefits. In the first case, ESA 79 specifies that they be recorded on an accrual basis, in other words at the time goods and services are produced, sold, or imported. Consequently, any change in the payment due date of taxes in this case, though affecting the cash balances in public budgets, should not be included in the calculation of taxes recorded in national accounts and the determination of the government deficit. This situation applies to Sweden and Portugal, which permitted Sweden to reclassify its national accounts to show an increase of 0.6 percent of its deficit for 1996, and by 0.36 for Portugal during the same year, as these VAT taxes could not be included to reduce the government's deficit. In the second case, of taxes on salaries, etc. these should be recorded at the payment due date established by law, and should be included in the deficit calculation. Temporary administrative adjustments in tax payment dates, though improving the government's cash balances, should not affect the government's deficit position.

A.1.3   Decisions Related to the Classification of Units

1. *Classification of National Bodies Acting on Behalf of the European Commission:* In the case of those national institutional units that are engaged in market regulation and the distribution of subsidies, such as the Irish Intervention Agency, if their activities cannot be divided along these lines, then these units will be classified in the sector General Government, which will influence the government's deficit and debt calculation, when their costs incurred in

market regulation compared to total costs are less than 80 percent. This decision increased Ireland's 1997 debt by 1 percent of GDP.

2. *Pension Funds:* Pension funds that finance benefits primarily on a pay-as-you-go basis and to a minor extent on a capital funding basis have to be classified in the subsector S63 "Social Security Funds" of General Government sector S60. The classification criteria are that these funds are institutional units, as they have a complete set of accounts, have autonomy of decision, and pay benefits to the insured without reference to the individual exposure of risk, where these employment-based pension schemes are built on a collective financial balance principle.

References

Abrams, B. and W. R. Dougan (1986). "The Effects of Constitutional Restraints on Government Spending," *Public Choice*, 49(1), 101–16.

Alderman, Liz (2002). "Fiscal Fisticuffs for Europe?" *International Herald Tribune*. May 14, p. 13.

Allen, R. G. D. (1980). *An Introduction to National Statistical Accounts*. London: Macmillan Press.

Almunia, Joaquin (2004). "Press Conference on Public Communications," Brussels, June 24, speech/04/330.

Arnold, R. Douglas (1979). *Congress and the Bureaucracy: A Theory of Influence*. New Haven: Yale University Press.

Artis, Michael J. and Marco Buti (2001). "Setting Medium-Term Fiscal Targets in the EMU," *Public Finance & Management* 1(1), 34–57.

Associated Press (1999). "All Commissioners of European Union Give Resignations," *New York Times*. March 17, p. A1.

Atkins, Ralph (1997a). "Budget Concerns May Spur Telekom Sell-Off," *Financial Times*. May 15, p. 2.

——(1997b). "Waigel Resolves Bundesbank Row," *Financial Times*. June 20, p. 2.

——(1998). "Euro Doubts Raised in Bonn," *Financial Times*. March 12, p. 3.

Atkins, Ralph and Michael Smith (1997). "Germany Set for Unexpected Windfall," *Financial Times*. August 21, p. 2.

Ausubel, J. and D. Victor (1992). "Verification of International Environmental Agreements," *Annual Review of Energy and the Environment*, 17, 1–43.

Ballman, Alexander, David Epstein, and Sharyn O'Halloran (2002). "Delegation, Comitology, and the Separation of Powers in the European Union," *International Organization*, 56(3), 551–74.

Banchoff, T. (1997). "German Policy Towards the European Union: The Effects of Historical Memory," *German History*, 6(1), 60–76.

Banks, Martin (2003). "Whistleblower Claims Trigger Eurostat Fraud Investigation," *European Voice*, June 20–6, p. 1.

Barber, Lionel (1997a). "Brussels to Clarify Stance on Deficits," *Financial Times*. February 1–2, p. 2.

——(1997b). "Boost for Italy's Bid to be in First EMU Wave," *Financial Times*. February 4, p. 4.

——(1997c). "Watchdog Approves Italy's Tax Route to EMU Target," *Financial Times*. February 22–3, p. 24.

——(1997d). "Brussels Cautious on Germany's Gold Ploy," *Financial Times*. May 17–18, p. 2.

——(1997e). "Budget Deficit Error Deals Blow to Finns," *Financial Times*. July 28, p. 2.

Barber, Lionel and James Blitz (1998). "Italy Loses Gold Profits Battle," *Financial Times*. January 28, p. 1.

Barber, Tony (2000a). "Euro-Zone's Output Growth Shows Signs of Peaking," *Financial Times*. July 4, p. 2.

——(2000b). "Economic Indicators Cast a Pall Over the Euro-Zone's Prospects," *Financial Times*. September 27, p. 2.

Barber, Tony and James Blitz (1999). "Prodi's Rhetoric Highlights Public Disunity on Euro," *Financial Times*. June 23, p. 2.

Bates, Robert H. (1988). "Contra Contractarianism: Some Reflections on the New Institutionalism," *Politics & Society*, 16 (2–3), 387–401.

Beetsma, R. and H. Uhlig (1999). "An Analysis of the Stability and Growth Pact," *Economic Journal*, 109, 546–71.

Bendor, Jonathan, Serge Taylor, and Roland Van Gaalen (1985). "Bureaucratic Expertise Versus Legislative Authority: A Model of Deception and Monitoring in Budgeting," *American Political Science Review*, 79(4), 1041–60.

Bendor, Jonathan, A. Glazer, and T. Hammond (2001). "Theories of Delegation," *Annual Review of Political Science*, 4, 235–69.

Benoit, Bertrand (2003). "Surprise at Eichel's 'Emotional Response,'" *Financial Times*. November 26, p. 4.

Benoit, Bertrand and Daniel Dombey (2003). "Schroder Drops Budget Pledge," *Financial Times*. May 12, p. 3.

Benoit, Bertrand and Haig Simonian (2000). "German Mobile Phone Auction Raises $46bn," *Financial Times*. August 18, p. 1.

Betts, Paul (2002). "France Backs Tax Cuts At the Expense of Balanced Budget," *Financial Times*. September 25, p. 6.

Bini-Smaghi, L., T. Pado-Schioppa, and F. Papadia (1994). "The Transition to EMU in the Maastricht Treaty," Princeton Studies in International Finance, Essay 194.

Blau, Peter M. and W. R. Scott (1962). *Formal Organizations: A Comparative Approach*. Scranton: Chandler.

Blitz, James (2000a). "Italy Set for Mobile Phone Bonanza," *Financial Times*. June 19, p. 2.

——(2000b). "Italian Deficit Reduction on Tract Despite 3G Debacle," *Financial Times*. November 2, p. 4.

——(2001a). "Italy Looks to Real Estate Sales to Meet Budget Targets," *Financial Times*. September 11, p. 2.

——(2001b). "Italy Rebuts Swap Contract Claims," *Financial Times*. November 6, p. 6.

——(2002). "UK Wants Tougher Rules on European Government Borrowing," *Financial Times*. October 21, p. 2.

Borzel, Tanja A. and Thomas Risse (2003). "Conceptualizing the Domestic Impact of Europe," in Kenneth Featherstone and Claudio M. Radaelli (eds.), *The Politics of Europeanization*. New York: Oxford University Press, pp. 57–80.

Bream, Rebecca (2002). "Asset-Backed Proves Port in Storm," *Financial Times*. October 9, p. 24.

Briffault, R. (1996). *Balancing Acts: The Reality Behind State Balanced Budget Requirements*. New York: Twentieth Century Fund Press.

Brown, John Murray, Nichoas Timmins, and Peter Wise (2004). "Brussels Acts to Exclude Private Finance for Public Works from Stability Pact Rules," *Financial Times*. February 7, p. 2.

Buchan, David (1996). "The Magic of Maastrichtian Mathematics," *Financial Times*. September 19, p. 3.

——(1997). "Jospin Raps Germany over Criteria 'Fudge,'" *Financial Times*. May 29, p. 2.

Buck, Tobias (2003a). "Comment and Analysis: 'To Safeguard the Interests of the Institution'—but was Action Taken Quickly Enough?" *Financial Times*. June 17, FT.com website.

—— (2003b). "Eurostat Faces Paris Corruption Probe," *Financial Times*, May 16, p. 1.

——(2003c). "Four Companies Suspected in Eurostat Affair Lose Contracts," *The Financial Times*. July 24, p. 4.

Buck, Tobias and George Parker (2003a). "Eurostat Scandal Draws in Prodi and Kinnock," *Financial Times*. June 17, p. 1.

——(2003b). "Brussels Attacked Over Alleged Fraud," *Financial Times*. June 18, p. 1.

——(2003c). "Brussels Widens Fraud Probe," *Financial Times*. July 17, p. 1.

Buck, Tobias, George Parker, and John Prideaux (2003). "Brussels Finally Moves to Quell Critics Over Financial Scandals at Eurostat," *Financial Times*. July 10, p. 3.

Buckley, Neil (1997). "Belgium Accused of Cooking Books on Debt," *Financial Times*. January 19, p. 2.

Buerkle, Tom (1996). "Germany Grows 'Suspicious' Over EMU," *International Hearald Tribune*. November 11, p. 5.

——(2000). "Mobile Auction Frenzy Wanes Across Europe," *International Hearld Tribune*. July 12, p. 1.

Buiter, W. H., G. Corsetti, and N. Roubini (1992). "'Excessive Deficits': Sense and Nonsense in the Treaty of Maastricht," Center for Economic Policy Research Paper 750.

Bunch, B. (1991). "The Effect of Constitutional Debt Limits on State Governments," *Public Choice*, 68(1), 57–69.

Bush, Janet (1996). "Why Further Euro-Fudge Will Sweeten Path to EMU," *The Times*. September 10, p. 31.

Caporale, Guglielmo Maria (1992). "Fiscal Solvency in Europe: Budget Deficits and Government Debt Under European Monetary Union," *National Institute Economic Review*, 5(1), 69–77.

Carpenter, Daniel P. (2001). *The Forging of Bureaucratic Autonomy*. Princeton: Princeton University Press.

Casella, A. (1999). "Tradable Deficit Permits: Efficient Implementation of the Stability Pact in the European Monetary Union," *Economic Policy*, 29, 323–61.

Castle, Stephen (2003). "New Fraud Inquiry Into Missing EU Money," *Independent*. June 18, FT.com web site.

Chapman, Peter (2003). "Infrastructure Finance Guidelines Promised," *European Voice*. October 23–9, p. 38.

Chayes, Abram and Antonia Handler Chayes (1991). "Compliance Without Enforcement: State Behavior Under Regulatory Treaties," *Negotiation Journal* 7(3), July, 311–40.

——(1993). "On Compliance," *International Organization*, 47(2) (Spring), 175–205.

——(1995). *The New Sovereignty: Compliance with International Regulatory Agreements*. Cambridge, MA: Harvard University Press.

Chiorazzo, V. and L. Spaventa (1999). "The Prodigal Son or a Confidence Trickster? How Italy Got into EMU," in D. Cobham and G. Zis (eds.), *From EMS to EMU: 1979 to 1999 and Beyond*. London: Macmillan, pp. 129–55.

Christiansen, Thomas and Emil Kirchner (eds.) (2000). *Europe in Change: Committee Governance in the European Union.* Manchester: Manchester University Press.

Cohen, B. J. (1993). "Beyond EMU: The Problem of Sustainability," *Economics and Politics,* 5(2), 187–203.

"Commission Faces Vote of Censure from MEPs," Euobserver.com. April 20, 2004.

Commission of the European Communities (1997). "Commission's Recommendation for the Broad Guidelines of the Economic Policies of the Member States and of the Community." Brussels, March 23, Com (97) 168.

Cook, Brian J. and B. Dan Wood (1989). "Principal-Agent Models of Political Control of Bureaucracy,"*American Political Science Review,* 83(3), 965–78.

Council of Economic and Financial Affairs (2003). "2546th Council Meeting," C/03/320. Brussels. November 25.

Council of Economic and Finance Ministers (2002). "Statement by the Council (ECOFIN) on the Budgetary Situation of Germany," Brussels. February 12.

Council of the European Union (1996). "Council Recommendation on the Broad Guidelines of the Economic Policies of the Member States and of the Community". Brussels, July 1, 8577/96.

—— (1997). "Council Recommendation on the Broad Guidelines of the Economic Policies of the Member States and of the Community". Brussels, July 3, 9669/97, pp. 10–13.

—— (2000). "Statement for the Council Minutes," Interinstitutional File: 00/0196 (CNS). Brussels. February 17.

Cowles, Maria Green, James Caporaso, and Thomas Risse (eds.) (2001). *Transforming Europe: Europeanization and Domestic Change.* Ithaca: Cornell University Press.

Cramb, Gordon (1997). "Dutch Express Alarm at German Gold Scheme," *Financial Times.* May 23, p. 1.

Crooks, Ed (2003). "Eurozone Enforcer Prepares to Strike First Blow," *Financial Times.* September 3, p. 6.

Dai, Xinyuan (1998a). "Information Systems of Treaty Regimes," unpublished manuscript.

——(1998b). "International Institutions, Domestic Constitutencies and Compliance with Environmental Agreements," unpublished manuscript.

——(1998c). "International Institutions and National Compliance: The Domestic Constituency Mechanism," unpublished manuscript.

Dalsgaard, T. and A. de Serres (1999). "Estimating Prudent Budgetary Margins for 11 EU Countries: A Simulated SVAR Model Approach," Economics Department Working Papers No. 216, OECD, ECO/WKP (99)8.

Delors, Jacques (2001). Interview with Jacques Delors, March 30.

De Michelis, Alberto (2000). "Subject: Amendments to ESA 95 (SWAPS)," Luxembourg: Eurostat. February 4.

De Michelis, Alberto and Alain Chantraine (2003). *Memoirs of Eurostat: Fifty Years Serving Europe.* Luxembourg: Office for Official Publications of the European Communities.

Dinan, Desmond (1999). *Ever Closer Union.* Boulder: Lynne Rienner.

Dombey, Daniel and Gavin Jones (2002). "Eurostat Warns Portugal Deficit May Be Higher," *Financial Times.* March 22, p. 2.

Downs, George W., D. M. Rocke, and P. N. Barsoom (1996). "Is the Good News About Compliance Good News About Cooperation?" *International Organization*, 50(3) (Summer), 389–406.

Drozdiak, William (1997*a*). "Kohl Defies Central Bank by Revaluing Gold," *Washington Post*. May 30, p. A28.

——(1997*b*). "Germany Unnveils Plan to Reduce Deficit in Preparation for Common Currency," *Washington Post*. June 20, p. A24.

Duchatczek, Wolfgang (1996). "Statement of Wolfgang Duchatczek (Chairman of the CMFB), Delivered by John Kidgell (Vice Chairman), on the 'France Telecom' Case," November 27/8.

——(1997). "Report on Statistical Work Concerning the Excessive Deficit Procedure," November 2.

Duffield, John S. (2003). "The Limits of Rational Design,'" *International Organization*, 57 (3), 411–30.

Dupuis, Jean-Pierre (1998). "The Reliability of the National Accounts in the Context of the Excessive Deficit Procedure," Seventh Naitonal Accounts Seminar, National Accounts Association, Paris.

Dyson, Kenneth (2002). "Introduction: EMU as Integration, Europeanization, Convergence," in Kenneth Dyson (ed.), *European States and the Euro*. New York: Oxford University Press, pp. 1–30.

——(2004). "Economic Policies: From Pace-Setter to Beleaguered Player," in Kenneth Dyson and Klaus H. Goetz (eds.), *Germany, Europe and the Politics of Constraint*. New York: Oxford University Press, pp. 3–35.

Dyson, Kenneth and Kevin Featherstone (1999). *The Road to Maastricht: Negotiating Economic and Monetary Union*. Oxford: Oxford University Press.

Dyson, Kenneth and Klaus H. Goetz (eds.) (2004). *Germany, Europe and the Politics of Constraint*. New York: Oxford University Press.

Economic Policy Committee (2001). "Report on Potential Output and the Output Gap," ECFIN/EPC/670/01/en. Brussels. October 25.

Ehrlich, Peter (2000). "Germany Expects DM2obn from Auction," *Financial Times*. June 19, p. 2.

Eichengreen, Barry (1992). "Should the Maastricht Treaty Be Saved?" Princeton Studies in International Finance, Essay 74.

——(1996*a*). "A More Perfect Union? The Logic of Economic Integreation," Princeton Studies in International Finance, Essay 198.

——(1996*b*). "Sensible EMU: How to Avoid a Maastricht Catastrophe," *The International Economy*, 3(1), 16–7.

Eichengreen, Barry and J. Frieden (eds.) (1994). *The Political Economy of Monetary Unification*. Boulder: Westview Press.

Eichengreen, Barry and C. Wyplosz (1998). "The Stability Pact: More Than a Minor Nuisance?" *Economic Policy*, 26, 67–113.

Eijffinger, Sylvester C. W. and Jokob de Haan (2000). *European Monetary and Fiscal Policy*. New York: Oxford University Press.

Elgie, Robert (2002). "The Politics of the European Central Bank: Principal-Agent Theory and the Democratic Deficit," *Journal of European Public Policy*, 9(2), 186–200.

"EU Faults Irish Inflation Policy" (2001). *International Herald Tribune*. February 13, p. 11.

"EU Ruling Raises Italy's Deficit Level" (2002). *International Herald Tribune*. July 5, p. 12.

"EU Reprimands Portugal Over Budget Deficit" (2002). *International Herald Tribune*. November 6, p. 11.

Euobserver (2003a). "Sobles Hits Back At France," September 30.

——(2003b). "Ireland Set to Leave Euro Rules Alone," December 19.

European Commission (1998). "Convergence Report 1998: Prepared in Accordance with Article 109j(1) of the Treaty," Brussels.

——(2002). "Report From the Commission: Excessive Deficit in Portugal—Report Prepared in Accordance With Art. 104.3 of the Treaty," ECFIN/436/02-en. Brussels. September 9.

"EMU: Who's Going to Make It?" (1996). *Financial Times*, November 26, p. 2.

European Commission (2003a). "Report of the Eurostat Task Forces (TFES), Summary and Conclusions," Brussels. September.

——(2003b). "Summary of the Eurostat Cases Now Closed," Brussels: European Anti-Fraud Office (OLAF), September 24.

——(2003c). "Eurostat Briefing Note: Based on Second Interim Progress Report by the Internal Audit Service, European Commission," Brussels. September 24.

——(2003d). "Commission Asks France to Take New Measures to Reduce the Budget Deficit in 2004," IP/03/1420. Brussels. October 21.

——(2004). "Commission Sets Out Strategy for Economic Policy Coordination and Surveillance," IP/04/35. Brussels.

European Commission: Directorate-General for Economic and Financial Affairs (2002). *European Economy: Public Finances in EMU 2002, No. 3/2002*. Brussels: European Communities.

——(2003). *Public Finances in EMU, 2003*. Brussels.

European Commission and Council of the European Union (2001). "Report: The Contribution of Public Finances to Growth and Employment: Improving Quality and Sustainability," Brussels. 6997/01. March 12.

European Convention (2003). "Draft Treaty Establishing a Constitution for Europe," Brussels, July 18, Part III, Title III, Chapter II, Section 1, Articles 70–76.

European Court of Justice (2004). "Judgement of the Court of Justice in Case C-27/04," Luxembourg, July 13, Press Release No. 57/04.

European Monetary Institute (1998). "Convergence Report: Report Required by Article 109j of the Treaty Establishing the European Community," Frankfurt.

European Parliament (2004). *Motion of Censure*, B5-0189/2004, Brussels. April 16.

Eurostat (1979). *European System of Integrated Economic Accounts, ESA*. Luxembourg: Eurostat.

—— (1996). *European System of Accounts, ESA 1995*. Luxembourg: Office for Official Publications of the European Communities, p. 72.

——(1998a). "Statistics on Convergence Criteria: Assessment by Eurostat," Luxembourg: Eurostat.

——(1998b). *Eurostat, Our Corporate Plan*. Luxembourg: Eurostat.

—— (1998c). "Excessive Deficit Procedure: Statistical Aspects: Mission Report in Italy," February 2.

——(2000a). "Some Options Concerning Swaps for General Government in ESA 95," Luxembourg: Eurostat. March 9.

—— (2000b). *ESA95 Manual on Government Deficit and Debt*, Chapter 11.3 Capital Injections, Luxembourg, p. 47–54.

Eurostat News Release (1997a). "Deficit & Debt: Eurostat Rules on Accounting Issues," Luxembourg: Eurostat Press Office. No. 10/97. Feburary 3.

——(1997b). "Accounting Rules: Eurostat Takes Further Decisions on Deficit and Debt," Luxembourg: Eurostat Press Office. No. 16/97. February 21.

——(1997c). "Accounting Rules: Complementary Decisions of Eurostat on Deficit and Debt," Luxembourg: Eurostat Press Office. No. 24/97. March 26.

——(1997d). "New Decisions of Eurostat on Deficit and Debt," Luxembourg: Eurostat Press Office. No. 88/97. December 17.

——(1998). "New Decisions of Eurostat on Deficit and Debt," Luxembourg: Eurostat Press Office. No. 05/98. January 27.

——(2000a). "Euro-Zone Government Deficit at -1.2% and Debt at 72.2% of GDP in 1999," Luxembourg: Eurostat Press Office. N. 34/2000. March 13.

——(2000b). "Eurostat Decision on the Allocation of Mobile Phone Licences (UMTS)," Luxembourg: Eurostat Press Office. No. 81/2000. July 14.

——(2002). "Securitisation Operations Undertaken by General Government," Luxembourg: Eurostat Press Office. No. 80/2002. July 3.

——(2003a). "Euro-Zone Government Deficit at 2.2% of GDP and Public Debt at 69.1% of GDP," Luxembourg: Eurostat Press Office. No. 30/2003. March 17.

——(2003b). "Liquidation of the EFTA Industrial Development Fund for Portugal," Luxembourg: Eurostat Press Office. No. 97/2003. August 21.

——(2003c). "Capital Injections by Government Units Into Public Corporations," Luxembourg: Eurostat Press Office. No. 89/2003. August 21.

——(2003d). "Payments to Government by Public Corporations in the Context of the Transfer to Government of Their Unfunded Pensions Obligations," Luxembourg: Eurostat Press Office. No. 120/2003. October 21.

——(2003e). "Treatment of Public-Private Partnerships," Luxembourg: Eurostat Press Office. N. 18/2004. February 11.

——(2004a). "Classification of Funded Pension Schemes in Case of Government Responsibility or Guarantee," Luxembourg: Eurostat Press Office. N. 30/2004. March 2.

——(2004b). "Greek Government Deficit at 3.2% of GDP and Public Debt at 103.0% of GDP," Luxembourg: Eurostat Press Office. No. 62/2004. May 7.

"Eurostat Rules on Booking Pension Fund Transfers" (2003). *Reuters Limited*. October 21.

"Eurostat Pension Fund Rule Confirms Belgium's View" (2003). *Reuters Limited*. October 22.

Falkner, Gerda (1999). "Interest Groups in a Multi-Level Polity: The Impact of European Integration on National Systems," Robert Schuman Centre for Advanced Studies, EUI Working Paper RSC 99/34.

Featherstone, Kenneth and Claudio M. Radaelli (eds.) (2003). *The Politics of Europeanization*. New York: Oxford University Press.

Feigenbaum, Harvery, Jeffrey Henig, and Chris Hamnett (1999). *Shrinking the State: The Political Underpinnings of Privitization*. New York: Cambridge University Press.

Fitchett, Joseph (2000). "France Is Torn Over Potential Windfall," *International Herald Tribune*. May 31, p. 1.

Forhlich, Norman, Joe A. Oppenheimer, and Oran R. Young (1971). *Political Leadership and Collective Goods*. Princeton: Princeton University Press.

"France Lifts Outlook for Deficit to 2.8% of GDP," (2002). *International Herald Tribune*. November 21, p. 11.

Franchet, Yves (1996). "Note for the Attention of the Chairman of CMFB," November 5.

——(2000). "Eurostat and the Trade-Off Between Rapidity, Accuracy and Comparability: Past Objectives and Future Challenges," Luxembourg: Eurostat.

——(2002a). "Note for the Attention of Mr. Pedro Solbes, Subject: Portugal—Debt and Deficit Issues," Luxembourg: Eurostat. February 21.

——(2002b). "Eurostat's New Rules on Securitisation Transactions," *Financial Times*. July 6, p. 6.

——(2002c). "Note A L' Attention de Monsieur P. Solbes, Membre De La Commission, Objet: Procedure de deficit excessif—cas du Portugal," Luxembourg: Eurostat. February 5.

——(2002d). "Report on the Greek EDP Notification of September 2002," Luxembourg: Eurostat. September 20.

——(2003a). Letter to Jean-Michel Charpin, Director-General INSEE. "Dontation en capital dans RFF," Luxembourg: Eurostat. March 4.

——(2003b). Letter to Jean-Michel Charpin, Director-General INSEE. "Notification PDE de la France—1 mars 2003 Communiqué de presse Eurostat," Luxembourg: Eurostat. March 13.

Fuller, Thomas (2002). "Rift Widens On EU Deficits," *International Herald Tribune*. September 26, p. 11.

Gallagher, Nancy W. (1999). *The Politics of Verification*. Baltimore: Johns Hopkins University Press.

George, Nicholas and George Parker (2002). "Finns Insist EU Pact Must Be Protected," *Financial Times*. September 4, p. 2.

Giovannini, Enrico (2003). "The France Telecom Affair : A Night at the Bundesbank," in Alberto De Michelis and Alain Chantraine (eds.), *Memoirs of Eurostat: Fifty Years Serving Europe*. Luxembourg: Office for Official Publications of the European Communities, 144.

Glatzel, Dieter (1998). "The Excessive Deficit Procedure: Statistical Measurement of Debt and Deficit," Luxembourg.

——(2002). "EDP Notification—Austria," Luxembourg: Eurostat. September 12.

Graham, Robert (1996a). "Italy Levies 'Euro-tax' in Drive to Meet EMU Targets," *Financial Times*. November 20, p. 2.

——(1996b). "Government Passes Maastricht Milestone," *Financial Times*. November 18, p. 2.

—— (1996c), "Italy is Pressed to Rethink Euro-tax," *Financial Times*. November 28, p. 3.

——(1997). "Prodi Dodges Tough Budget Decisions," *Financial Times*. April 1, p. 2.

——(2000). "Jospin Under Pressure to Boost Social Spending," *Financial Times*. November 8, p. 6.

——(2001a). "Jospin Opts to Increase Budget," *Financial Times*. July 18, p. 2.

——(2001b). "France to Create 50,000 Temporary Jobs," *Financial Times*. October 3, p. 7.

——(2001c). "Fabius to Introduce Fiscal Stimulus," *Financial Times*. October 16, p. 4.

Greenwood, John, Robert Pyper, and David Wilson (2002). *New Public Administration in Britain*, 3rd edn. London: Routledge.

Grey, Stephen (2003). "Kinnock Under Fire for Rebuffing Second Fraud Whistleblower," *Sunday Times*. March 16, p. 20.

Guerrera, Francesco (2003). "France May Ignore Order to Cut Deficit," *Financial Times*. January 22, p. 4.

Guerrera, Francesco and Jo Johnson (2003). "France Refuses to Take Steps to Curb Budget Deficit," *Financial Times*. February 26, p. 8.

Haas, Peter M. (1992). "Introduction: Epistemic Communities and International Policy Coordination," *International Organization*, 46(1), 1–36.

——(1998). "Compliance with EU Directives: Insights from International Relations and Comparative Politics," *Journal of European Public Policy*, 5(1), 17–37.

Hallerberg, Mark (1999). "The Importance of Domestic Political Institutions: Why and How Belgium and Italy Qualified for EMU," unpublished manuscript.

——(2001). "EU Institutions and Fiscal Policy Coordination, 1991–2001," unpublished manuscript.

——*Domestic Budgets in a United Europe: Fiscal Governance from the End of Bretton Woods to EMU*. Ithaca: Cornell University Press, 2004.

Hallett, Andrew Hughes and Peter McAdams (1996). "Fiscal Deficit Reduction in Line with the Maastricht Criteria for Monetary Union: An Empirical Analysis," Center for Economic Policy Research, Paper 1351.

Hansen, Jorgen Drud and Jan Guldager Jorgensen (1999). "How to Play Safe in Fiscal Policy Under the Stability and Growth Pact," *European Union Review*, 4(3), 37–52.

Harlow, Carol (2002). *Accountability in the European Union*. New York: Oxford University Press.

Harnischfeger, Uta (1999). "German Deficit Falling 'Faster'," *Financial Times*. July 5, p. 3.

Hartvig, Hans Peter and Miguel Diaz-Llanos La Roche (2002). "Subject: Portugal—Derogation on the Application of Regulation (EC)2516/2000," Brussels: European Commission Legal Service, May 6.

Heaton-Harris, Chris (2003). "Brussels Must Stop Burying Bad News," *Financial Times*. September 22, FT.com web site.

Hix, Simon (1999). *The Political System of the European Union*. New York: Palgrave.

Hollingsworth, Katheryn and Fidelma White (1999). *Audit, Accountability and Government*. New York: Oxford University Press.

Hooghe, Liesbet (2001). *The European Commission and the Integration of Europe*. New York: Cambridge University Press.

Huber, John D. and Charles R. Shipan (2003). *Deliberate Discretion? The Institutional Foundations of Bureaucratic Autonomy*. New York: Cambridge University Press.

Hulverscheidt, Claus and Daniel Dombey (2001). "German Finance Chief Hints At Changes to Key European Pact," *Financial Times*. August 17, p. 12.

Inter-Secretariat Working Group on National Accounts (1993). *System of National Accounts*, 1993. Brussels: United Nations Publications.

Italianer, Alexander (1993). "Mastering Maastricht: EMU Issues and How They Were Settled", in Klaus Gretschmann (ed.), *Economic and Monetary Union: Implications for National Policy-Makers*. Dordrecht: Martinus Nijhoff, 51–113.

Jakob, Barbara (1998). "Making the Most of Diminishing Resources," *Sigma: The Bulletin of European Statistics*, March, p. 36.

James, Barry (2002). "France to Cut Taxes Despite Jump In Deficit," *International Herald Tribune*. June 21, p. 11.

Jones, Larry R. and K. J. Euske (1991). "Strategic Misrepresentation in Budgeting," *Journal of Public Administration Research and Theory*, 4(1), 437–60.

Jones, Tim (2000). "Lisbon Summit to Sanction Tighter EU Budget Surveillance," *European Voice*. March 9–15, p. 1.

Kapner, Fred and George Parker (2002). "Angry Italy Agrees to EU Guidelines on Accounts," *Financial Times*. July 5, p. 2.

Kaufman, Herbert (1960). *The Forest Ranger: A Study in Administrative Behavior*. Baltimore: Johns Hopkins University Press.

Kendrick, John W. (1972). *Economic Accounts and Their Uses*. New York: McGraw-Hill.

Kenen, Peter B. (1995). *Economic and Monetary Union in Europe*. Cambridge: Cambridge University Press.

——(ed.) (1996). "Making EMU Happen, Problems and Proposals, A Symposium," Princeton Studies in International Finance, Essay 199.

Kidgell, John (1996). "Procedures for Handling Transactions That are Not Clearly Defined in ESA," December.

Kiewiet, D. Roderick and Mathew D. McCubbins (1991). *The Logic of Delegation*. Chicago: University of Chicago Press.

Kingdon, John (1995). *Agendas, Alternatives, and Public Policies*. New York: HarperCollins.

Knill, Christoph (2001). *The Europeanisation of National Administrations: Patterns of Institutional Change and Persistence*. New York: Cambridge University Press.

Koremenos, Barbara, Charles Lipson, and Duncan Snidal (2001). "The Rational Design of International Institutions," *International Organization*, 55(4), 761–99.

Kraan, Dirk-Jan (1996). *Budgetary Decisions*. New York: Cambridge University Press.

Laffan, Brigid (1997). *The Finances of the European Union*. New York: St. Martin's Press.

Landler, Mark (2002). "EU Faces Major Test on Deficit in Portugal," *International Herald Tribune*. July 27–8, p. 1.

Landler, Mark and Paul Melleur (2003). "EU Warns Berlin, Paris, and Rome," *International Herald Tribune*. January 9, p. 1.

Lequesne, Christian (2000). "The European Commission: A Balancing Act Between Autonomy and Dependence," in Karlheinz Neunreither and Antje Wiener (eds.), *European Integration After Amsterdam*. New York: Oxford University, pp. 37–51.

Lex Column (1996). "Roman Numerals," *Financial Times*. November 20, p. 18.

Lindner, Johannes (2001). "Linking Institutions with Outcomes: An Institutionalist Assessment of the EU Budgetary Procedure," Paper for the ECSA Seventh Biennial International Conference, May 31–June 2.

Mahoney, James (2000). "Path Dependence in Historical Sociology," *Theory and Society*, 29, 507–48.

Major, Tony (2002) "ECB Mounts Defense of 'Indispensible' Stability Pact," *Financial Times*. October 25, p. 6.

Majone, Giandomenico (2001). "Two Logics of Delegation: Agency and Fiduciary Relations in EU Governance," *European Union Politics*, 2(1), 103–22.

Mallett, Victor (2002a). "France Set To Break Pledge on Balanced Budget Target," *Financial Times*. May 12, p. 1.

——(2002b). "French Deficit 'Likely To Remain Beyond 2006,'" *Financial Times*. September 26, p. 4.

Mallet, Victor and George Parker (2003). "France 'To Breach Deficit Limit This Year,'" *Financial Times*. February 5, p. 4.

Manchau, Wolfgang (1997). "Row Creates Dilemma for Financial Markets," *Financial Times*. May 30, p. 2.

Marshall, Matt (1997). "Germany Scuttles Controversial Plan for Gold Reserves," *Wall Street Journal*. June 4, p. A15.

Mavroidis, Petros C. (1992). "Surveillance Schemes: The GATT's New Trade Policy Review Mechanism," *Michigan Journal of International Law*, 13(2), 374–414.

McCubbins, Matthew D. and T. Schwartz (1984). "Congressional Oversight Overlooked: Police Patrols Versus Fire Alarms," *American Journal of Political Science*, 2(1), 165–79.

McNamara, Kathleen R. (1998). *The Currency of Ideas: Monetary Policy in the European Union*. Ithaca: Cornell University Press.

Meganck, Bart (2002a). "Government Real Estate in Austria," Luxembourg: Eurostat. July 2.

——(2002b). "Note for the Attention of Mr. Cabral, Director, Directorate B, ECFIN, Subject: Portugal—Excessive Deficit Procedure," Luxembourg: Eurostat. April 10.

——(2002c). Letter to Professor Doctor Paulo Gomes, President Instituto Nacional de Estatistica. "Subject: Statistical Aspects for the Excessive Deficit Procedure," Luxembourg: Eurostat. May 3.

Meller, Paul (2003). "EU Orders France to Cut Its Deficit," *International Herald Tribune*. May 8, p. 1.

Merritt, Giles (2003). "Scandal May Topple Prodi's Team," *International Herald Tribune*. August 7, p. 6.

Meyers, Roy T. (1994). *Strategic Budgeting*. Ann Arbor: University of Michigan Press.

Minkkinen, P. and H. Patomaki (1997). *The Politics of Economic and Monetary Union*. Dordecht: Kluwer Academic.

Missale, Alessandro (2001). "Optimal Debt Management with a Stability and Growth Pact," *Public Finance & Management*, 1(1), 58–91.

Mitchell, Ronald B. (1993). "Compliance Theory: A Synthesis," *Review of European Community and Institutional Environmental Law*, 2(4), 327–34.

——(1994a). *International Oil Pollution At Sea: Environmental Policy and Treaty Compliance*. Cambridge, MA: MIT Press.

——(1994b). "Regime Design Matters: International Oil Pollution and Treaty Compliance," *International Organization*, 48(3), 425–58.

——(1998). "Sources of Transparency: Information Systems in International Regimes," *International Studies Quarterly*, 42 (1), 109–30.

Mitchell, Ronald B. and Patricia M. Keibackh (2001). "Situation Structure and Institutional Design: Reciprocity, Coercion, and Exchange," *International Organization*, 55(4), 891–917.

Moe, Terry (1985). "Control and Feedback in Economic Regulation: The Case of the NLRB," *American Political Science Review*, 79(4), 1094–116.

——(1987). "An Assessment of the Positive Theory of 'Congressional Dominance,'" *Legislative Studies Quarterly*, 12(4), 475–520.

Monnet, Jean (1978). *Memoirs*. New York: Doubleday.

Moravcsik, Andrew (1998). *The Choice for Europe*. Ithaca: Cornell University Press.

——(1999). "A New Statecraft? Supranational Entrepreneurs and International Cooperation," *International Organization*, 53(2), 267–306.

Moulton, Brent R. and Eugene P. Seskin (2003). "Preview of the 2003 Comprehensive Revision of the National Income and Product Accounts," *Survey of Current Business*, June, 17–34.

Munchau, Wolfgang (2003). "A Treaty to Undermine the Eurozone," *Financial Times*. December 1, p. 15.

——(2004). "Europe Needs a Strategy, Not Looser Fiscal Rules," *Financial Times*. May 24, p. 13.

National Council on Statistical Information (1994). "Report of Working Group, Calculation of the Criteria of Convergence," Paris.

National Institute for Statistics and Economic Studies (1998). "Level of Cooperation with Maastricht Criteria," Paris.

Norman, Peter (1997a). "German Turmoil Over Gold Plan," *Financial Times*. May 17–18, p. 1.

——(1997b). "Waigel Gambles with Reputation for Prudence," *Financial Times*. May 17–18, p. 2.

——(1997c). "Prospects for EMU Thrown Into Confusion," *Financial Times*. May 29, p. 1.

——(2001a). "EU Reprimands Ireland Over 'Inflationary' Budget," *Financial Times*. February 13, p. 1.

——(2001b) "Rome 'Did Not Cheat Over Deficit,'" *Financial Times*. November 6, p. 6.

——(2002a). "Germany May Take Its Own Medicine," *Financial Times*. January 20, p. 2.

——(2002b). "EU Avoids Vote in Compromise Over Finances," *Financial Times*. February 13, p. 2.

Norman, Peter (2002c). "Protagonists Each Claim Satisfaction From Accord," *Financial Times*. February 13, p. 2.

Norman, Peter, Andrew Fisher, and Wolfgang Manchau (1997). "Germany's Rift on EMU Deepens," *Financial Times*. May 30, p. 1.

Normanton, E. L. (1966). *The Accountability and Audit of Governments: A Comparative Study*. Oxford: Manchester University Press.

North, Douglass C. (1990). *Institutions, Institutional Change and Economic Performance*. New York: Cambridge University Press.

Nugent, Neill (2001). *The European Commission*. New York: Palgrave.

Ogul, Morris (1976). *Congress Oversees the Bureaucracy*. Pittsburgh: University of Pittsburgh Press.

O'Loughlin, Carleen (1971). *National Economic Accounting*. New York: Pergamon Press.

Olson, Mancur, Jr. (1973). *The Logic of Collective Action*. Cambridge, MA: Harvard University Press.

"'Olympics' Cost Pushes Greece Over EU Deficit Limits" (2004). *International Herald Tribune*. May 8–9, p. 11.

Ostrom, Elinor (1990). *Governing the Commons*. New York: Cambridge University Press.

O'Toole, Laurence, Jr. (1997a). "Treating Networks Seriously: Practical and Research-Based Agendas in Public Administration," *Public Administration Review*, 57(1), 45–52.

——(1997b). "The Implications for Democracy in a Networked Bureaucratic World," *Journal of Public Administration Research and Theory*, 7(3), 443–59.

Parker, George (2002). "Finns Insist EU Pact Must Be Protected," *Financial Times*. September 4, p. 2.

——(2003a). "Passing the Buck on Eurostat," *Financial Times*. June 18, FT.com Web site.

——(2003b). "Greece Warns on Easing of Stability Pact," *Financial Times*. July 30, p. 3.

——(2003c). "Brussels Widens Fraud Probe", *Financial Times*. July 17, p. 1.

——(2004). "EU Ministers Will Not Rewrite Pact Until 2005," *Financial Times*. April 3–4, p. 2.

Parker, George, Ian Bickerton, and Tony Major (2002). "Brussels Plan Upsets Smaller Countries," *Financial Times*. September 26, p. 4.

Parker, George, Tobias Buck, and John Prideaux (2003). "Prodi Orders Disciplinary Action for Directors," *Financial Times*. July 10, p. 3.

Parker, George and Robert Graham (2003). "France Could Be in Deficit For Three Years," *Financial Times*. April 3, p. 4.

Parker, George and Raphael Minder (2003). "Brussels Seeks to Limit Fallout Amid Eurostat Affair," *Financial Times*. September 24, p. 5.

Parker, George and Haig Simonian (2004). "EU Nations Call For Delay to Fiscal Reforms," *Financial Times*. February 2, p. 2.

Parker, George, Haig Simonian, and Tony Major (2003). "Brussels to Warn Schroder Over Deficit Rule Breach," *Financial Times*. January 8, p. 4.

Parker, George, Haig Simonian, Victor Mallet, and Tony Barber (2003). "EU Orders Berlin to Curb Budget Deficit," *Financial Times*. January 9, p. 4.

Parry, John N. (1997). "Spanish Reputation Falls In Hole," *The European*. May 29–June 4, p. 4.

Paterson Tony and Victor Smart (1997). "Has Germany Kissed the Strong Euro Goodbye?" *The European*. May 22–8, p. 1.

Pearson, Lea (2003). "Eurostat Ruling May Resolve French Row," *The Times*. October 23, p. 23.

Peterson, John and Elizabeth Bomberg (1999). *Decision-Making in the European Union*. New York: St. Martin's Press.

Pfanner, Eric (2003a). "France, Foe of Unilateralism, Stands Alone on EU Debt," *International Herald Tribune*. February 27, p. 5.

——(2003b). "EU Warns France on Breaching Deficit Limit," *International Herald Tribune*. March 8–9, p. 15.

Pierson, Paul (1996). *Dismantling the Welfare State? Reagan, Thatcher, and the Politics of Retrenchment*. New York: Cambridge University Press.

——(1998). "The Path to European Integration: A Historical-Institutionalist Analysis," in Wayne Sandholtz and Alex Stone Sweet (eds.), *European Integration and Supranational Governance*. New York: Oxford University Press, pp. 27–59.

——(2000). "Increasing Returns, Path Dependence, and the Study of Politics," *American Political Science Review*, 94(2), 251–67.

Pierson, Paul and Theda Skocpol (2000). "Historical Institutionalism in Contemporary Political Science," in Ira Katznelson and Helen V. Milner (eds.), *Political Science: The State of the Discipline*. New York: W. W. Norton & Company, pp. 693–721.

Pollack, Mark A. (1997). "Delegation, Agency, and Agenda Setting in European Community," *International Organization*, 51(1), 99–134.

——(2002). "Learning from the Americanists (Again): Theory and Method in the Study of Delegation," *West European Politics*, 25(1), 200–19.

——(2003). *The Engines of European Integration: Delegation, Agency, and Agenda Setting in the EU*. New York: Oxford University Press.

"Portugal Says Eurostat Backs Deficit-Cutting Move," (2003). *Reuters Limited*. October 21.

Poterba, James M. (1994). "State Responses to Fiscal Crises: The Effects of Budgetary Institutions and Politics," *Journal of Political Economy*, 102, 799–821.

——(1995). "Balanced Budget Rules and Fiscal Policy: Evidence from the States," *National Tax Journal*, 48, 329–36.

——(1996). "Budget Institutions and Fiscal Policy in the U.S. States," *American Economic Review*, 86, 395–400.

Poterba, James M. and Jurgen von Hagen (1999). *Fiscal Institutions and Fiscal Performance*. Chicago: University of Chicago Press.

"President Assails Jospin's Economic Principles," (2001). *International Herald Tribune*. July 16, p. 7.

Prodi, Romano (2003). "'The Eurostat Case,' Statement of the President of the European Commission," Conference of the Presidents of the European Parliament, Strasbourg. Brussels: European Commission. September 25.

"Public Deficit Is Flirting with EU Limit," (2003). *International Herald Tribune*. February 5, p. 10.

Raab, Jorg (2002). "Where Do Policy Networks Come From?" *Journal of Public Administration Research and Theory*, 12(4), 581–622.

Radaelli, Claudio M. (2003). "The Europeanization of Public Policy," in Kenneth Featherstone and Claudio M. Radaelli (eds.), *The Politics of Europeanization*. New York: Oxford University Press, pp. 27–56.

Richardson, Jeremy (1996). "Policy-Making in the EU: Interests, Ideas and Garbage Cans of Primeval Soup," in Jeremy J. Richardson (ed.), *European Union: Power and Policy Making*. London: Routledge, pp. 3–23.

Risse, Thomas, Maria Green Cowles, and James Caparaso (2001). "Europeanization and Domestic Change: Introduction," in Maria Green Cowles, James Caporaso, and Thomas Risse (eds.), *Transforming Europe: Europeanization and Domestic Change*. Ithaca: Cornell University Press, pp. 1–20.

"Roll Over, Enron," (2002). *The Economist*. August 3, p. 42.

Rosamond, Ben (2000). *Theories of European Integration*. New York: St. Martin's Press.

Ruggles, Nancy D. and Richard Ruggles (1999). *National Accounting and Economic Policy: The United States and UN Systems*. Cheltenham, Edward Elgar.

Sandholtz, Wayne and Alec Stone Sweet (eds.) (1998). *European Integration and Supranational Governance*. New York: Oxford University Press.

Savage, James D. (2000). "A Decade of Deficits and Debt: Japanese Fiscal Policy and the Rise and Fall of the Fiscal Structural Reform Act of 1997," *Public Budgeting & Finance*, 20(1), 55–84.

——(2001). "Budgetary Collective Action Problems: Convergence and Compliance Under the Maastricht Treaty on European Union," *Public Administration Review*, 61(1), 43–53.

——(2002). "The Origins of Budgetary Preferences: The Dodge Line and the Balanced Budget Norm in Japan," *Administration & Society*, 34(3), 261–84.

Sbragia, Alberta (2001). "Italy Pays for Europe: Political Leadership, Political Choice, and Institutional Adaptation," in Maria Green Cowles, James Caporaso, and Thomas Risse (eds.), *Transforming Europe*. Ithaca: Cornell University Press, pp. 79–96.

Schick, Allen (1983). "Incremental Budgeting in a Decremental Age," *Policy Sciences*, 16, 1–25.

——(1986). "Macro-Budgetary Adaptations to Fiscal Stress in Industrialized Democracies," *Public Administration Review*, 46, 124–34.

——(1988). "Micro-Budetary Adaptations to Fiscal Stress in Industrialized Democracies," *Public Administration Review*, 48, 523–33.

——(1990). "Budgeting for Results: Recent Developments in Five Industrialized Countries," *Public Administration Review*, 50(1), 26–34.

Schmid, John (2002a). "EU to Scold Berlin, But Gently," *International Herald Tribune*. January 31, p. 2.

——(2002b). "EU Rebukes Germay as Deficit Nears Limit," *International Herald Tribune*. January 31, p. 9.

——(2002c). "Berlin Will Partly Dodge EU Deficit Warning," *International Herald Tribune*. February 12, p. 1.

Schneider, Steffen (2000). "A man Still Brimming with Enthusiasm about His job . . ." *Sigma: The Bulletin of European Statistics*, February, p. 45.

Setear, John (1996). "An Iterative Perspective on Treaties: A Synthesis of International Relations Theory and International Law," *Harvard International Law*, 37(1), 139–230.

——(1997). "Responses to Breach of Treaty and Rationalist International Relations Theory: The Rules of Release and Remediation in the Law of Treaties and the Law of State Responsiblity," *Virginia Law Review*, 83(1), 1–126.

Simmons, Beth (1998). "International Law and State Behavior," *Annual Review of Political Science*, 1, 75–93.

——(2000). "International Law and State Behavior: Commitment and Compliance in International Monetary Affairs," *American Political Science Review*, 94(4), 819–35.

Simonian, Haig (2000a). "Eichel Predicts Future Budget Surpluses Could Cut Debt," *Financial Times*. November 10, p. 6.

——(2000b). "Germany to Fund Extra Spending With Mobiles Cash," *Financial Times*. October 13, p. 2.

——(2001). "Germany Slips Into Recession in Third Quarter," *Financial Times*. November 23, p. 6.

Simonian, Haig and Gerrit Weismann (2001). "Germany Revises Down Its Deficit Forecasts," *Financial Times*. November 27, p. 6.

Smaghi, L. B. and C. Casini (2000). "Monetary and Fiscal Policy Co-operation: Institutions and Procedures in EMU," *Journal of Common Market Studies*, 38(3), 375–91.

Smith, Mitchell P. (2000). "The European Commission: Diminishing Returns to Entrepreneurship," in Maria Green Cowles and Michael Smith (eds.), *State of the European Union: Risks, Reform, Resistance, and Revival*. New York: Oxford University Press, pp. 207–27.

Snidal, Duncan (1985). "Coordination Versus Prisoners' Dilemma: Implications for International Cooperation and Regimes," *American Political Science Review*, 79 (4), 923–42.

Sobles, Pedro (2002). "Statement by Commissioner Solbes on the Portugese Deficit Data," Brussels: EU Press Release IP/02/1168. July 7.

Steil, Benn (2002). "Enron and Italy," *Financial Times*. July 21, p. 13.

Stoiber, E. (1997). "Defender of a Decimal Point," *Financial Times*. August 7, p. 13.

Strauch, Rolf R. and Jurgen von Hagen (eds.) (2000). *Institutions, Politics, and Fiscal Policy*. Dordrecht: Kluwer Academic.

Stuvel, G. (1986). *National Accounts Analysis*. London: Macmillan Press.

Sweet, Alec Stone and Wayne Sandholtz (1998). "Integration, Supranational Governance, and the Institutionalization of the European Polity," in Wayne Sandholtz and Alec Stone Sweet (eds.), *European Integration and Suprantational Governance*. New York: Oxford University Press, pp. 1–26.

Sweet, Alex Stone, Wayne Sandholtz, and Neil Fligstein (eds.) (2001). *The Institutionalization of Europe*. New York: Oxford University Press.

Tallberg, Jonas (2000). "The Anatomy of Autonomy: An Institutional Account of Variation in Supranational Influence," *Journal of Common Market Studies*, 38(5), 843–64.

——(2002a). "Delegation to Supranational Institutions: Why, How, and with What Consequences?" *West European Politics*, 25(1), 23–46.

——(2002b). "Paths to Compliance: Enforcement, Management, and the European Union," *International Organization*, 56(3), 609–43.

Tanzi, Vito and Ludger Schuknecht (2000). *Public Spending in the 20th Century*. New York: Cambridge University Press.

Thatcher, Mark (2002). "Delegation to Independent Regulatory Agencies: Pressures, Functions, and Contextual Mediation," *West European Politics*, 25(1), 125–47.

Thatcher, Mark and Alec Stone Sweet (2002). "Theory and Practice of Delegation to Non-Majoritarian Institutions," *West European Politics*, 25(1), 1–22.

Thomas, Craig (1997). "Public Management as Interagency Cooperation: Testing Epistemic Community Theory at the Domestic Level," *Journal of Public Administration Research and Theory*, 7(2), 221–46.

Tsebelis, George (1990). *Nested Games: Rational Choice in Comparative Politics*. Berkeley: University of California Press.

——(2002). *Veto Players: How Political Institutions Work*. Princeton: Princeton University Press.

Underal, Arild (1998). "Explaining Compliance and Defection: Three Models," *European Journal of International Relations*, 4(1), 5–30.

Verdun, Amy (1999). "The Role of the Delors Committee in the Creation of EMU: An Epistemic Community?" *Journal of Economic Public Policy*, 6(2), 308–28.

——(2002). "Merging Neofunctionalism and Intergovernmentalism: Lessons from EMU," in Amy Verdun (ed.), *The Euro: European Integration Theory and Economic and Monetary Union*. New York: Rowman & Littlefield, pp. 9–28.

Vinocur, John (2002). "Pure Politics Drove EU to Be Lenient on Berlin," *International Herald Tribune*. February 13, p. 1.

von Hagen, Jurgen (1991). "A Note on the Empirical Effectiveness of Formal Fiscal Restraints," *Journal of Public Economics*, 44, 199–210.

——(1992). "Budgeting Procedures and Fiscal Performance in the European Communities," *Economic Papers*, 96, 1–79.

von Hagen, Jurgen and I. J. Harden (1994). "National Budget Proceesses and Fiscal Performance," *European Economic Reports and Studies*, 3(2), 311–408.

von Hagen, Jurgen and Rolf Strauch (1999). "Tumbling Giant: Germany's Experience with the Maastricht Fiscal Criteria," in D. Cobham and G. Zis (eds.), *From EMS to EMU: 1979 to 1999 and Beyond*. London: Macmillan, pp. 70–94.

Watson, Alison M. S. (1997). *Aspects of European Monetary Integration*. New York: St. Martins.

Webb, Eugene J., Donald T. Campbell, Richard D. Schwartz, and Lee Sechrest (1966). *Unobtrusive Measures: Nonreactive Research in the Social Sciences*. Chicago: Rand McNally.

White, Joseph and Aaron Wildavsky (1989). *The Deficit and the Public Interest*. Berkeley: University of California Press.

Wildavsky, Aaron (1980). *How to Limit Government Spending*. Berkeley: University of California Press.

——(1984). *The Politics of the Budgetary Process*. Boston: Little, Brown.

Wildavsky, Aaron and Larry R. Jones (1994). "Budgetary Control in a Decentralized System: Meeting the Criteria for Fiscal Stability in the European Union," *Public Budgeting & Finance*, 14(4), 7–22.

Wildavsky, Aaron and Eduardo Zipico-Goni (eds.) (1993). *National Budgeting for Economic and Monetary Union*. Dordrecht: Martinus Nijhoff.

Williamson, Hugh (2002). "Berlin Attacked Over Stance On Deficit," *Financial Times*. February 13, p. 2.

Wise, Peter (2002a). "Portugal Gets No Reprieve at Home Over Budget Deficit," *International Herald Tribune*. February 13, p. 2.

——(2002b). "Candidates in Portuguese Polls Turn Guns on Budget Dilemma," *Financial Times*. March 4, p. 2.

——(2003). "Portugal Learns to Love Stability Pact," *Financial Times*. January 29, p. 4.

Wood, B. Dan (1988). "Principals, Bureaucrats, and Responsiveness in Clean Air Enforcements," *American Political Science Review*, 83(3), 965–78.

Wright, John (1995). "Big Job to Finish," *Sigma: The Bulletin of European Statistics*, Summer, p. 31.

—— (1996). "Wind of Change at Statistics Sweden," *Sigma: The Bulletin of European Statistics*, winter, pp. 38–46.

—— (1999a). "EU Support for Portuguese Statistics Has Been 'Decisive,' " *Sigma: The Bulletin of European Statistics*, February, p. 39.

—— (1999b). "Crucial Role of CMFB," *Sigma: The Bulletin of European Statistics*, March, p. 13.

Young, Oran (1979). *Compliance and Public Authority: A Theory with International Applications*. Baltimore: Johns Hopkins University Press.

——(1999). "Comment on Andrew Moravcsik, 'A New Statecraft? Supranational Entrepreneurs and International Cooperation,'" *International Organization*, 53(4), 805–09.

Index

Organizations are referred to under the main entry in full, but subsequently under their acronyms, e.g. EMU (Economic and Monetary Union). Notes and tables are designated by n and t in bold.